THE MAFIA

Charles Luciano, FBI 62920.

THE MAFIA

CORRUPTION, VIOLENCE AND DEGRADATION

AL CIMINO

ARCTURUS

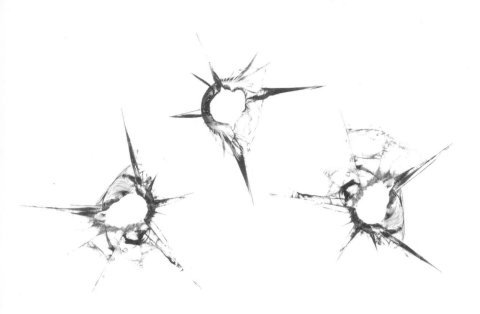

Picture credits

Shutterstock: 6, 12, 14, 20, 98, 167, 172, 179, 193, 210, 265, 277, 281, 309, 317, 318, 322, 335
Corbis: 7, 10, 16 (x2), 32, 42, 44-5, 54, 63, 78, 81, 102 (t), 111, 112, 113, 115, 116, 118, 131, 135, 139, 146, 149, 165, 180, 202, 203, 221, 225, 235, 252, 254, 260, 268, 271, 276, 279, 287, 293, 297, 302-3, 304, 307, 314, 316, 321, 324, 326, 327, 329, 331, 332, 339, 340-1, 347 **Getty Images:** 9, 11, 17, 28, 41, 46, 49, 66, 68, 69, 75, 76, 77, 82, 83, 84, 87, 88, 89, 90, 102 (b), 107, 110, 114, 119, 122, 124-5, 134, 140, 152, 154, 158, 163, 175, 183, 186, 189, 197, 201, 204, 213, 214, 216. 217, 218, 223, 227, 228, 229, 231, 232, 238, 239, 240, 242, 244, 250, 253, 257, 258, 264, 282, 285, 288, 310, 311, 323, 325, 333, 336, 337, 345 **Topfoto:** 23, 52, 56, 65, 144, 169 **ED Archives:** 25, 35, 38, 67, 91, 92, 93, 94, 97, 100, 121, 128, 132 (x2), 136, 142, 211, 212, 261, 280, 286, 292, 294, 312, 315 **New York Public Library:** 61 **PA:** 166, 177, 266, 270, 273, 275, 291, 296, 298 **Rex Features:** 208 **Kobal Collection:** 305

ARCTURUS

This edition published in 2015 by Arcturus Publishing Limited
26/27 Bickels Yard, 151–153 Bermondsey Street,
London SE1 3HA

ISBN: 978-1-78404-865-5
AD004766UK

Printed in China

CONTENTS

Introduction 6

Chapter 1 **The Sicilian Vespers** 10

Chapter 2 **The Black Hand** 32

Chapter 3 **Prohibition** 66

Chapter 4 **The Castellammarese War** 98

Chapter 5 **The Commission** 116

Chapter 6 **The Mafia Versus Mussolini** 142

Chapter 7 **The Teacher** 166

Chapter 8 **The Mafia Wars** 178

Chapter 9 **Little Doll** 202

Chapter 10 **The Strip and the Broadwalk** 210

Chapter 11 **The Pizza Connection** 232

Chapter 12 **The Ice Man** 252

Chapter 13 **The Snake** 260

Chapter 14 **Baby Shacks** 266

Chapter 15 **Skinny Joey** 270

Chapter 16 **The Gentle Don** 276

Chapter 17 **The Last Don** 280

Chapter 18 **The Lost Don** 286

Chapter 19 **The Sixth Family** 292

Chapter 20 **The Charnel House** 298

Chapter 21 **Casino** 304

Chapter 22 **Gaspipe** 310

Chapter 23 **Diabolik** 316

Chapter 24 **Pentiti** 322

Epilogue 345

Index 348

INTRODUCTION

Valley of the Temples, Sicily, 1786 – travellers feared journeys at night, but daytime could be dangerous too

The Italian criminal societies that are now collectively known as the Mafia gradually evolved on the island of Sicily. Gangs of bandits had probably roamed the island for centuries. They would perhaps have survived by rustling cattle or kidnapping for ransom. By the 18th century the names of some of the gangs and their leaders began to be recorded, but there was still little or no communication between them.

Then somewhere around the middle of the 19th century these isolated bands discovered a common purpose when they began to unite against the island's hated Bourbon rulers.

It was at about this time, also, that they began to be referred to as the Mafia. By the 1860s traditional banditry had given way to a gangster culture that permeated the whole of Sicilian society.

The Mafia took on roles such as tax collection or law enforcement and it also began to control the island's financial system. Anyone who opposed the Mafia was dealt with in swift and bloody fashion, so people began to fear it. As a result, members of the Mafia became immune from prosecution and they were able to ensure that politicians of their choice were elected. The Mafia became even more resistant to authority when it began to collude with the Church. Finally, a savage code of honour, the *omèrta*, ensured that all disciplinary matters were dealt with within the society, rather than by the authorities. Members were also required to observe a strict code of silence. Any infringement of these rules was punishable by death.

The influence of the Mafia soon spread far beyond the shores of Italy and Sicily. In the early 20th century thousands of organized crime figures entered the United States, often illegally. Soon the tentacles of the Mafia entwined themselves around every aspect of American life. And because of its central role in the drug trafficking industry, the Mafia quickly spread its web across Britain, Canada and Australia.

In 1970, the Racketeer Influenced and Corrupt Organizations Act (RICO) was passed in the United States. This provided for extended criminal penalties for acts performed as part of an ongoing criminal enterprise, such as the Mafia. Significantly, it became possible to prosecute Mafia bosses who had ordered an offence, as well as those who had actually committed it.

Under RICO any member of the mob – a popular name for the Mafia – could be sentenced to twenty years' imprisonment and fined $25,000 if they had committed any two of 27 federal and eight state crimes, which included murder, gambling, extortion, kidnapping, bribery, robbery, drug trafficking,

Opposing the Mafia has always been a risky business. In May 1992, Judge Giovanni Falcone died in his car after a roadside bomb exploded

counterfeiting, fraud, embezzlement, money laundering and arson. Convictions for these crimes served as evidence for a new crime – racketeering to benefit an illegal enterprise.

Individuals harmed by these criminal enterprises could collect triple damages and those charged under RICO laws could be placed under a restraining order to seize their assets to prevent their dispersal.

These harsh new laws have put many of the old-style Mafia bosses away for good and have done much to impoverish the mob. However, there are always young mobsters waiting to fill the shoes of the older generation and there are always fresh rackets they can get into. As retired FBI agent David W. Breen said: 'They're like the Chinese army – you kill one and there are ten others to take his place.'

In Italy, inroads were made into the power of the Mafia by the Maxi Trial of 1986, which saw hundreds of gangsters in the dock. More were tried in absentia and went underground. Mafia wars also thinned out the ranks.

Those imprisoned were held under restrictions outlined in Article 41-bis of the Prison Administration Act. They could be held in solitary confinement, refused the use of the telephone, banned from sending or receiving money and denied visits from family members. This meant that it was impossible to go on running a criminal organization from prison. However, with the Mafia shackled, its rivals flourished, leading to the rise of the Camorra in Naples, the 'Ndrangheta in Calabria and the Sacra Corona Unita in Puglia.

Among Italians and Italian-Americans there seems to be no shortage of young men who want to live 'the life'. This means that you have pockets full of money when others are worried about paying their bills. It gives you standing in society. These days, it also means flash cars, flash suits, bling, beautiful women and fine champagne.

On the other hand you must have no scruples. You must be able to turn your hand to any form of crime, no matter what the consequences are for others. You must be willing to kill friend, foe – and innocent bystanders – without qualm and be prepared to torture others to death if that is what you are told to do. Equally you must accept that your closest associates are likely to do that to you, too. Few Mafiosi have died in their beds of natural causes.

The Mafia tells the stories of a number of characters who have accepted this pact with the devil. Though many Mafia members might well be ruthless, antisocial criminals, their arguably 'glamorous' lifestyle has captured the public imagination, both in real life and fiction. Thousands of ordinary, law-abiding citizens have flocked to see movies such as *The Godfather* and *Goodfellas* and many well-known personalities have been flattered by the attentions of prominent mobsters.

The traditional Mafia organization might now be in decline, but criminals will always find a way. In the United States, the Russian Mafia and the Yakuza – the Japanese Mafia – are moving in, while old Mafia families such as the Lucchese are making new alliances with African-American gangs such as the Bloods.

The Mafia is full of blood-chilling characters: Don Vito Cascio Ferro, the New York mobster who lured Joe Petrosino to his death in Palermo; Al Capone, who ran Chicago during the Prohibition era; Lucky Luciano, who escaped death and then life imprisonment by lending Mafia support to the war effort; Don Calogero Vizzini, who eliminated the enemy when the Allies invaded Sicily; Vito Genovese, who made money from both sides during the war; Meyer Lansky, the racketeer who never spent a day in jail; hitmen Louis 'Lepke' Buchalter and Albert Anastasia, who ran Murder, Inc.; Benjamin 'Bugsy' Siegel, who turned Las Vegas into the home of gambling; Giuseppe 'Joe Bananas' Bonanno, who crossed the Five Families and walked away with his life; Tommaso Buscetta, the 'Don of the Two Worlds'; Salvatore 'Totò' Riina, 'boss of bosses'; John Gotti, 'The Teflon Don'; Bernardo 'The Tractor' Provenzano, who hid out under cover for 43 years. The list goes on.

These were extraordinary men who lived through extraordinary times, times that are rapidly disappearing. *The Mafia* tells the story of their lives, their families, their codes, their crimes and their cold-blooded murders.

While the story of the Mafia may not be over, it is a long and enthralling tale which is drenched in blood and scored with betrayal.

The body of Nunzio Giuliano, 57, lies in a Neapolitan street on 21 March 2005. Giuliano was reportedly an important member of the Naples Mafia, known as the Camorra

Chapter 1

THE SICILIAN VESPERS

Above: **Joseph 'Joe Bananas' Bonanno walks through a group of reporters, New York City, 1966**

Left: **The Sicilian Vespers, 1282**

Giuseppe Bonanno grew up in the Mafia stronghold of Castellammare del Golfo. He went on to become the head of one of New York's Five Families, where he was known as 'Joe Bananas'. As a child he was told the story of the Sicilian Vespers.

In the 13th century, Sicily was under French domination. As the people of Palermo made their way to evening worship – vespers – during Easter week of 1282, there were tax collectors waiting outside the churches. Their job was to arrest those who were in arrears. They handcuffed debtors and dragged them away to jail, publicly shaming them by slapping their faces – an intolerable insult to a Sicilian.

A young lady of rare beauty, who was soon to be married, was going to church with her mother when a French soldier named Droetto grabbed hold of her, under the pretext of helping the tax collectors. He then dragged the girl behind the church and raped her. Her distraught mother ran through the streets, crying: 'Ma fia, ma fia!' ('My daughter, my daughter', in the Sicilian dialect). The girl's fiancé found Droetto and stabbed him to death. Meanwhile, the mother's cry, 'Ma fia', raced through the streets of Palermo and onwards throughout Sicily. According to Bonanno, 'Ma fia' became the rallying cry of the resistance movement, who declared that it was an acronym for 'Morte alla Francia, Italia anela' ('Death to France, Italy cries out').

This story is based on historical truth. There was indeed an insurrection called the Sicilian Vespers that began on Easter Monday 1282, with French soldiers being killed at vespers in the church of Santo Spirito in Sicily. However, scholars have dismissed the notion that the incident represented the beginning of the

The street urchins of Palermo acclaim the arrival of Garibaldi in 1860

rival states. At that time, Sicily and Naples – then jointly known as the Kingdom of the Two Sicilies – were under the control of the Bourbon dynasty, a royal family that also ruled in France and Spain. Then in 1860 the Italian patriot Giuseppe Garibaldi and 1,000 of his followers, wearing their distinctive red shirts, landed in Sicily. Although the Red Shirts were vastly outnumbered by the Bourbon army, the men of Sicily rallied to Garibaldi – not because they wanted a united Italy, but because they wanted to get rid of the Bourbons. With Garibaldi's aid, Sicily was liberated. Garibaldi and his Red Shirts then crossed the Strait of Messina and went on to unite Italy under King Victor Emmanuel of Savoy. But the people of Sicily soon discovered that they had merely swapped one external ruler for another. Nothing else had changed.

According to Bonanno, the concept of Italian nationhood never stirred Sicilians deeply.

'It was a vague concept that required men to give their highest loyalty to an abstract entity, the nation, rather than to their families, which were flesh and blood. It would require young men to fight foreign wars on behalf of the national state, to fight strangers from whom one had never received a personal affront or injury, to fight people one didn't even know… Sicilians are among the most idealistic people on earth, but they are not abstract. They like things on a human scale. Even in the smallest business transactions, they like to deal with each other man to man, eyeball to eyeball. It is no different when they fight. They take

Mafia. But that did not worry Bonanno, who was less concerned by the veracity of the story than the Sicilian spirit it exemplified.

Bonanno also told the story of another insurrection that was supposedly related to the origins of the Mafia, but this time his account might have been closer to the truth. In his grandfather's time Italy had yet to be unified, because it was still a patchwork of

fighting very personally. They believe in personal, not abstract, honour.'

THE ORIGINS OF THE MAFIA

The ferocious independence of the Sicilians is rooted in their history. Because of its position in the centre of the Mediterranean, Sicily has been invaded repeatedly – by Phoenicians, Greeks, Romans, Byzantines, Ostrogoths, Crusaders, Arabs and Normans and by the French, the Spanish and the British. Bonanno also talked of Sicilians forming secret societies in the 15th century, in order to protect themselves from Catalan marauders. With no independent state to depend on, this left the Sicilians fiercely loyal to their extended families. They had little regard for the law that was largely imposed on them by outsiders and crime was thought to be an expression of patriotism, a show of resistance to the occupier. Executed criminals were considered martyrs. Their bones were kept in shrines and the sick and the poor offered prayers to them, in which they requested their intercession.

Sicily had been a feudal society since Norman times. Although the peasants were given the right to own land in the early 19th century, three-quarters of the land was still owned by aristocrats by the beginning of the 20th century. They spent their time in their palaces in Palermo if they did not live abroad and they hired private armies, or *mafie*, to protect their property against the bandits who abounded. There were no roads and few officers of the law in the countryside, so the bandits and the *mafie* came to an understanding. After joining forces, they supported themselves by demanding the traditional *u pizzu* (later *pizzo*), or protection money. It even had to be paid to the police.

This levy was based on the system whereby landowners were entitled to take a certain amount of grain from the peasants at harvest time. *Pizzu* means 'beak' in Sicilian and the expression *fari vagnari u pizzu* means 'to wet one's beak' or, more colloquially, 'to wet your whistle' – traditionally with a glass of wine, or any other light refreshment that was offered in recognition of a service rendered. Sicilian criminals embraced this principle on practical grounds. Instead of asking for a large amount of money that risked bankrupting the victim, it was better to ask for a smaller amount, one that the victim could afford, and then return later for more money. *Pizzu* soon became prison slang for extortion. A Sicilian dictionary of 1857 gives only one meaning – 'beak' – but the 1868 edition also mentions the criminal usage of the word.

'With no independent state to depend on, this left the Sicilians fiercely loyal to their extended families. They had little regard for the law that was largely imposed on them by outsiders'

Calascibetta, an ancient hilltop town in the very heart of Sicily

The names of Sicilian gangs such as the black-hooded Beati Paoli were first recorded in the 18th century, along with those of individual bandits like Don Sferlazza, a seminarist who turned outlaw over a family vendetta. As a priest, however, he was immune to the law. These bandits survived by cattle-rustling and kidnapping for ransom.

Sicily's gangs first came together in 1848, during a rebellion against the island's Bourbon rulers. One gang of thirty to forty men was led by a peasant woman known as 'Testa di Lana' ('Wool Head') and three of her sons. Two of her other sons had been killed by the Bourbon authorities, leaving her with a consuming hatred of the police force. During the uprising,

she led a 4,000-strong mob against the convent of St Anna, where a number of Bourbon police officers were being held. After a summary trial, those officers who had carried out their duties in a compassionate and considerate way were acquitted by acclamation but any who were condemned by the crowd were shot. However, when a provisional government was established, it was decided that Testa di Lana was a threat to social order, so she was imprisoned in the fortress of Castellammare. She was released when the Bourbons regained control of the island, but after that she and her family were kept under constant surveillance.

The Sicilian state had virtually collapsed in the political turmoil and gangs such as the Little Shepherds and the Cut-Throats were in cahoots with the police. Giuseppe Scordato, the illiterate peasant boss from Bagheria, and Salvatore di Miceli from Monreale, were taken on as tax collectors and coastguards and became rich, while law enforcement at Misilmeri, outside Palermo, was handed over to the famous bandit Chinnici. Such men flourished in the liberal environment that accompanied the unification of Italy in 1861. People feared them, they could deliver the vote to any politician who would do business with them and nervous jurors guaranteed them immunity from prosecution. They also

'The Sicilian state had virtually collapsed and gangs like the Little Shepherds and the Cut-Throats were in cahoots with the police'

controlled the financial system – the directors of the newly-founded Bank of Sicily lived in fear of kidnap and murder. The tentacles of the gangsters exerted a stranglehold on the whole of society, as the British consul in Palermo recorded in the 1860s.

'Secret societies are all-powerful. Camorre and *maffie*, self-elected juntas, share the earnings of the workmen, keep up intercourse with outcasts and take malefactors under their wing and protection.'

Then in 1863 the gangsters acquired a glamorous image when the Sicilian actor Giuseppe Rizzotto wrote a popular play called *I mafiusi di la Vicaria* (The Mafiosi of Vicaria). The play was set in Palermo's central prison and the characters were Palermo street thugs. It was such a success that Rizzotto added two acts and put on a new production called simply *I Mafiusi*.

Mafiusi is the plural of *mafiusu*, which means 'swagger'. It can also be translated as 'boldness' or 'bravado' and when used pejoratively it describes a bully. Some think it derives from the Arabic slang word *mahyas*, meaning 'aggressive boasting, bragging', or *marfud*, meaning 'rejected', while others consider that it descends from the Arabic word *mu'afah*, meaning 'exempt from the law', or *mahfal*, meaning 'a meeting or gathering'. And in Norman French there is the verb *se*

méfier, which means 'to beware'. Then there is the proper name Maufer, with which the medieval Knights Templar used to refer to the 'God of Evil'.

Sicilian gangsters not only flourished under the liberalism of the newly united Italy but they also befriended those that opposed it. The *maffie* protected the citrus estates of absentee aristocrats and they also colluded with the Church, which sought to preserve the old order. In the 1870s, a Tuscan member of parliament wrote the following account.

'There is a story about a former priest who became the crime leader in a town near Palermo and administered the last rites to some of his own victims. After a certain number of these stories the perfume of orange

and lemon blossoms starts to smell of corpses.'

The collusion between the Church and the Mafia continued. So much so that in the late 1940s the bandit Salvatore Giuliano attended tea parties at the archbishop's palace, after being given leave from the Ucciardone jail in Palermo. When the top Mafia boss Tommaso Buscetta turned against the Cosa Nostra ('Our Thing') in 1983 and became a *pentito* (informer), the current archbishop condemned him as an enemy of Sicily.

For the authorities, the Cosa Nostra was always a problem. In 1864, Niccolò Turrisi Colonna, head of the Palermo National Guard, wrote that a 'sect of thieves' operated across Sicily. It had been in existence for about 20 years and was a largely rural phenomenon, comprising cattle thieves, smugglers, wealthy farmers and their guards. However, it was widely suspected that Colonna was protecting important mafiosi in Palermo at the time. He went on to say that the brightest young people in the countryside were joining. They made money from protection rackets and had

The Via Maqueda in Palermo, Sicily, at the turn of the last century. Much of Palermo was built with Mafia money

little or no fear of the authorities. According to Colonna, members of the sect had special signals with which to recognize each other, they scorned the law and they had a code of loyalty and non-interaction with the police which he called *umirtà* (humility). He went on to explain the concept in detail.

'In its rules, this evil sect regards any citizen who approaches the *carabiniere* [military policeman] and talks to him, or even exchanges a word of a greeting with him, as a villain to be punished with death. Such a man is guilty of a horrendous crime against "humility"... "Humility" involves respect and devotion towards the sect. No one must commit any act that could directly or indirectly harm members' interests. No one should provide the police or judiciary with facts that help uncover any crime whatsoever.'

This was the origin of *omertà* – a savage code of honour which meant that mafiosi never, under any circumstances, spoke to the authorities to settle a grievance. Victims and their families had the right to avenge any wrong, while anyone breaking the code of silence would be dealt with by the Mafia itself. Colonna knew about this because he was part of it. The captain of his National Guard was Antonino Giammona, boss of a village named Uditore, just outside Palermo.

The Mafia became increasingly organized when, in the late 1800s, various 'families' or *cosche* in western Sicily joined together in a loose confederation. They enforced a brutal code. Death was the punishment for any infringement and corpses were symbolically mutilated as a warning to others. A corpse with a missing tongue signified that the victim had violated the *omertà*; a body with a hand chopped off denoted a petty thief; and a cadaver with its own severed genitals stuffed into its mouth was a sign that the dead man had 'dishonoured' the wife of a member.

In 1865 the prefect of Palermo sent a dispatch to Rome, in which he described how a number of men from the town of Monreale forced their way into Palermo and declared the city an independent republic. They held out for over a week while they repulsed a government attack and then they withdrew after burning the police and tax records. These rebels were known as *mafiusi* or, in the Italian spelling, *mafiosi*. The word then came into general usage. One police report described a fashionable young mafioso.

'[He] wears a brightly coloured shirt, keeps his hat at a rakish angle, has his well pomaded hair combed so that a curl falls on his forehead; his moustache is well trimmed. When he walks he swings his hips, and with his cigar in his mouth and his walking-stick in his hand, he keeps his long knife well hidden.'

BEYOND THE LAW

But the criminal conspiracy was much more sinister than that. In 1872, Dr Gaspare Galati inherited a ten-acre lemon and tangerine farm in Malaspina, just 15 minutes' walk from Palermo. The previous owner had been his brother-in-law, who had died from a heart attack after receiving threatening letters. Dr Galati's estate came with a warden, Benedetto Carollo, who creamed 20 to 25 per cent off the sale price of its produce, and many thought that Carollo had been responsible for the letters. In a bid to avoid trouble Dr Galati tried to lease the property, but Carollo put off prospective tenants, so the new owner sacked him.

Galati's friends, who otherwise knew nothing of his business, advised him to take Carollo back. But Galati was unwilling to be bullied, so he hired a new warden, who was shot in the back. Digging his heels in, Galati engaged yet another manager. He then received threatening letters asking him why he had hired an 'abject spy' in place of a 'man of honour'. Galati took the letters to the police, who did nothing. He then discovered that Carollo was an associate of Colonna's friend, Antonino Giammona.

Born into poverty as a peasant, Giammona used his participation in the revolts of 1848 and 1860 to win important friends. By 1875, he owned property worth some 150,000 lire, according to the chief of police in Palermo. More importantly, he was a criminal who was suspected of providing fugitives with shelter before murdering them. He was also being paid to carry out business on behalf of a man from Corleone, who had fled to the United States in order to escape prosecution. It was clear that Giammona was attempting to take control of the citrus business – not just on Galati's estate, but in the entire district. Then the new warden was shot in broad daylight. Badly injured and thinking he was about to die, he managed to identify his attackers to a local magistrate and Carollo was arrested. However, when Dr Galati managed to nurse the warden back to health, the man made peace with Giammona and the case was dropped.

This event was followed by a celebration feast in Uditore, after which Dr Galati abandoned his property and fled to Naples. He then wrote a letter to the Minister of the Interior in Rome, in which he described the situation in Uditore, a village with just 800 inhabitants. In 1874 alone at least 23 people had been murdered, including two women and two children, and a further ten inhabitants had been seriously injured. Yet the police had done nothing to investigate. The minister of the interior ordered the chief of police in Palermo to look into the matter. In the meantime, Carollo went hunting on Galati's land, accompanied by a judge from the Palermo court of appeal.

Palermo's chief of police sent an official reply to the Minister of the Interior, in which he described the initiation ceremony for a 'man of honour'. In the presence of a number of bosses and underbosses, the *padrino* or godfather would prick the initiate's finger and smear the blood on the image of a saint.

'In 1874 at least 23 people had been murdered, including two women and two children, and a further ten had been seriously injured. Yet the police had done nothing...'

As the novitiate undertook an oath of loyalty, the picture was burnt and the ashes were scattered, symbolizing the fate of all traitors. The same ceremony was used a hundred years later. It seems to have been borrowed from the Carbonari, or 'charcoal burners', a revolutionary Masonic sect that came to Italy with Napoleon's army.

Members would be identified by a 'man of honour', who would say: 'He is a friend of ours' or 'You two are the same as me'. If two members met, and they were unknown to each other, they would strike up a conversation about having a toothache. They would then go on to say where and when it started, which was the code for where and when they were initiated, or 'made'.

THE BROTHERHOOD

In 1876 a Mafia case hit the international newspaper headlines. John Forester Rose, the English manager of a sulphur company, was kidnapped. A ransom was paid and he was released. *The Times* said that he had been well treated, but the American press later reported that his wife had paid up only after she had received her husband's ears in the mail. It was also clear that the kidnappers had contacts in the upper echelons of society in Palermo and that the ransom was paid through a Mafia intermediary.

INITIATION

'Marsala tied my index finger of my right hand tightly with a string. He pricked the finger with a pin. The blood dripped on the image of a female saint. He burned the image, divided it into two portions and gave me one. We ground up our portions in our hands and then threw the result into the air.

As part of the ceremony I swore that I would remain a member of the Society that has as its *capo* Don Vito Vita, and its aim is to commit crimes against persons and property. I was told that the Society has affiliates in other towns, each town with its own capo, and if an affiliate does not carry out his assigned duties he would be judged by the Society and condemned to death. Then they taught me the mode of recognizing other affiliates.'

Testimony from the police interrogation of Leo Pellegrino, from the village of Sciacca, Agrigento province, 15 March 1876.

CRACKDOWN

Italy's minister of the interior, Giovanni Nicotera, concluded that the upper classes in Sicily were 'heavily compromised with the Mafia', so he instituted a crackdown. During the campaign, Mr Rose's kidnapper was shot and within a year Nicotera declared that the bandits had been totally defeated – but in fact only a few troublemakers had been shopped. While 12 death sentences were handed down to members of the Piazza Montalto family, the Stuppagghieri walked free. Those with the right political connections escaped conviction, while the rest were told to keep high-profile crimes like kidnapping down to a politically acceptable level. Nicotera was removed from office a month after he had proclaimed victory. Meanwhile, Mafia-backed politicians did deals with Rome in order to obtain the money to build roads, hospitals, schools and other public works. Over the years that followed Nicotera's departure there were high-profile trials of groups such as the Stuppagghieri, or 'Fuse Burners', in Monreale, the Fontana Nuova, or 'New Source', in Misilmeri and the Fratellanza, or 'Brotherhood', in Bagheria.

In 1883, a man was shot dead by two hooded assassins at a christening in Favara, a major centre of sulphur mining in southwest Sicily. The guests claimed that they did not recognize the killers, but on the following day a member of the rival gang was found dead. He had been shot in the back and his right ear was missing. Armed groups roamed the streets and it seemed that violence was about to erupt, but then the crisis dissipated.

A few weeks later, a railway worker went to the police and reported that he had been approached by the Fratellanza, but it seemed to him that the organization had criminal intentions. More than 200 people were arrested. Many confessed and the skeletons of victims were found discarded in caves, old wells and disused mine shafts.

The Brotherhood, it transpired, had been formed from two rival gangs in Favara in an attempt to keep the peace after the murder of the christening guest. It was significant that the first murder took place at a christening – an occasion at which a family adopts a new godfather. Like the 'sect' before it, the Brotherhood had an initiation ceremony that involved the smearing of blood on a sacred image, which was then burnt while an oath was being said.

'I swear on my honour to be faithful to the Brotherhood, as the Brotherhood is faithful to me. As this saint and these few drops of blood can never be returned to their original state, so I can never leave the Brotherhood.'

Its 500 members in the surrounding towns also identified one another through a conversation about a toothache. The prototype Mafia had even managed to spread to Favara, a town that was separated from Palermo by 60 miles of terrible roads.

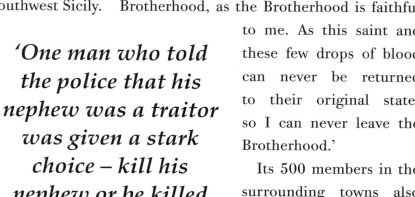

'One man who told the police that his nephew was a traitor was given a stark choice – kill his nephew or be killed himself... Then he lured his nephew into a trap where other members of the Brotherhood could kill him'

Just like the Cosa Nostra a hundred years later, the Brotherhood was divided into *decine* – groups of ten men. Each *decina* would be led by a *capodecina*. Above the *capodecina* was the *sottocapo* or underboss, and above him was the *capo* or boss and his *consigliere* or adviser. A member's duty to the Brotherhood came before family loyalty. One man who told the police that his nephew was a traitor was given a stark choice – kill his nephew or be killed himself. He agreed that his nephew must die and he made a toast: 'Wine is sweet, but the blood of a man is sweeter.' Then he lured his nephew into a trap where other members of the Brotherhood could kill him. Later the man led the police to a ruined castle where the body of his garrotted nephew had been hidden. Afterwards he hanged himself.

Two years after the Brotherhood had been discovered, 107 men stood in the dock of the specially adapted church of St Anne in Agrigento. They were chained in four lines. Although some claimed that confessions had been extracted from them under torture, they were all convicted and imprisoned.

In 1886, policeman Giuseppe Alongi wrote *The Maffia in its factors and its manifestations; study of the dangerous classes of Sicily*, in which he condemned the 'unbounded egoism' and 'exaggerated sense of themselves' possessed by the mafiosi as well as their 'capacity for violent, tenacious disdain and hatred... until vendetta is achieved'. However, he also revealed another side to their characters.

'These people are imaginative and their villages hot; their day-to-day language is mellifluous, exaggerated, full of images. Yet the maffioso's language is short, sober, clipped. The true maffioso dresses modestly. He makes himself seem naïve, stupidly attentive to what you are saying. He endures insults and slaps with patience. Then, the same evening, he shoots you.' Four years later, he published a similar study of the Neapolitan Camorra.

THE CASE OF THE FOUR MISSING MEN

Official reports also confirmed the existence of the Mafia. One came from the chief of police of Palermo, Ermanno Sangiorgi, who was from Romagna and had been sent to Sicily to investigate Dr Galati's complaints.

He organized the roundup of the Brotherhood in Favara and in 1898 he reported that eight Mafia gangs were operating in the vicinity of Palermo.

Sangiorgi's investigation centred on what the newspapers called the 'case of the four missing men'. In October 1897, the police found a farm building just north of Palermo, whose interior was riddled with bullet holes and caked with blood. A nauseating odour emanated from a cave nearby. It came from the decomposing bodies of four men. Each had died from multiple gunshot wounds. When Sangiorgi arrived in Sicily in the following year, the case was still unsolved and the Mafia war was raging.

The first breakthrough came when Giuseppa Di Sano, a woman who ran a grocery store, came forward. For a start, the local commander of the *carabinieri* had been wooing her 18-year-old daughter Emanuela. This did not go down well in a community that was opposed to law and order.

The local women started spreading rumours about her and boycotting her shop and then the sons of a local businessman tried to pay her with counterfeit money. After a series of veiled threats a hole appeared in a wall across the road from Giuseppa's shop, which provided a clear line of fire. At eight o'clock on the evening of 27 December 1896 a shot was fired, which felled Giuseppa. Emanuela

THE SICILIAN VESPERS 23

Camorra members at the start of the 20th century – today, there are some 111 Camorra clans around Naples. See page 29

rushed to her assistance, but she was killed instantly by a second bullet. Sangiorgi decided that this was a Mafia killing.

Two weeks before the incident a raid had been made on a counterfeiting factory, where Giuseppa's husband had worked as a handyman. The local men of honour, led by Vincenzo D'Alba, the brother of one of the mafiosi who was arrested in the raid, decided that Giuseppa had broken the *omertà*, so they informed the *carabinieri*. The hole in the wall had been deliberately obvious, so that everyone could see the sentence being carried out. However, Giuseppa did not die when she was shot and she was willing to testify. Then after talking to detectives she noticed another hole in the wall.

A man named Giuseppe 'Pidduzzo' Buscemi was questioned. He had an alibi but he hinted that Vincenzo D'Alba was the man the police were after, so he was arrested. Vincenzo's cousin, Antonio D'Alba, protested that Buscemi had clearly breached the *omertà*, so he was tried by the local men of honour. At his trial, Buscemi claimed that he had implicated D'Alba in order to protect the Mafia as a whole and he declared that he intended to change his story at a later date, in order to confuse the police further. He was acquitted. However, as things worked out, Buscemi's godfather, Tommaso D'Aleo, began to suspect that Antonio D'Alba was attempting to muscle in on one of his protection rackets. Soon afterwards another trial was held, this time in secret. After Antonio D'Alba had been sentenced to death *in absentia* he was taken to the farmhouse, where he was shot.

FRIENDS IN HIGH PLACES

As his investigations progressed, Sangiorgi discovered that the Mafia's influence spread to the very top of society, including such notaries as the shipping magnate and industrialist Ignazio Florio Jnr., a regular host to the crowned heads of Europe, and Joshua Whitaker, the head of an English Marsala wine dynasty that had founded the Palermo Football and Cricket Club. These two men were so distinguished that they received invitations to Queen Victoria's funeral in 1901.

In early 1897, Florio and his wife awoke to find that several valuable art objects had been stolen from their villa. Florio immediately chastised his gardener Francesco Noto. Noto and his younger brother Pietro were the *capo* and the underboss of the local Mafia clan, who had been hired to provide security.

Some time earlier, mafiosi under the command of the Noto brothers had kidnapped Whitaker's 10-year-old daughter Audrey. Knowing the ways of the island, Whitaker promptly paid up and the child was returned unharmed. However, two of the gang members, Giuseppe Caruso and Vincenzo Lo Porto – carriage drivers who also worked for the Florios – were unhappy with their share of the spoils.

They decided to respond with a *sfregio* – a scar or dishonour. Stealing from the Florios' villa was a deliberate insult to the Notos, who were supposed to protect it. The Notos resolved the problem by giving the thieves more of the ransom and the stolen items were returned,

> *'Two of the gang members were unhappy with their share of the spoils. They decided to respond with a* sfregio *– a scar or dishonour'*

but that was not the end of it. A meeting of the *capos* of the eight Palermo clans condemned Caruso and Lo Porto, which meant they were next in line to visit the farmhouse. The fourth man to meet his death in the farmhouse was another young mafioso, who was accused of stealing from his boss.

After Lo Porto had been killed, his widow appealed to Ignazio Florio's mother, the Baroness Giovanna d'Ondes Trigona, for help to rear her son – only to be refused on the grounds that her husband and Caruso had been thieves. This experience drove the two men's widows to talk to the police. When they did so Sangiorgi began to wonder how

complicit Florio had been in the murder of the gang members. The Baroness Trigona, he reasoned, would make a formidable witness, but there was no way he could make her take the stand. The Mafia did all they could to halt the investigation. First of all, the brother of one of the carriage drivers was driven to suicide over the suspicion that he had spoken to the police. One mafioso did manage to give evidence, after which the authorities assisted him to emigrate to the United States. However, an assassin traced him to New Orleans and poisoned him.

Then in October 1899 the regional *capo*, Francesco Siino, was shot and wounded.

A map of Sicily from 1900 showing Mafia influence – the darker the shading, the greater the presence

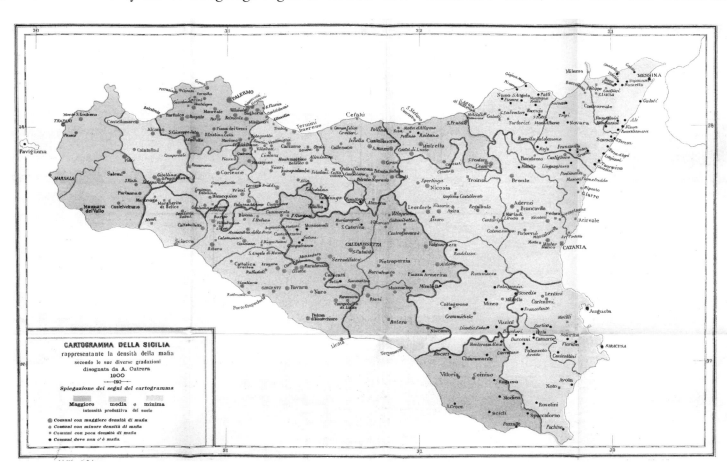

Sangiorgi arranged for Siino's wife to confront his would-be assassin. Thinking that her husband was close to death, she fell into a rage and accused the attacker of a series of murders. And once his wife started talking, Siino did too. Others also defected. It appeared that a war had been going on between the Siino family and that of Antonino Giammona, the Mafia boss in the Galati case, who was by then 78 years old. This showed that the Mafia was not a fly-by-night operation, but had a long history.

In April 1900, Sangiorgi began rounding up hundreds of suspected mafiosi. During the following year, 89 went on trial for criminal association in the case of the four missing men. But the chief prosecutor decided that the evidence against the other mafiosi that Sangiorgi had identified – including Antonino Giammona – was not strong enough. Indeed, the chief prosecutor, who was from Naples, even denied the existence of the Mafia.

'Until 1882 only two per cent of the population of Sicily could vote, then the franchise was widened to include a quarter of the adult male population, making election rigging much more expensive'

Then Siino recanted, Joshua Whitaker denied that his daughter had been kidnapped and Ignazio Florio did not turn up at court. Instead he sent a statement denying that he had ever discussed the burglary with the Noto brothers. Nevertheless, 32 mafiosi were convicted of forming a criminal association.

These included the Noto brothers, Tommaso D'Aleo and Antonino Giammona's son. But given the time they had already spent in jail, most were released immediately. Sangiorgi was sanguine. People condemned the Mafia in the evening, he said, and then defended it in the morning. The problem, he realized, was political so he began to investigate Don Raffaele Palizzolo, who was a notorious counsellor for the commune of Palermo and a member of the Sicilian parliament.

THE NOTARBARTOLO AFFAIR

Until 1882 only two per cent of the population of Sicily had been eligible to vote, but then the franchise was widened to include a quarter of the adult male population, making election rigging much more expensive. Nevertheless Don Raffaele Palizzolo continued to dispense preferment from his bed in the Palazzo Villarosa. He did it every morning for 40 years. He could obtain gun licences, curtail police investigations, secure a promotion or get a child's grades in school improved. Just as easily, he arranged for his friend Don Francesco Crispi to become prime minister. However, he had an enemy in the former mayor of Palermo, Emanuele Notarbartolo.

In 1890, Notarbartolo retired as director of the Bank of Sicily and returned to his heavily fortified estate near the Mafia town of Caccamo. The bank then became involved in a fraudulent share-dealing operation which involved stock in Ignazio Florio's shipping firm, Navigazione Generale Italiana (NGI). Notarbartolo was recalled to the bank, where he was sure to uncover the fraud. On 1 February 1893 he boarded the train to Palermo, having taken the precaution of taking a loaded rifle with him. When the train entered a tunnel he was set upon by two men with knives, who stabbed him to death and threw his body out of the carriage as it crossed a bridge. The body was found, but the case took seven years to come to trial. By then it had become a national scandal. The trial was held in Milan to prevent witnesses being intimidated, but only two employees of the railway company, the brakeman and the ticket collector, were present. But then Notarbartolo's son Leopoldo, a naval officer, took the stand and accused Palizzolo of orchestrating his father's death.

There had been long-standing animosity between Palizzolo and Leopoldo's father. When Notarbartolo had become mayor he had forced Palizzolo to repay money set aside to buy bread for the poor and Palizzolo had never forgotten it. Eleven years before his death Notarbartolo was kidnapped. He suspected Palizzolo for a couple of good reasons. At election time Palizzolo depended on support from the Mafia town of Caccamo and the kidnappers had been arrested near Palizzolo's estate.

During his time at the bank, Notarbartolo discovered that large sums were being lent in the names of children, dead men and fictitious figures, but when he tried to stop this, he was opposed by Palizzolo, who was a governor. And when Notarbartolo notified the authorities in Rome, Palizzolo ensured that his report was stolen from the Ministry of Commerce. The bank's general council then read the document behind Notarbartolo's back and he was forced to resign. Palizzolo was one of those who benefited from the fraud yet he had never been questioned, in spite of the fact that Leopoldo had related all of the facts to the authorities.

Sangiorgi moved quickly. A police inspector who had been accused of concealing evidence was arrested in the courtroom and the Chamber of Deputies in Rome suspended Palizzolo's parliamentary immunity.

The telegraph line to Palermo [*Cont.* p.30]

> '*He boarded the train to Palermo with a loaded rifle. When the train entered a tunnel he was set upon by two men with knives, who stabbed him to death and threw his body out of the carriage as it crossed a bridge*'

THE CAMORRA AND THE 'NDRANGHETA

November 2006: Camorra boss Antonio Bianco is arrested in the Melito district of Naples, then suffering from a tidal wave of serious crime

The House of Bourbon ruled Naples until 1860, apart from a period at the beginning of the 19th century when a short-lived republic emerged in the wake of the French Revolution. Although the Neapolitan Republic fell apart within a year, a power vacuum existed until the Bourbon restoration in 1815.

It was at this time that the Camorra sprang up in Naples. An indigenous opposition group similar to the Mafia, it is thought that its origins might lie in the Garduña, a secret society founded in Spain in the 15th century and introduced by the officials of the Spanish king. In 1735 there is mention of a gaming house called *Camorra avanti palazzo,* or *Camorra in front of the palace.* The name seems to be a concatenation of *'capo'* meaning boss and *'morra',* which was a popular street game. *Camorra* was the word that was used for the rake-off taken by the *camorristi* who delivered goods around the city. So it was another word for extortion.

In 1820 there were police records of the Camorra holding disciplinary meetings and by 1842 it had established its own initiation rites. Its adherents also collected money for the families of members in prison. After the 1848 revolt the organization made a pact with the liberal opposition, who wanted it to incite the poor to rise against the monarchy.

Despite its growing influence the Camorra remained a decentralized body, with local power being wielded by individual clans. Like the Mafia, its members maintained a code of silence, the *omertà.*

After the unification of Italy in 1861, measures were introduced to suppress the Camorra. Nevertheless, some Camorra members served as elected representatives until the Neapolitan elections of 1901. Then, in 1911, 20 alleged Camorristi were brought to trial including one man, said to be their chief, who had to be extradited from the United States. Harsh sentences were handed down and more Camorristi then fled to the United States, where they carried on blood feuds with the Mafia throughout the 1920s. But the gangsters of Neapolitan descent gradually joined the Mafia-led structure of organized crime in the United States.

was interrupted while the vote was taken, in case he absconded. Sangiorgi then arrested him. While he was in jail Palizzolo stood for election again, in the hope of renewing his immunity.

Giuseppe Fontana was one of the men who was suspected of murdering Notarbartolo. As the net closed in he sought the protection of the owner of the estate he guarded, who was a prince and a member of parliament. The prince then dictated the conditions under which Fontana would surrender. He was taken to Sangiorgi's house in the prince's carriage and the prince's lawyers were present when he was questioned. He was then conducted, without handcuffs, to a comfortable cell. Fontana had already been acquitted of four murders due to 'insufficient evidence', so this was nothing new to him.

Palizzolo and Fontana went on trial in Bologna in 1902 and 503 witnesses were heard. These included three former government ministers, seven senators, eleven current members of parliament and five police chiefs. The lawyers had to be separated several times to prevent them from coming to blows. One delivered a speech that lasted for eight days while another spoke for four-and-a-half days. Rumours spread that the Mafia were going to assassinate one of Notarbartolo's lawyers,

'Palizzolo and Fontana went on trial in Bologna in 1902 and 503 witnesses were heard. The lawyers had to be separated several times to prevent them from coming to blows'

even though the courtroom was surrounded by policemen and half a company of infantry.

Another 45 *carabinieri* formed up around the dock with fixed bayonets. In the end, Palizzolo and Fontana were convicted amid scenes of jubilation. They were led away still protesting their innocence.

However, Ignazio Florio's newspaper, *L'Ora*, questioned the verdict. Six months later it was overturned in Rome by the Court of Cassation, Italy's highest appeal court, and a retrial was ordered. This took place in Florence. This time Palizzolo and Fontana were acquitted. Palizzolo returned to a hero's welcome in Palermo, while Fontana and his family emigrated to New York, where he continued his life of crime.

Leopoldo Notarbartolo had to sell his father's estates to pay his lawyers' bills. He stayed on in the navy, rising to become an admiral, and spent his time at sea writing his father's biography.

In the 1970s, after a bitter internecine war that cost 400 lives, the Camorra joined the Mafia in its drug-smuggling activities. It also controlled cigarette smuggling, garbage dumping, industrial waste disposal and construction.

The reconstruction of the Campania region after the 1980 earthquake was particularly lucrative. Other Camorra activities include money laundering, extortion, people trafficking, prostitution, robbery, blackmail, kidnapping, political corruption and counterfeiting.

More recently, the organization has formed alliances with Nigerian drug gangs and the Albanian Mafia. There are also Camorra affiliates in Cleveland, Los Angeles, Albany, Springfield, Massachusetts and Aberdeen, Scotland.

With the decline in the status of the Mafia since the Maxi Trial of the 1980s the Camorra became the most powerful gang in Italy, though it is rivalled by Calabria's 'Ndrangheta, whose name derives from the Greek word for courage or virtue. Some people believe that the 'Ndrangheta is descended from the Spanish Garduña, but the FBI maintains that it was formed in the 1860s by Sicilian mafiosi banished from the island by the Italian government.

The 'Ndrangheta also maintains the omertà and engages in drug trafficking, murder, bombings, counterfeiting, gambling, frauds, thefts, labour racketeering, loan-sharking and the smuggling of illegal aliens. Its cells are loosely connected by blood relations and marriages and it has affiliates in New York and Florida.

> '*In the 1970s, Camorristo Raffaele Cutolo wanted to expand into Puglia, a move he oversaw from jail. He was so powerful that he secured the release of a member of the regional government kidnapped by the Red Brigades*'

There is a Mafia-like organization in the Puglia region called the Sacra Corona Unita, or the 'United Sacred Crown'.

In the 1970s, Camorristo Raffaele Cutolo wanted to expand into Puglia, a move he oversaw from jail. By 1981 he was so powerful that it is said that he secured the release of Ciro Cirillo, a Christian Democrat member of the regional government who had been kidnapped by the Red Brigades.

However, he gained such notoriety that his political supporters distanced themselves from him. His faction, the *Nuova Camorra Organizzata*, lost the Camorra war and the Puglia branch broke free. Based in Brindisi, it specializes in smuggling cigarettes, drugs, arms and immigrants from Albania, Croatia and other ex-Communist states, though it is also involved in money laundering, extortion and political corruption.

The government policy of banishing leading Sicilian mafiosi to northern Italy encouraged the original criminal syndicates to organize themselves more efficiently. This was particularly true of the Veneto region in the northeast, where the existing criminal groups became known collectively as the Mala del Brenta.

≋ Chapter 2 ≋

THE BLACK HAND

As early as 1878, a gang of Sicilian immigrants was operating a flourishing extortion racket among the southern Italian residents of San Francisco. It called itself '*La Maffia*'. The San Francisco *Examiner* described its members as 'a neat little tea party of Sicilian brigands... a villainous gang' whose objective was 'the extortion of money from their countrymen by a system of blackmail, which includes attacks on character and threats to kill'. Their activities were curtailed when the body of a Sicilian immigrant called Catalani was found near Sausalito. Evidence pointed to Salvatore Messino, Ignazio Trapani, Rosario Meli and Giuseppe Bianchi. They were arrested and eventually convicted – but not of murder, only of robbing Catalani prior to his death.

In 1880 12,354 Italians emigrated to the United States and by 1890 the number had reached 52,003. Italian immigrants poured into the United States in ever-increasing numbers: 100,135 by 1900, 230,622 by 1903 and 285,731 by 1907. From 1903 until the First World War, an average of 200,000 Italians emigrated to the United States every year. New York became the second most populous Italian city after Naples. One quarter of the population of America's largest city – more than half a million people – was Italian. The figure rose to one million in 1920. Most of the immigrants were from the south of Italy and Sicily. Out of their depth in their new land, and bewildered by its strange language, the incomers flocked together in the 'Little Italies' of New York, Philadelphia, Chicago, New Orleans and other cities. In many cases, people moved *en masse* from their towns and villages and set up almost identical communities in their adopted land. They brought with them their old loyalties – and their old vendettas.

Mafiosi and Camorristi often entered the United States on false papers. These were supplied by the Italian authorities, who were only too happy to rid themselves of criminals

'Mafiosi and Camorristi often entered the US on false papers supplied by the Italian authorities, who were happy to rid themselves of criminals'

they could neither catch nor imprison.

Even the criminals who had been jailed and released had good reason to travel to America, because ex-convicts in Italy were placed under *Sorveglianza Speciale* – 'Special Surveillance'.

There was a strict nightly curfew, they were barred from visiting drinking establishments, they could not carry guns, they had to report regularly to the police and they had to seek permission to take employment. Criminals who were on the run also found sanctuary in the United States.

In their closed communities, the Italian immigrants found themselves living in a microcosm of the society they had left behind in Europe. Sicilians in particular clung to their

Gang members in an alley known as 'Bandits' Roost' in Manhattan's Little Italy around 1900. Only the brave passed by this way

distrust of the law and authority in general.

The US mafiosi exploited this fact by turning to their traditional occupation – extortion. They preyed on bankers, barbers, contractors and merchants – fellow Italians who already understood the ways of the Mafia.

On 3 August 1903 Nicolo Cappiello, a prosperous contractor living in Brooklyn, received a letter:

> *'If you don't meet us at Seventy-second Street and Thirteenth Avenue, Brooklyn, tomorrow afternoon, your house will be dynamited and your family killed. The same fate awaits you in the event of your betraying our purposes to the police.'*

The note was adorned with three black crosses surmounted by a skull and crossbones, and signed '*Mano Nera*', or 'Black Hand'. When Cappiello tried ignoring the letter, he got another one two days later:

> *'You did not meet us as ordered in our first letter. If you still refuse to accede to our terms, but wish to preserve the lives of your family, you can do so by sacrificing your own life. Walk in Sixteenth Street, near Seventh Avenue, between the hours of four and five tonight.'*

The letter concluded with the line: 'Beware of *Mano Nera*'.

Opposite: **Typical New York market at the turn of the last century: early banana importers and distributors were mostly Italian immigrants**

After Capiello had ignored this second letter, several men visited his house. Some were old friends and others claimed to be agents of the Black Hand. They told him that a price of $10,000 had been put on his head, but if he handed over $1,000 they would do their best to persuade the blackmailers to spare his life. Capiello delivered the money on 26 August, but within a few days four men returned for an additional $3,000. Convinced that the gang intended to rob him of his entire fortune – which amounted to around $100,000 – bit by bit, he went to the police. Five men – three friends and two Black Handers – were arrested, tried and convicted.

Capiello and the extortionists were Neapolitan and Brooklyn was largely the province of the Camorra. Until then, the newspapers had written about the criminal activities of *La Società Cammorristi*, the *Mala Vita* and the Mafia. But after 1903 the *New York Herald* and the Italian-language *Bollettino della Sera* began to use 'Black Hand' as a catch-all term for Italian criminal gangs. Respectable Italian-Americans preferred it that way.

For some time, they had petitioned the newspapers not to bandy the name 'Mafia' around because it applied only to a small band of Sicilian thugs.

From then on, letters demanding money were regularly adorned with a crudely drawn Black Hand symbol. On 24 May 1911, Tano Sferrazzo of 307 East 45th Street in New York City received a letter that read:

'Various men of my society as you know well will demand some money because we need it in our urgent business and you finally have never consented to satisfy us to fulfil your duty… Money or death. If you want to save your life, tomorrow 25 May at 10 pm take the Third Avenue train, go to 129th Street, walk towards Second Avenue. Walk as far as the First Avenue Bridge that leads you to the Bronx, walk up and down the bridge for a while; two men will then present themselves and will ask you, where are you going? To them you will give not less than $200. Signed Black Hand.'

Sometimes the extortionists were apprehended. This letter appeared as an exhibit in the trial of Salvatore Romano, who had been indicted, along with Antonio Lecchi and Pasquale Lopipero, at the Court of General Sessions in New York on 22 September 1911. Another letter was equally threatening:

'This is the second time that I have warned you. Sunday at ten o'clock in the morning at the corner of Second Street and Third Avenue, bring three hundred dollars without fail. Otherwise we will set fire to you and blow you up with a bomb. Consider this matter well, for this is the last warning I will give you. I sign the Black Hand.'

Black Hand gangs also appeared in Pittsburgh. On 27 May 1908, Mr G. Satarano received a menacing letter:

'You please you know the company of the Black Hands. I want you to send $2,000, all gold money. You will find some friend to tell you about it. Send it to head man, Johnstown. We don't want you to tell no person that talks too much. If you report about this letter we will kill you. We will kill you with a steel knife. You and your family. Give me money right away, for I want to use it. And remember, keep it quiet – Black Hand.'

That same year, an Italian-American in Philadelphia also received a threatening letter, which read:

'You will never see Italy again if you do not give $1,000 to the person that pinches you after he salutes you. (I say one thousand.) Carry it with you always and remember I am more powerful than the police and your God – Black Hand.'

In St Louis, another immigrant received a letter that addressed him as 'Dear Friend'. It read:

'This is your second letter. You did not answer or come. What have you in your head? You know what you did in Brooklyn and that you went to Italy and then returned to Dago Hill [the Italian quarter] to hide yourself. You can go to hell to hide but we will find you. It will be very bad for you and your family if you do not come to an understanding. So come Thursday night at ten o'clock. If you do not come we will cut you up in pieces. How will that be, you dirty false face. So we will wait for you. Best regards, good bye.'

Under these words were two pictures – one of a man in a coffin; the other of a skull and crossbones. There was also a postscript:

'So this will be your appearance if you do not do as we tell you. The way the blood flows in my veins is the way the blood will flow from your veins.'

In Chicago 'Most Gentle Mr Silvani' received an anonymous letter from the Black Hand that read:

'Hoping that the present will not impress you too much, you will be so good as to send me $2,000 if your life is dear to you. So I beg you warmly to put them on the door within four days. But not, I swear this week's time not even the dust of your family will exist. With regards, believe me to be your friend.'

Detective Lt. Petrosino (left), Inspector Carey and Inspector McCafferty escorting Mafia hitman 'Petto the Ox' (2nd left) to court

Usually these letters used a mockingly deferential form of Sicilian, though sometimes they were more blunt:

'You got some cash. I need $1,000. You place the $100 bills in an envelope and place it underneath a board in the north-east corner of 69th Street and Euclid Avenue at eleven o'clock tonight. If you place the money there you will live. If you don't, you die. If you report this to the police, I'll kill you when I get out. They may save the money, but they won't save your life.'

Most people paid up. They felt that the authorities could not protect them, especially if they spoke no English. Instead, they armed themselves. According to a police report: 'Ninety-five out of every one hundred Italians are armed with some sort of deadly weapon.'

THE ITALIAN SQUAD

The police took the situation seriously in New York. First of all, they set up a special Italian Squad under Detective Sergeant Giuseppe 'Joe' Petrosino. An immigrant from the Salerno region, Petrosino had dealt with extortion rackets earlier in his career with the NYPD. In 1902, he accompanied prosperous wholesale tailor Stephen Carmenciti to a rendezvous at which he had arranged to pay $150 to an extortion gang calling itself the 'Holy House'. Carmenciti lived on East 103rd Street in the Italian neighbourhood

of East Harlem. Two Holy House members – Carmine Mursuneso of East 106th Street and Joseph Mascarello of East 107th Street – were arrested, but they were acquitted when Carmenciti refused to testify, fearing for the safety of his family.

'Most people paid up. They felt that the authorities could not protect them, especially if they spoke no English'

Petrosino rose to prominence in 1903, when the corpse of a man with 17 stab wounds was found in a barrel on a piece of waste ground near Little Italy, on Manhattan's Lower East Side. His throat had been cut so savagely that his head was nearly severed from his body and his genitals had been cut off and stuffed into his mouth. The case was reminiscent of a murder that had taken place in the previous year, when the partially dismembered body of a grocer named Giuseppe Catania had been found in a sack on the beach at Bay Ridge, Brooklyn. The murderers had not been found, but they seemed to be exacting revenge for a trial in Palermo, some 20 years before, where Catania's testimony had sent a number of men to jail for 20 years.

The body in the barrel was not immediately identified, but Petrosino believed that he had seen the victim at the trial of counterfeiter Giuseppe De Priemo. The detective travelled to Sing Sing to interview the prisoner. When De Priemo was shown a photograph of the dead man he immediately identified him as his brother-in-law, Benedetto Madonia. The victim had been a member of a counterfeiting gang who had been in hiding in Buffalo, Upstate New York.

He had recently visited De Priemo with a man named Tomasso Petto – known on the streets as 'Petto the Ox'.

According to De Priemo, his brother-in-law always carried a watch with distinctive markings. The watch was found after a number of pawn shops had been checked. It had been pawned for one dollar by a man answering to Petto's description. When the police went to question Petto in the Prince Street Saloon he pulled a stiletto, but the officers managed to grapple him to the ground. Once he was restrained, they searched him and found another knife, a pistol and a pawn ticket for the watch. Petto denied murdering Madonia or getting the watch from him.

An Italian named 'John' had given it to him, he said. He did not know the man's last name, though they had been friends for three years.

According to the Secret Service – then part of the United States Treasury – Madonia's role in the counterfeiting ring had been to distribute forged bills to dealers around the country. However, he had been suspected of double-dealing after some of the money had gone missing, so he had been put to death.

The gang was led by Giuseppe Morello – aka 'Clutch Hand', 'Little Finger' or 'One Finger Jack', because his deformed right hand resembled a claw – and his underboss and brother-in-law Ignazio Saietta – aka 'Lupo the Wolf'. Both men were from Corleone, Sicily. Giuseppe's two brothers, Nicolo and Ciro were also gang members, along with their two half-brothers Ciro and Vincenzo Terranova. Tomasso Petto was the gang's strong-arm man. Physically powerful but not very bright, Petto could not resist stealing the only valuable – and traceable – item in Madonia's possession. He went on trial for murder, but the case against him collapsed after Madonia's wife, son and brother-in-law refused to testify against him. In August 1904 he was implicated in the kidnapping of Morello gang member Vito Laduca, though no charges were ever filed. The following year, he was found dead outside his home. There were 62 stab wounds in his body. Giuseppe De Priemo – then out of jail – was suspected, but no arrests were made and Petto's murderer was never found.

Another man who was involved with the Lupo-Morello gang was the Sicilian Don Vito Cascio Ferro. When he first travelled to New York in 1901 he was already a seasoned criminal. It was said that he was the first mafioso 'of respect' to set foot in America, so he was feted in Sicilian-American criminal circles. He brought with him the *u pizzu*, or 'protection money', concept – no one who could afford it was to escape paying *u pizzu* to the *Onorata Società*. Ferro was a known counterfeiter, who was suspected of being involved in the murder of Madonia. He fled to New Orleans in order to escape arrest and then went back to Sicily, leaving Lupo [*Cont.* p.47]

Vito Cascio Ferro, the first mafioso 'of respect' to set foot in America

Mugshots of Ignazio Saietta, aka 'Lupo the Wolf'

LUPO THE WOLF

Ignazio Lupo was born in Palermo, Sicily to Rocco Lupo and Onofrio Saietta. He was known as Ignazio Lupo and 'Lupo the Wolf', but also Ignazio Saietta, his mother's maiden name. From the age of ten he worked in a grocery store in Palermo. At the tender age of 21, he shot and killed a business rival named Salvatore Morello. Although he was convicted of 'deliberate and willful murder', Lupo had already fled.

Arriving in New York in 1898, he opened a grocery store on East 72nd Street in Manhattan with a cousin named Saietta. After a brief sojourn in Brooklyn, he moved back to Manhattan where he set up a small import business on Prince Street. Across the road was a saloon owned by Giuseppe 'the Clutch Hand' Morello, another immigrant from Corleone, Sicily and head of the Morello crime family.

In 1903, Lupo married Salvatrice Terranova,

half-sister to Morello. Her brothers Vincenzo and Ciro Terranova and Nicolo Morello were also part of the Morello gang. Lupo became underboss. His name – Lupo – means 'wolf' in Italian, so that's why he was known as Lupo the Wolf. Together they became the leading Mafia family in New York City.

Lupo developed a fearsome reputation and was suspected of being involved in at least 60 murders. Legend has it that he ran a 'murder factory' in a stable on East 108th Street in New York with Giuseppe Morello, where victims were hung on meat hooks or burned in furnaces. It has also been reported that honest members of New York's Italian community crossed themselves when his name was mentioned. Despite all of this, he would only serve time for counterfeiting and lesser crimes.

He was the last person seen with Brooklyn grocer Giuseppe Catania, whose body was found in the river under the Bay Bridge with its throat cut from ear to ear. The body was badly mutilated. No warrants were issued in the case.

Only a year later he was arrested along with other members of the Morello gang when Benedetto Madonia's body was discovered in a barrel of sawdust. Barrel murders were a speciality of the Morellos. A search of his apartment revealed a dagger and three pistols, but most members of the gang, including Lupo, were released due to lack of evidence. Tomasso Petto was the only gang member to be charged with Madonia's murder, but the prosecution failed to secure a conviction due to the unwillingness of Madonia's family to testify.

Two years later, Petto was found dead outside his home with 62 stab wounds in his body.

Lupo was re-arrested on counterfeiting charges, but these too were eventually dropped. In January 1904, he was arrested for carrying a concealed weapon described as 'a big blue-barreled revolver of the latest kind'. Later that year, he was arrested for the kidnapping of Antonio Bozzuffi, the son of wealthy Italian banker John Bozzuffi who had previously had dealings with the Morello gang. However, brought face to face with

'Lupo developed a fearsome reputation and was suspected of at least 60 murders'

Lupo in court, Antonio Bozzuffi said he did not recognize him.

THE WOLF VANISHES

In December 1908, Lupo's business went bankrupt in suspicious circumstances and he disappeared along with Antonio Passananti, another member of the Morello gang who had paid Lupo large sums of money while running his wholesale wine business into the ground. When the wine importer Salvatore Manzella then went bankrupt, he claimed his business had collapsed because Lupo had been extorting large amounts from him over the previous three years. Manzella had been afraid for his life if he did not keep paying up.

Lupo hid out under the name Joseph La Presti in upstate New York, not far from the farm of Morello-gang forger Salvatore Cina. After moving back to Brooklyn, Lupo walked into the receiver's office with his attorney and claimed that his business had failed because he had been blackmailed. He was arrested for extortion in the Manzella case, but was released when Manzella failed to appear at his arraignment. Lupo was then immediately re-arrested for counterfeiting.

In 1909 Giuseppe Morello and Ignazio Saietta were sentenced to 30 years for counterfeiting and 12 smaller fry were sentenced to shorter terms. The $2 and $5 bills that had been printed in Salerno had been shipped over to New York in boxes that supposedly contained olive oil, cheese, wine, macaroni, spaghetti and other prime Italian produce. They were sold for 30 or 40 cents apiece to agents who then distributed them round the country. Both Lupo and Morello were paroled in 1920, just in time to benefit from the opportunities offered by Prohibition. By the 1930s, though, Lupo's status as a mobster had diminished. Barred from the Mafia leadership, and stripped of all of his operations by the Commission, he was left with a small Italian lottery in Brooklyn. To get back something of his former lifestyle, he began running a protection racket involving bakers. This led to him ending up in jail again. He died in 1947, a shadow of his former self, almost unnoticed by the world.

With a shotgun wrapped in a towel, Vito Corleone (Robert De Niro) eliminates the much-feared Don Fanucci in The Godfather, Part II. The character of New York racketeer Don Fanucci, who terrorizes the inhabitants of Little Italy in the movie, was loosely based on Lupo the Wolf

The Italian Squad of the New York City police force headed by Detective Lt. Petrosino (standing left in hat). They did undercover work against the Mafia. All members were Italian, with the exception of a single Irish cop who spoke Italian

and the others to continue the collection of the *pizzu*. Ferro took with him a photograph of Joe Petrosino, which he carried in his wallet.

Despite the formation of the NYPD Italian Squad, extortion remained rife in New York.

When two plain-clothed policemen were killed by a young man freshly arrived from Palermo, the police combed the city for Italians carrying concealed weapons.

The county coroner received a letter of protest signed by 200 Italian women, who complained that Italians were being picked on. It was the Sicilians who were to blame, they said in the letter:

> *'The Sicilian is a blood-thirsty man. He belongs to the Black Hand. He exercises blackmail, is a dynamiter and, by blood, a coward... We must suppress the immigration from Sicily. Then you will see if the Italians in America will not be mentioned any more criminally.'*

But most New York policemen, being Irish, could not tell the difference between a Sicilian and an Italian.

Petrosino's Italian Squad enjoyed some successes. During the round-up, it arrested Enrico 'Erricone' Alfano, 'Generalissimo of the Camorra', who was deported back to Italy to stand trial. As a result, Petrosino was hailed by the newspapers as the 'Italian Sherlock Holmes'. The arrest caused 'an enormous sensation among the members of the Neapolitan Camorra' and it was reported that 'the Black Hand condemned Petrosino to death'.

At 6.30 pm on 23 January 1908, a bomb went off outside the bank of Pasquale Pati & Sons at 240 Elizabeth Street in the heart of Manhattan's Little Italy. The bank had an unusual gimmick – it displayed $40,000 in gold and bills behind its windows in order to prove its solvency. Although the bomb blew out the windows, their valuable contents were recovered. Pati's neighbour Paolo Bononolo, who owned the building adjoining the bank, 242 Elizabeth Street, thought the bomb was directed at him because he had received several Black Hand letters. He also owned a tenement at 512 East 13th Street, which adjoined a house in which a bomb had gone off two days earlier. Then Pati finally admitted that he had received Black Hand threats too. They had come from Lupo the Wolf.

After the bombing a meeting was called at 178 Park Row, above the offices of the *Bollettino della Sera*. Taking their cue from the White Hand Society, which had been formed three months earlier in Chicago in order to combat the Black Hand, those attending set up the Associazione de Vigilanza e Protezione Italiana. The editor of the *Bollettino*, Frank L. Frugone, became the association's president and it soon had over 300 members. It did no good. On 1 February, the Senna Brothers grocery store at 244 Elizabeth Street was blown up and three nights later a bomb exploded in the hallway of La Sovoia restaurant and saloon at 234 Elizabeth Street. Then on 26 March the

bombers hit Bononolo's bank at 246 Elizabeth Street. The bomb blew a hole in the wall of Bononolo's quarters, burying his wife and two daughters under the debris. All of the windows in the building above were smashed and the terrified tenants ran out into the street, where the crowds were crying, *'Mano Nera!'*

Bononolo gave a shaky statement to the police:

> *'This has happened because I did not heed their warnings. For five years, scarcely a month has gone by when I have not received one or more Black Hand letters. They asked for sums ranging from $1 to $1,000, but nothing ever happened, and recently I had paid no attention to their threats. This is to warn me. Next time I shall be killed.'*

Even so Bononolo was refused permission to carry a pistol. Meanwhile Pati had armed himself. He had made representations to the Mafia that he should be left alone, due to his connections to the Camorra. When some men arrived at the bank asking for money, Pati and his son shot and killed one of them. Pati was congratulated by the police as a 'brave man and the first of his race to face the Black Hand issue squarely', but then he secretly relocated – for fear of Mafia reprisals, it was said. In fact, he made off with the deposits after a run on the bank had been prompted by the Black Hand threats. It was then discovered that the

Joseph Petrosino

man he had shot had actually been an innocent depositor, who was there to withdraw his money. Four years later, the police were still looking for Pati.

In Chicago, the White Hand Society gained the support of the city's leading Italian-language newspapers, *L'Italia* and *La Tribuna Italiana Transatlantica*, as well as the Italian ambassador in Washington and the Italian minister of foreign affairs in Rome. Its organizers declared 'war without truce, war without quarter' against the Black Hand

and looked forward to the day when there would be *Mano Bianca* groups 'in all the cities that contain large Italian colonies, which suspect the existence of Mafiosi or Camorristi in their midst'. Indeed, a group of leading White Handers had a shoot-out with some Black Handers in the Pennsylvania Railroad yards in Pittsburgh on 9 December 1907.

By January 1908, the White Hand Society decided to claim that they had driven ten of the worst Italian criminals out of Chicago.

However, the *Mano Nera* fought back. On 28 February, the president of Chicago's White Hand Society, Dr Carlo Volini, received a sinister letter:

> 'The supreme council of the Black Hand has voted that you must die. You have not heeded our warnings in the past, but you must heed this. Your killing has been assigned and the man waits for you.'

Volini was not killed, but support for the *Mano Bianca* soon began to ebb away. The Italian immigrants no longer believed that they could be any more effective than the authorities. Then an Irish outfit calling themselves the White Hand Gang fought the Italians for

> *'Dynamiting was a favourite Black Hand method of enforcement. There was a great deal of construction work in New York and some workmen used to help themselves to sticks of dynamite'*

control of the waterfront in Brooklyn. They disappeared after their leaders were killed in a docklands 'speakeasy'. The police suspected Al Capone, who was visiting from Chicago.

In July 1908, Petrosino's men arrested a man they claimed was the Black Hand's principal bomb-maker and they raided a saloon on East 11th Street which was supposedly the gang's headquarters. But it soon became clear that the problem was far from over. Only a few days later the following letter appeared in *The New York Times*:

> 'My name is Salvatore Spinelli. My parents in Italy came from a decent family. I came here eighteen years ago and went to work as a house painter, like my father. I started a family and I have been an American citizen for thirteen years. I had a house at 314 East Eleventh St and another one at 316, which I rented out. At this point the "Black Hand" came into my life and asked me for seven thousand dollars. I told them to go to hell and the bandits tried to blow up my house. Then I asked the police for help and refused more demands, but the "Black Hand" set off one, two, three, four, five bombs in my

houses. Things went to pieces. From thirty-two tenants I am down to six. I owe a thousand dollars interest that is due next month and I cannot pay. I am a ruined man. My family lives in fear. There is a policeman on guard in front of my house, but what can he do? My brother Francesco and I do guard duty at the windows with guns night and day. My wife and children have not left the house for weeks. How long can this go on?'

Dynamiting was a favourite Black Hand method of enforcement. There was a great deal of construction work going on in New York at the time and some of the workmen used to help themselves to sticks of dynamite. As late as 1917, long after strict laws had been introduced, the police commissioner warned that the 'workmen at the 14th Street subway are getting away with two or three sticks of dynamite daily'.

The Pittsburgh police did somewhat better than their New York counterparts. They were credited with 'the break up of the best organized blackmailing bands in the history of the Black Hand'.

In one of their raids, they had found 'carefully written by-laws, with a definite scale of spoil division and with many horrible oaths'. On another raid they found what appeared to be a 'school of the Black Hand', where two young Italians had 'actually been practising with daggers on dummy figures'.

Giuseppe Petrosino, now a lieutenant, then learnt of a new, more sophisticated extortion method that was spreading through the community. A shopkeeper in Elizabeth Street told him that three men entered his shop and informed him that they knew he had received Black Hand letters. They offered him protection from the Black Hand threats for a small, regular fee. This was a typical Mafia tactic. *U pizzu* had arrived in New York.

New York was treated to a colourful Italian visitor in the summer of 1908, when Mafia politician Don Raffaele Palizzolo visited the city. He was hailed as 'the political boss of Palermo; indeed, the uncrowned king of Sicily' and was greeted as an honoured guest by the Italian community. However, Palizzolo's power was waning in Sicily, so his visit to New York was a fund-raiser. Although he posed as an enemy of the Black Hand and the Mafia, stories circulated that he was actually the 'king of the Mafia'. Palizzolo's freedom of action was curtailed when Petrosino shadowed him and he headed home sooner than planned. According to New York's mayor, George B. McClellan, Palizzolo shook his fist at Petrosino, who had followed him to the pier, and shouted: 'If you ever come to Palermo, God help you.'

PETROSINO'S ASSASSINATION

During 1908, New York police commissioner Theodore A. Bingham compiled a record of all Black Hand-related crimes. Some 424 cases had been reported, including 44 bombings. As

DOCKS   POLICE

HARBOR PRECINCT A

Joseph Petrosino encountered the long arm of the Black Hand when he ventured to Palermo. Here, a guard of honour salutes his courage with drawn batons, as his funeral cortege sets off for the graveyard

a result, a new undercover squad was formed under Petrosino. It was funded by some of the Italian merchants who had been extortion targets.

According to Petrosino, the only way to thwart the Mafia was to cut it off at the roots, so he decided to go to Sicily. However, the news leaked out prematurely. On 5 February 1909 *L'Araldo Italiano*, a New York Italian-language

newspaper, published a story about Petrosino's forthcoming departure, in which it listed his itinerary and wished him well in his mission. Then on 20 February *The New York Times* reported that Petrosino had been given a roving commission to wipe out the Black Hand and had disappeared from police headquarters.

The *Herald* followed by reporting that he was on his way to Sicily. Petrosino left the country a few days later under an assumed name, but the purser on the Italian liner *Duca di Genova* recognized him. When he reached Rome he met the editor of *L'Araldo*, who was in Italy to cover the aftermath of the earthquake that had hit Messina on 28 December 1908. The two men went to a restaurant where they bumped into Giovanni Branchi, the former Italian consul general in New York.

The United States ambassador arranged a meeting with Francesco Leonardi, the head of the national police force, who furnished him with a letter of introduction to his subordinates, in which he ordered them to furnish Petrosino with all possible assistance. Petrosino then made a short detour to Padula, his home town, where his brother showed him an Italian newspaper that carried a reprint of the *Herald* story. His secret mission was not so secret any more. On the train to Naples he was recognized by a captain in the *carabinieri*. From there, Petrosino took a steamer to Palermo, arriving on the morning of 28 February.

He registered at a hotel under a false name and then called the United States consul, William H. Bishop. Bishop was the only person he confided his plans to, though he had made contact with a supposed 'informant' in Palermo. The police lieutenant then went

> *'Petrosino registered at a hotel under a false name... then made an entry in his notebook on 11 March: "Have already met criminals who recognized me from New York. I am on dangerous ground"'*

to a bank and opened an account in his own name, so that he could have his mail directed there. After that he went to the courthouse and started searching the criminal records for wanted mafiosi. His aim was to have them deported.

He made an entry in his notebook on 11 March: 'Have already met criminals who recognized me from New York. I am on dangerous ground.'

On the following day he made another note: 'Vito Cascio Ferro, born in Sambuca Zabut, resident of Bisaquino, Province of Palermo, dreaded criminal.'

After having dinner at a café, where he was seen talking briefly to two men, he went to the Piazza Marina. A few minutes later, shots were heard. Petrosino's dead body was found near the Garibaldi Gardens, in the centre of the square.

News of Petrosino's assassination caused a sensation in New York. After his body was shipped back, an estimated 250,000 people turned out for his funeral. But the popular acclaim surrounding Petrosino did little to dent the power of the Black Hand. A few weeks later a personal friend of Petrosino's, Pioggio Puccio, was also shot and killed. Puccio had helped organize Petrosino's funeral, followed by a benefit for Petrosino's

Five-time Italian PM Giovanni Giolitti, who was in his third term at the time Petrosino was killed. His lax administration was described by historian Gaetano Salvemini as 'the prime ministry of the underworld'

widow at the Academy of Music. The benefit itself was not a great success because 'the majority of those who promised to take part at the last moment sent excuses'. In fact, almost everyone involved with the benefit, including Puccio, had received threatening letters. Soon afterwards, an Italian grocer on Spring Street received a letter demanding money, which read: 'Petrosino is dead, but the Black Hand still lives.' He took it to the police.

Days later, the tenement in which he lived was burnt down with the loss of nine lives.

In Sicily, William H. Bishop felt that he was being 'delayed and hindered' by the authorities in his efforts to investigate the murder. However, in April he issued a report calling for the indictment of 15 men, including Vito Cascio Ferro, who had risen to become the *capo di capi* in Palermo since his return from the United States. His system of collecting *u pizzu* had been extended to those outside commerce. Everyone – lawyers, landowners, civil servants – paid this 'tax' to the Mafia one way or another. Even lovers had to pay a *cannila*, or 'candle', tribute, which allowed the man to walk up and down beneath his sweetheart's window.

Just before the murder of Petrosino, two of the men connected with the Barrel Murder (pages 39-40) had returned unexpectedly to Sicily. They were soon arrested. Vito Cascio Ferro was picked up a few days later.

However, Ferro had a cast-iron alibi supplied by the Honourable Domenico De Michele Ferrantelli, who had recently been elected to the chamber of deputies. Ferrantelli was a supporter of Giovanni Giolitti, whose administration was described by historian Gaetano Salvemini as 'the prime ministry of the underworld'. The suspects were freed on bail and two years later all charges were dismissed.

Don Vito Cascio Ferro's criminal career continued to flourish until 1926, when he fell foul of Mussolini. Unwilling to compromise with the Fascists, he was arrested on trumped-up charges. Throughout his short trial Don Vito maintained a disdainful silence.

At the end of the proceedings he was asked whether he had anything to add. His statement was courteous but dismissive.

'Gentlemen, since you have been unable to find any evidence for the numerous crimes I really have committed, you are reduced to condemning me for the only one I have not.'

While he was in prison he was treated with respect by the other inmates and he made it his business to help needy prisoners and their families. Much of the respect that was given to Don Vito came from the one and only murder he did admit to – that of Giuseppe Petrosino.

'In my entire life,' he said, 'I killed only one person and that I did disinterestedly.'

Later, the whole story came out. On the day of the murder, Don Vito had been invited to lunch by Deputy Ferrantelli. In the middle of the meal, the Mafia *capo* absented himself for a short time. Borrowing his host's carriage he drove to the Piazza Marina, where he waited outside the Courts of Justice.

When Petrosino arrived, Don Vito despatched him with a single shot then got back into the carriage and returned to Ferrantelli's house to finish lunch. When Don Vito was later charged, Ferrantelli testified that he had been in his home all the time, so Petrosino's killer walked free.

Don Vito saw it as a matter of honour that he should kill Petrosino personally. Although other candidates have been put up, it is now widely accepted that while Passananti and Costantino had perhaps orchestrated the situation it was Don Vito who actually pulled the trigger.

The Mafia *capo di capi* was finally sentenced to life imprisonment in 1930. While he was incarcerated he carved a motto in one of the passages leading to the prison infirmary: *'Vicaria, malatia i nicissitati: si vidi lu cori di l'amicu'* ('In prison, sickness or need, one finds the heart of a true friend'). For many years, these words gave comfort to inmates and warders alike.

It is not known how Don Vito died. According to anti-Mafia journalist Michele Pantaleone, he died 'of a broken heart after a few years'. Officially, he died in 1945 at the age of 83. However, Petrosino's biographer Arrigo Petacco believes that he died in 1943, after the Allied invasion of Sicily.

'Fascism had collapsed, the Allied armies were moving north along the peninsula and the Flying Fortresses were attacking without respite. So the prison authorities had ordered

THE MORELLO–TERRANOVA FAMILY

The police stand over another gang-war victim, Naples, c.1890. At this point, organized crime had existed in Italy for nearly a hundred years

Calogero Morello, Giuseppe's father, married Angela Piazza in Corleone, Sicily, in 1865, but he died in 1872, leaving Giuseppe fatherless at the age of five. In the following year Giuseppe's mother married Bernardo Terranova, also from Corleone, and they had four children – a daughter named Salvatrice and three sons, whose names were Vincenzo, Ciro and Nicolo.

Bernardo was a 'man of honour' and a soldier in the Corleonesi clan. Giuseppe followed in his footsteps in the 1880s. He rose quickly through the ranks, but when he became implicated in a counterfeiting investigation in 1893 the Morello–Terranova family emigrated to the United States, settling in East Harlem, New York. In the late 1890s, Salvatrice married Ignazio Saietta – aka 'Lupo the Wolf' – a Black Hand extortionist also from Corleone, who joined the Morello crime family as Giuseppe's underboss. As soon as they were old enough, Giuseppe's Terranova brothers – Vincenzo ('Vincent'), Ciro ('The Artichoke

King') and Nicolo ('Nick') – joined what was originally known as the 116th Street Mob or Morello gang.

They worked in a counterfeiting ring with Cascio Ferro, which specialized in printing $5 bills in Sicily and smuggling them into the United States. At the same time they were implicated in the Barrel Murders. Then in 1909, Giuseppe Morello and Lupo the Wolf went to jail. While Giuseppe was away, the gang was run by his half-brothers – Vincenzo, Ciro and Nicolo Terranova.

The Morello gang was the forerunner of the Genovese crime family, the oldest of New York's 'Five Families'. One of its early members was the ambitious Giuseppe 'Joe the Boss' Masseria. It was also to become the breeding ground for future leaders of the Five Families, such as Charles 'Lucky' Luciano, Frank 'the Prime Minister' Costello, Vito Genovese and Giuseppe 'Joe Adonis' Doto.

the evacuation of the penitentiary of Pozzuoli, which was too exposed to bombardment. In a few hours all the inmates were moved except one; Don Vito, who was forgotten in his cell. He died of thirst and terror in the gloomy, abandoned penitentiary, like the villain in some old serial story.'

For many years afterwards it was an honour to occupy Don Vito's prison bed. Other inmates

treated it with respect. Later, it would be occupied briefly by another famous mafioso Don Calogero Vizzini, better known as Don Calò, who lent Mafia assistance to the Allied invasion.

Meanwhile, back in New York the Secret Service rounded up the Lupo–Morello gang. In 1909 Giuseppe Morello and Ignazio Saietta were sentenced to 30 years for counterfeiting and 12 smaller fry were sentenced to shorter terms. Morello's sentence was commuted in

1920 and Saietta was released on parole in the same year. His sentence was conditionally commuted in 1921 and he went back to Italy for around two years on 'family business'. When he returned to the United States the Mafia doors were closed to him. After running minor rackets he ended up in jail again in 1935 and was released in 1946.

THE MAFIA-CAMORRA WAR

While Lupo and Morello and many of their gang were in jail, a Neapolitan named Giosue Gallucci became 'King of Harlem's Little Italy'. He ran all of the gambling and prostitution in the area and was thought to be worth $500,000. Giosue lived just two blocks from the Morellos at 318 East 109th Street, above a bakery and stables, where his brother Gennaro had been killed in September 1909. His sister joined him in claiming that Gennaro had been shot by an unidentified gunman, but the police received letters that accused Giosue himself of being the killer.

On 2 September 1912 Gallucci's bodyguard, Antonio Zaraca, was shot dead while playing cards in a café on 109th Street. Aniello 'Zopo the Gimp' Prisco was arrested for the crime. He had already been tried and acquitted for the murder of the widow Pasquarelli Spinelli at the so-called 'murder stable' on 108th Street,

'Buonomo usually wore a chainmail vest, but on 13 April he went out without it. Unfortunately, it was the day on which he was shot. As he died he made a grim prediction…'

which was the scene of a series of murders during the Mafia-Camorra war. As usual, Prisco walked free. It was the fourth time he had been acquitted on a murder charge, usually because of the non-appearance of a prosecution witness.

But he was still answerable to Gallucci.

On 12 December Prisco was due to meet Gallucci at a barber's shop belonging to the Neapolitan Del Gaudio brothers on East 104th Street. Gallucci did not turn up, but he sent word that Prisco should meet him at his bakery on 109th Street. When Prisco arrived, he was shot dead by Gallucci's nephew, John Russomano. Gallucci told the police that Russomano had shot Prisco in self-defence because Prisco was blackmailing him. Russomano was released without charge.

In February 1913 Russomano was shot in the arm outside his home, which was across the road from the bakery on 109th Street, and his bodyguard, Capalongo, was killed. The unidentified gunman got away, but Amadio Buonomo, a friend of Prisco's, was thought to have been responsible. Buonomo usually wore a chainmail vest, but on 13 April he went out without it. Unfortunately, it was the day on which he was shot in Jefferson Park. As he died he made a grim prediction: 'I knew they would get me, but my friends will get them…

this feud will go on until all of them are wiped out of existence.'

The police rounded up 40 Italians, including Gallucci, Russomano and Gallucci's bodyguard, Generossi 'Joe Chuck' Nazzaro, who was also known for wearing a steel vest. They were all charged with carrying concealed weapons. Gallucci was the only one who walked free. Russomano went down for seven years, while Nazzaro was locked up for ten months. When he got out, Nazzaro sold his café on 108th Street to Carmine Mollica. Soon after, Mollica was killed. Nazzaro was arrested again, but was later released.

Tension grew between Gallucci and the Del Gaudio brothers and then Nicolo Del Gaudio was shot and killed on 114th Street. Gallucci was blamed, but it later appeared that the Morello gang had something to do with the killing. Understandably, Nicolo's brother Gaetano did not feel safe after his brother had died so he hired Johnny 'Lefty' Esposito as his bodyguard. Esposito had previously worked for Gallucci.

Several attempts were made on Gallucci's life but he escaped unharmed until 7 May 1915. Shortly before 10 pm, Gallucci was in the coffee shop that he had just bought for his son Luca when four men came in and started shooting. Gallucci was hit in the neck and Luca was hit in the stomach. Giosue Gallucci died that evening in hospital and Luca only survived until the following day, in spite of the fact that he had managed to stagger back to the family home.

It seems that the Morellos had planned the killings with the help of Buonomo's uncle, Pellegrino Morano, who was the head of a Neapolitan gang on Coney Island. The killers were thought to be Joe 'Chuck' Nazzaro, Tony Romano and Andrea Ricci, a powerful figure in the Brooklyn Camorra. Giosue Gallucci's gambling and prostitution empire then passed to the Morello gang. With Giuseppe Morello and Lupo the Wolf in jail, it was being run by Giuseppe's half-brothers, Vincenzo, Ciro and Nicolo Terranova.

At that time relations were good between the East Harlem Mafia, led by the Morellos, and the Brooklyn Camorra – particularly the Navy Street gang that was being run by Leopoldo Lauritano and Alessandro Vollero. Each year the Morellos would head over to Brooklyn for a 'smoker' hosted by Andrea Ricci.

Following the murder of Giosue Gallucci, the Morellos planned to take over all of the gambling in the whole of Manhattan. They had already driven local gaming boss Joe

> *'Gallucci was in the coffee shop that he had just bought for his son Luca when four men came in and started shooting. Gallucci was hit in the neck and Luca was hit in the stomach...'*

DeMarco out of East Harlem. DeMarco had tried to kill Nicolo Terranova and now the Morellos were trying to kill him. First of all he was shot in the neck on 112th Street, but surgeons in the Harlem Hospital managed to save his life. Then two men with sawn-off shotguns attacked him while he was in a barber's shop on East 106th Street. More than a dozen slugs entered his body, but again he survived.

DeMarco finally took the hint and moved downtown, where he muscled in on several of the Brooklyn gangs' gambling joints around Mulberry Street. In July 1916, Nicolo and Ciro Terranova, Steve LaSalle and Giuseppe Verizzano travelled to Navy Street to discuss DeMarco's murder. The Morellos' gunmen were too well known by DeMarco to get near him but Verizzano, who worked for DeMarco, said he could get Navy Street hitmen into his new gambling joint on James Street.

On the afternoon of 20 July, Tom Pagano, John 'The Painter' Fetto and Lefty Esposito – who was now with the Navy Street gang – arrived at James Street where the doorman Nick Sassi – another friend of the Navy Street gang – let them in. DeMarco was playing cards. It was Verizzano's job to point him out to the gunmen, while Sassi and Rocco Valenti, another Navy Street accomplice, were on hand to help them escape. However, Pagano and Esposito misread Verizzano's signal and they shot and killed Charles Lombardi instead. Verizzano rectified the mistake by taking out DeMarco himself and the gunmen then escaped through a window into Oliver Street.

That evening Nicolo, Ciro and Vincenzo Terranova, Steve LaSalle and Verizzano travelled to Navy Street to congratulate Leopoldo Lauritano. They gave him $50 to pass on to the gunmen. However, bad blood was brewing between the Brooklyn camorristi and Manhattan's mafiosi. Camorra leader Pellegrino Morano had been running a numbers racket in Harlem, but the Morellos were demanding such a high rake-off that it was not profitable. Added to that Alessandro Vollero, another Brooklyn camorristi, had been upset by the death of

Opposite: **The Navy Street gang in the backyard of their Brooklyn HQ: they were Neapolitans, one of two major branches of the Camorra active in New York City in 1916**

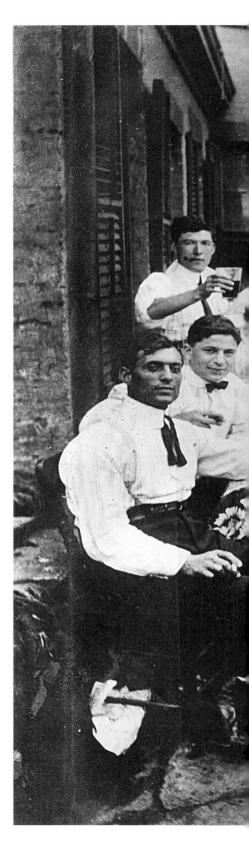

Nicolo Del Gaudio. Together they decided to kill the Morellos and take over the rackets in Harlem.

On 7 September 1916, Nicolo Terranova and Camillo 'Charles' Ubriaco were in Brooklyn for a meeting with the Navy Street gang when they were ambushed on Myrtle Avenue. Terranova was shot dead by Tom Pagano and Ubriaco was killed by Tom Carillo and Lefty Esposito. One of the detectives sent to investigate was Michael Mealli, who was on the Navy Street payroll. He arrested Rocco Valente, who had been found in a pool hall with a loaded pistol. Alessandro Vollero was also arrested. He appeared in a police line-up, but was later released.

On 5 October 1916, Ricci surrendered himself to the police, but only to give himself an alibi for the following day, when Alphonso 'The Butcher' Sgroia and Mike Notaro shot Verizzano dead in the Italian Gardens restaurant in the Occidental Hotel on Broome Street. A week later the body of Joe DeMarco's brother Salvatore was found on a piece of waste ground on Washington Avenue in Astoria. His throat had been cut and his head had been smashed in. The newspapers reported that he was about to tell the police all he knew about his brother's killers.

In just over a month four associates of the Morello gang had been murdered by the Camorra in Philadelphia, which led the Navy Street gang to think that they could take over the Morellos' rackets in East Harlem. But the Terranovas were not letting go so easily. On 8 November 1916, Esposito was killed on 108th Street. Then on 30 November, Gaetano Del Gaudio was serving coffee to two men in his restaurant on 1st Avenue when he was hit by a shotgun blast through the window. As he lay dying in Flower Hospital he said he knew his killer, but he refused to name him.

After the murder of Joe DeMarco on 20 July, Joe Nazzaro had aligned himself with the Navy Street gang. But Antonio 'Tony The Shoemaker' Paretti said that he had seen Nazzaro talking to the Morellos. On 16 March 1917 Nazzaro was lured out to the city of Yonkers by Alphonso Sgroia and the Paretti brothers, on the pretext that they were going to kill Frank Fevrola for speaking to the police. Instead Fevrola, Sgroia and the Parettis killed Nazzaro. His body was found under a trolley car on 16 March 1917. There was a bullet hole in his chest and another in his right shoulder. The corpse had been dragged 100 feet (30 m) by the vehicle before it stopped and it took half an hour to disentangle it. The police said Nazzaro was 'one of fifty or more men whose lives were sacrificed in a long-standing feud which it had been hoped ended on 7 May 1915, when Gallucci and his son Luca were murdered'.

In May 1917, Ralph 'The Barber' Daniello was in court facing robbery and abduction charges. Although he was acquitted he decided that it was not safe to stay in New York, so he eloped to Reno with his 16-year-old girlfriend, Amelia Valvo. As a member of the Navy Street gang he had helped set up the ambush of

BRONX

MANHATTAN

CIRO TERRANOVA

GUISEPPE *(Joe the Boss)* MASSERIE

QUEENS

110TH ST. and 1 ST AVi

FRANKIE YALE (YALE)

EAST 14TH ST

BROOKLYN

HUDSON RIVER

NEW JERSEY

ANTHONY *Little Augie* CARFANO

RED HOOK

NAVY ST.

UNION ST. and 4TH AVE

SCARFACE AL CAPONE

BAY RIDGE

RICHARD *(Peg Leg)* LONERGAN

CHARLES *(Vannie)* HIGGINS

W. L. *(wild Bill)* LOVETT

Crime map of New York featuring notorious racketeers – by the publication date (1933), five of those pictured had taken a 'one-way ride' (died) and Capone was in Federal prison

Nicolo Terranova and Charles Ubriaco and he had killed a man in a drug deal gone wrong.

But he soon ran short of cash in Reno so he asked his boss, Alessandro Vollero, to help him out. When Vollero failed to reply to any of his letters, Daniello grew bitter. His next letter was to the New York police. By the end of November 1917 he was back in Brooklyn telling the police everything he knew. His testimony cleared up 23 unsolved murders, including those of Nicolo Terranova and

Giosue Gallucci, which had been jointly committed by the Morellos and the Navy Street gang. He also revealed that most of Brooklyn's Italian police officers were taking bribes. This included Mike Mealli, who was reduced in rank and sent back out on the beat as a patrolman.

Vollero was condemned to death for the murders of Terranova and Ubriaco, though this was reduced to life imprisonment on appeal. Pellegrino Morano, leader of the

Coney Island gang, was handed a sentence of 20 years to life and Leopoldo Lauritano was jailed for 20 years after being found guilty of manslaughter. Released after seven and a half years, he was re-arrested on a charge of perjury and spent another five years in Sing Sing prison. Sgroia was sentenced to 12 years in Dannemora prison for the manslaughter of Nick Terranova. However, he went on to testify against Fevrola and Paretti, so his sentence was commuted and he was deported back to Italy. Esposito and Notaro were each given a prison sentence of from six to ten years.

Frank Fevrola was sentenced to death, largely because of the testimony his wife gave against him, but he was granted a retrial after his wife said she had been threatened and bribed by the police. He was reprieved seven hours before his scheduled execution and the punishment was eventually commuted.

Aniello Paretti was also sentenced to death, but the court of appeal ordered a retrial and the district attorney then dropped the case. He was released after 20 months in jail.

His brother Antonio Paretti fled to Italy, but he returned to the United States in March 1916.

Unlike Aniello he did not manage to escape the electric chair. He was put to death on 17 February 1927. One of the last men to visit him was the up-and-coming gangster Vito Genovese.

Vincenzo and Ciro Terranova were then arrested, along with a number of their followers. Most of them, including Vincenzo, were released after 'influence' was brought to bear, but Ciro stood trial for the murder of Verizzano on the strength of Daniello's testimony. At Ciro's trial, his attorney Martin Littleton argued that Daniello's evidence showed that the Morellos and the Navy Street gang regularly co-operated in criminal ventures.

They were, in fact, one gang. Under United States law no one could be convicted solely on the testimony of an accomplice, yet as a member of the Navy Street gang Daniello was exactly that – an accomplice. The prosecutors were nonplussed by this reasoning so Ciro Terranova walked free, receiving a rapturous reception back on East 116th Street.

In June 1918, Ralph Daniello pleaded guilty to his part in the murder of Nick Terranova. In recognition of his testimony in the other cases he was given a suspended sentence, but he begged the judge to keep him behind bars until the rest of the gang were jailed. A year after he was released, he got into a fight in a Coney Island bar and was sentenced to five years for assault.

When he was released he moved to Newark, where he bought a bar. Less than a month after his release, he was sitting in his saloon when a stranger approached.

'I've got you now,' the stranger said, pulling a gun. He fired three times, hitting Daniello in the belly. The former informant died in agony while the gunman sped away in a waiting car.

Without Daniello, the Camorra would almost certainly have won the Mafia–Camorra war, but now the leading camorristi were in

THE MAFIA RIOTS IN NEW ORLEANS

In 1881, a young detective named David C. Hennessy was investigating the high rate of homicide in New Orleans. His investigations led him to Giuseppe Esposito, who had been a member of the gang that had kidnapped John Forester Rose back in Sicily. After travelling to New Orleans via New York, he now led a band of 75 cut-throats who specialized in kidnapping and extortion. Esposito was arrested and deported to Italy where he was convicted of 18 murders and 100 counts of kidnapping and murder. He was sentenced to life imprisonment with hard labour. Soon afterwards, Hennessy was dismissed from the force.

He made a triumphant return, however, when he was appointed police chief after a victory by reformers in an 1888 election.

Under Hennessy's leadership the police began investigating instances of violence on the New Orleans waterfront. They discovered that two rival Mafia gangs – the Provenzanos and the Matrangas – were fighting for control. Hennessy's plan was to isolate one of the gangs, so the Provenzanos were arrested and tried for an attack on the Matrangas. Although the Provenzanos were convicted, they were granted a second trial after evidence of perjury was uncovered. The Provenzanos believed that Hennessy favoured the Matrangas and threats were made on his life. Shortly before the new trial, Hennessy was assassinated using the traditional Mafia method – a shotgun blast. His last words were said to be: 'The Dagos did it.'

jail and the others had fled. New York was left to the Mafia.

Hundreds of Italian immigrants were arrested and 19 were indicted. Allegations spread that the Sicilian Mafia was trying to take over the city.

When those indicted were acquitted there was a riot, urged on by the mayor's campaign manager, lawyer William S. Parkerson, who said:

'What protection or assurance of protection is there left us when the very head of our Police Department, our Chief of Police, is assassinated in our very midst by the Mafia Society and his assassins are turned loose on the community? Will every man here follow me and see the murder of Hennessy avenged? Are there men enough here to set aside the verdict of that infamous jury, every one of whom is a perjurer or a scoundrel?'

A mob stormed the jailhouse and six of the accused Italians were lynched, along with five other co-defendants who had not even been tried. But it did not stop there. Italy broke off diplomatic relations with the United States and there was even talk of war.

Chapter 3

PROHIBITION

When the Volstead Act banning the manufacture and sale of alcoholic beverages was passed in 1919, organized crime in America went mainstream. Until that point the mafiosi in the form of the Black Hand gangs simply preyed on other Italians, but after Prohibition came into being it is estimated that 75 per cent of the population of the United States became clients of the bootleggers. It was big business. There had been 16,000 saloons in New York before the Volstead Act. These were replaced by 32,000 'speakeasies' (illegal drinking establishments). Britain's alcohol exports to Canada rose six-fold and it was said that more intoxicating liquor was sent to Jamaica and Barbados than the population could possibly drink in a hundred years. During five years of Prohibition, 40 million gallons of wine and beer were seized. In 1925 alone, 173,000 illegal stills were impounded. This did nothing to stem the supply. And with the price of alcohol first doubling and then climbing to ten times what it had been before Prohibition, there was plenty of profit for the bootleggers.

But the Mafia did not have a monopoly on bootlegging. During Prohibition around 50 per cent of the bootleggers in New York were Jewish and only 25 per cent were Italian.

However, with the end of the Mafia–Camorra war the Sicilian Mafia families in

Right: **The 'wet block' in Congress. The 'dries', whipped on by the Methodists, the Baptists and other religious groups, believed drinking was not only a social evil but also a deadly sin. The 'wets' proclaimed that it was not the duty of government to enforce morality**

Left: **Clients of a New York speakeasy – there were an estimated 32,000 illegal drinking establishments in the city by 1930**

America allowed the Neapolitans to join their ranks and younger gangsters even worked with mobsters of other races. And it was Prohibition that secured the power and influence of the Mafia throughout American society for decades to come.

CAPONE'S EARLY DAYS

The man who symbolized the era was Al Capone. He was not a Sicilian and he did not belong to the Camorra, although he was of Neapolitan stock. In fact, he nursed a deep hatred of the Sicilians after his barber father became a target for Black Hand extortion. The young Capone hunted the two Sicilian culprits down and shot them dead.

Capone's parents had arrived in New York from Naples six years before he was born. After dropping out of school Capone fell under the influence of Johnny Torrio, a saloon and brothel keeper in Brooklyn. Torrio's lieutenant, Frankie Yale, ran the Harvard Inn in Coney Island and Capone went to work there as a doorman.

One evening Capone told gangster Frank Gallucio's sister that she had a nice ass. Gallucio demanded an apology but Capone refused, so the gangster pulled out a knife and slashed Capone's left cheek. The wound, which needed 30 stitches, gave Capone the nickname 'Scarface'. Gallucio sat down with the New York bosses after the incident and Capone was warned not to seek retribution for the injury.

Torrio's cousin Victoria Moresco was

America's most famous gangster Al Capone in characteristic pose

married to 'Big Jim' Colosimo. Together they ran a chain of brothels in Chicago. When a Black Hand gang led by 'Sunny Jim' Cosmano attempted to extort money from them, Colosimo called for Torrio's help. Within a month ten members of Cosmano's gang were dead, but he continued to demand money. Colosimo then agreed to pay him $10,000. However, when Cosmano and his Black Handers arrived to collect the money, Torrio and eight of his gunmen were waiting for them. There was a blaze of gunfire. Cosmano survived a shotgun blast to the stomach, inflicted by Torrio himself. He later fled the city after being smuggled out of the hospital.

In 1918 Colosimo persuaded Torrio to move permanently to Chicago so he could run the brothels there, leaving Frankie Yale to run the operation in New York. Torrio moved Colosimo's sleazy brothels upmarket, but behind the scenes the girls were kept there by force and he would not hesitate to kill them if they went to the police.

Capone was under investigation for murder in New York at the time, so he followed Torrio to Chicago and went to work as a doorman at

Ruthless gangster Johnny Torrio who was into bootlegging in a big way

the Four Deuces, a bordello. It is thought that he first caught syphilis there.

In 1920 Colosimo divorced Torrio's cousin and married Dale Winter, a singer at a club he owned. With the advent of Prohibition, Torrio was eager to move Colosimo's operation into bootlegging, but Dale was against it. Torrio did not take kindly to Colosimo's refusal. Just one month after the wedding, Torrio called Colosimo and asked him to come to the club. When he arrived, Colosimo was gunned down. Capone was the first to be suspected but the murder had actually been carried out by Frankie Yale. He avoided arrest because a waiter who had seen the hit refused to identify him.

With Colosimo out of the way, Torrio went into the bootlegging business in a big way, with Capone as his second-in-command. There were only two Italian bootlegging gangs at the time. Most of them were Irish and one was made up of all-American gangsters. From the beginning, however, Torrio's operation was one of the biggest. Astutely, he went into partnership with Joseph Stenson, the son of Chicago's leading brewing family. The company had converted its brewery to make 'near beer' – that is, beer with the alcohol removed – but Stenson supplied Torrio with the real stuff.

One of Torrio's competitors was Dean O'Banion, an Irish-American who had won a fearsome reputation in the newspaper circulation wars, where thugs were hired to beat up news vendors in order to keep rival publications off the news-stands. Together with two Polish Catholics – George 'Bugs' Moran and Earl 'Hymie' Weiss – O'Banion also imported whiskey from Canada. In order to give his operation a respectable front he bought into a florist's opposite Holy Name Cathedral, which also did good business at gangsters' funerals. Under an agreement with Torrio, O'Banion controlled the North Side of Chicago. He also supplied some of the thugs that supported Al Capone's mayoral candidate in the 1924 Cicero elections.

Chicago's Sicilian West Side was dominated by the six Genna brothers, who came from Marsala. After arriving in Chicago in 1910, the 'terrible Gennas' quickly established a reputation for violence. In 1920, they bought a licence to produce and sell industrial alcohol but they made whiskey and other spirits instead, paying the inhabitants of Little Italy $15 a day to run home stills. Their cheap liquor was coloured with coal-tar and creosote and fortified with wood alcohol and fuel oil, which sometimes made it lethal.

As if the Gennas' reputation were not fearsome enough, they also employed two enforcers, Alberto Anselmi and Giovanni Scalise, who had entered America illegally after a purge of the Sicilian Mafia. It was said that they greased their bullets with garlic, which was thought to give gangrene to anyone who was not killed instantly.

Few lived long enough to find out, however. Like the other bootleggers, the Gennas depended on the assistance of corrupt officials and police officers, who were among the regular customers of their liquor store.

The agreement between Torrio and O'Banion held up for three years and then Irish gangs began hijacking Torrio's trucks and smashing up his speakeasies. In an attempt to placate O'Banion, Torrio offered him some territory in Cicero and a quarter share in a casino called The Ship. O'Banion then persuaded the owners of a number of speakeasies in other parts of Chicago to move to Cicero, thereby altering the balance of power. Meanwhile the Gennas began moving in on O'Banion's territory on the North Side. In response, O'Banion ordered Angelo Genna to pay off the $30,000 debt he owed at The Ship. When he refused, O'Banion began hijacking the Gennas' deliveries.

The Gennas wanted to eliminate O'Banion, but first of all they needed the green light from the *Unione Siciliana*, a benefit society for Sicilian immigrants that worked as a front for the Mafia. But the president of its Chicago chapter, Mike Merlo, tried to keep the peace. Meanwhile O'Banion killed John Duffy, a Philadelphia hitman who had brought unwelcome attention to the gang by killing his own wife. He then tried to put the blame on Torrio and Capone.

At the time O'Banion was selling his stake in an illegal brewery to Torrio for $500,000, but while the deal was going through the police raided the brewery and Torrio was arrested. He already had convictions for breaking the Prohibition laws, so he faced a jail sentence.

On top of that, he had just paid half a million dollars for a useless brewery and O'Banion refused to compensate him.

Mike Merlo then died of cancer, which made it easier to go after O'Banion, so Torrio and the Gennas planned a joint hit. Frankie Yale was called in. Pretending to be the president of the New York chapter of the *Unione Siciliana*, he visited O'Banion's flower shop to order flowers for Merlo's funeral. On the following day he returned with Alberto Anselmi and Giovanni Scalise, who shot O'Banion dead on the spot. Chicago's gangsters then spent another $10,000 on flowers, including a basket from Al Capone.

'Hymie' Weiss was seen to cry like a baby at O'Banion's funeral. He then took charge of O'Banion's North Side gang and swore to revenge his dead boss. Figuring that Capone was behind the hit, Weiss, George 'Bugs' Moran and Vincent 'The Schemer' Drucci ambushed Capone's car outside a South Side restaurant, injuring his chauffeur. They were using the Thompson machine guns ('Tommy guns') that had recently been introduced to the Chicago underworld. Capone was unscathed but shaken, so he put in an order for a bulletproof car. A 1928 Cadillac, it would have 3,000 pounds of armour plating under the standard body, inch-thick bulletproof

windows, a siren and a flashing red light. Painted the same colour as Chicago police vehicles, it is also thought to have been the first private car with a police-band radio receiver. After the attack on Pearl Harbor it was used by President Roosevelt, who feared assassination by enemy agents.

> *'Frankie Yale visited O'Banion's flower shop to order flowers for Merlo's funeral. The following day he returned with Alberto Anselmi and Giovanni Scalise, who shot O'Banion dead on the spot'*

Weiss and his gunmen then went after Torrio. As he was returning from a shopping trip with his wife, gunfire from a .45 automatic and a .12-gauge shotgun hit him in the chest, arm, groin, legs and jaw. Torrio was lying injured on the pavement when Moran tried to finish him off by putting a .45 to his temple and pulling the trigger, but the gun misfired. At that point the police arrived and the would-be killers fled. From his hospital bed, Torrio handed over his entire operation to Capone. Throughout the police investigation, Torrio observed the *omertà*. He served time in jail for Volstead violations and then retired to Italy.

Weiss and the North Side gang were also pursuing the Gennas for their part in O'Banion's murder. On 26 May 1925, Angelo Genna was out driving when a large open car pulled up alongside his vehicle. In it were Weiss, Moran and Drucci, who immediately opened fire. Genna's car careered into a lamppost and a dozen more shots were fired into his defenceless body.

Nevertheless, the dying Genna was still conscious when he reached hospital. A policeman asked him who had attacked him but he said nothing.

Two and a half weeks later, Moran and Drucci were injured in a shootout with Alberto Anselmi, Giovanni Scalise and Mike 'The Devil' Genna. They were making off in a car driven, it is thought, by Samuzzo 'Samoots' Amatuna, when they were spotted by the police. In the ensuing car chase, the driver of Genna's car swerved to avoid a truck and the vehicle smashed into a lamppost.

When the police caught up with them, two patrolmen were cut down by gunfire. The gangsters then ran off, but Mike Genna was cornered. He turned his shotgun on another officer, but the gun failed to fire. Hit in the leg, he still managed to jump through the basement window of a nearby house.

As the police entered he fired a random shot from his .38, but it was all over – he was already dying from loss of blood on the way to hospital.

Even so, he had enough strength to kick the ambulance driver in the face. 'Take that, you son of a bitch,' he snarled.

After two more officers had died of their wounds, Anselmi and Scalise were arrested. Speaking through a translator they claimed

'On election day 1924, Capone brought in 200 thugs to beat up the Democrats; 100 police were drafted in to quell the riot'

they had acted in self-defence. They blamed the firefight on Genna, who was not there to defend himself. Nevertheless, Anselmi and Scalise were convicted of the manslaughter of Olsen and were sentenced to 14 years in prison. While they were inside they were beaten up and an attempt was made to poison Scalise with cyanide. A defence fund was set up by fellow Sicilians and Angelo Genna's brother-in-law Henry Spingola was killed when he refused to contribute. At subsequent trials the verdict was overturned and they were acquitted. They went to work for Al Capone as soon as they were freed.

Meanwhile, life was getting difficult for the Gennas. On 8 July 1925 Tony Genna was set up by his bodyguard Antonio 'Cavallero' Spano, who lured him to the corner of Grand Avenue and Curtis Street, where he was killed by two gunmen. Spano was killed the following year on the orders of Sicilian-born Giuseppe 'Joe' Aiello. His body was shipped back to Italy.

The surviving Gennas soon left town. James Genna went back to Italy with Johnny Torrio, but he was arrested for stealing jewels from the statue of the Madonna di Trapàni in the basilica of Maria Santissima Annunziata in his native Sicily. He served time with hard labour on Favignana, a small island off the west coast of Sicily. When he returned to Chicago in

1930, he was driving along with four former Genna gang members when another car pulled up alongside their vehicle and sprayed them with bullets. One of the gang members was killed and two others were injured. James Genna fled to Calumet City, where he died of natural causes in the following year.

TAKING CONTROL

With the Gennas now out of the picture, Capone united the Italian and Sicilian factions and took control of the South and West Sides of Chicago. Meanwhile Weiss, Moran and what was left of the O'Banion mob allied themselves with Jewish, Polish and German gangs so they could hold the North Side. Capone also held on to the political influence that had been built up by Colosimo and Torrio. One of his allies was Illinois governor Len Small, who pardoned or paroled over 1,000 convicted bootleggers and other felons. While he was governor, Small was indicted for embezzling $600,000 and running a money-laundering scheme when he had been state treasurer. His acquittal perhaps owed something to the fact that four of the jurors were subsequently hired as state employees.

Another of Capone's cronies was 'Big Bill' Thompson, the Republican mayor of Chicago from 1915 to 1923. During the Prohibition era he declared himself to be as 'wet as the Atlantic Ocean', which went down well with many people, especially bootleggers. However, when he abolished the Chicago police force's Morals Squad, leaving the city wide open to vice, he was ousted by Democrat reformer William Dever, who rode into power in 1923 on the backlash. Dever then targeted Capone, who simply transferred the remainder of his business to the self-governing suburb of Cicero. Capone had 161 saloons there, together with dozens of gambling houses and brothels. On election day in 1924, Capone brought in 200 thugs to beat up the Democrats. A hundred policemen were drafted in to quell the riot and a gunfight broke out. Al Capone escaped, but his brother Frank was killed and his cousin Charlie Fischetti was arrested. Nevertheless, Capone hung on to Cicero.

That November, Capone's only rival in Cicero, Eddie Tancl, was killed in a contrived gunfight with Myles O'Donnell and James Doherty. On 27 April 1926, Assistant State Attorney William McSwiggin unsuccessfully prosecuted O'Donnell and Doherty and the two killers walked free. Suspiciously, he went out for a drink with them in Cicero that same night, but the party was ambushed outside the Pony Inn. McSwiggin and two members of the O'Donnell gang were killed.

There were five grand jury investigations. Capone was a suspect, but he denied any involvement in McSwiggin's murder. He made a statement to the waiting reporters.

'Of course, I didn't kill him; I like the kid. Only the day before he was up at my place and when he went home I gave him a bottle of Scotch for his

old man. I paid McSwiggin and I paid him plenty, and I got what I was paying for.'

And pay he did. Out of his $100 million a year turnover, $30 million went in bribes to the police, public officials and politicians. In 1927, he gave 'Big Bill' Thompson $260,000 so that he could run for mayor again. Thompson beat Dever by 83,000 votes. Capone also added journalists to his payroll. In June 1930, the *Chicago Tribune's* top crime reporter, Alfred 'Jake' Lingle, was shot dead in the subway station of the Illinois Central Railroad. His editor swore revenge, but then it was discovered that Lingle had been bankrolled by Capone for years. He was a regular guest at Capone's Miami home and he had died wearing a diamond-encrusted belt buckle given to him by Capone.

Capone also curried favour with the public by doing good deeds. He supported striking miners in Pennsylvania and paid for the repair of a church roof. He also moved into labour unions and legitimate businesses, bringing people outside the Italian community into the Capone syndicate. He even tried to control the *Unione Siciliana*, which he could not join, being a Neapolitan. And he was unrepentant about his bootlegging.

'You can't cure thirst by law. I make my money by supplying a public demand. If I break the law my customers, who number hundreds of the best people in Chicago, are as guilty as I am. The only difference is that I sell and they buy... When I sell it is called bootlegging. When my patrons serve it on a silver tray, it's hospitality.'

WAR WITH THE NORTH SIDERS

The war between Capone's syndicate and the North Siders rumbled on. On 3 August 1926, the body of Anthony Cuiringione, aka Tommy Ross, was found in a cistern. The North Siders had kidnapped him several months before and tortured him to death, in an attempt to obtain information on Capone's routine. A week later, there was a shoot-out between Weiss, Drucci and some of Capone's men in broad daylight in front of the Standard Oil building. No one was killed, but Drucci was arrested.

On 20 September 1926, Capone was dining in the Hawthorne Hotel, his headquarters in Cicero, when eight carloads of North Siders drove by, spraying the restaurant with bullets. Capone emerged unscathed after being thrown to the ground by his bodyguard Frank Rio, but a veteran of the gunfight outside the Standard Oil building, Louis Barko, was hit, and a women got a piece of broken glass in her eye. Capone paid her medical bills and settled the account for repairs to the hotel.

Al Capone then tried to broker peace by setting up a meeting between Weiss, Drucci and his own representative Antonio 'The Scourge' Lombardo. Capone made his own contribution by telephone, which led some to

Mugshots of Al Capone and his trusted lieutenant, hitman Frankie Rio, a prime suspect in the St Valentine's Day massacre

believe that he was scared to meet Weiss face to face. Weiss demanded that Capone hand over Anselmi and Scalise for their part in the killing of O'Banion, but Capone refused. 'I wouldn't do that to a yellow dog,' he declared. Weiss then stormed out of the meeting and Capone decided that he must die.

On 11 October 1926, Weiss was machine-gunned on the steps of Holy Name Cathedral. Hit by ten bullets, he died on his way to hospital. One of his henchmen also died and three others were injured – they were only saved because the Tommy gun jammed on the thirty-ninth bullet. Drucci died on 4 April 1927. He was shot in the back of a squad car while trying to wrestle a gun from a detective who had arrested him after he had ransacked an election office.

Capone's residence and headquarters was the Metropole Hotel until 1928 and then he moved to the Lexington, one block to the north. It contained a shooting gallery that his men used for target practice, secret vaults where he kept his money and dozens of secret passages and stairways, including one behind his medicine chest. These led to hidden tunnels that ran to local taverns and whorehouses and provided escape routes in case of a raid by the police or rivals.

In 1929 Capone was able to celebrate the New Year in his new home on Palm Island, Miami. Not yet 30 years old, he was the undisputed king of the Chicago underworld. He ran his business in Chicago through daily telephone calls to his trusted aide, Jake 'Greasy Thumb' Guzik. Together they were

The body of Earl 'Hymie' Weiss lies lifeless outside Holy Name Cathedral

planning the final act in the Outfit's takeover of Chicago – the elimination of 'Bugs' Moran. Capone was still in Florida on 14 February when a Miami official called to ask him how much he had paid for his Palm Island home. Unwittingly, the official had provided the perfect alibi.

In the garage of the SMC Cartage Company on 2122 North Clark Street, six of Moran's top men were waiting for a delivery of whiskey. Capone's men, some disguised as policemen, then turned up but Moran was late. When he finally arrived he assumed the place was being raided, so he quietly made off. Capone's men then lined all of Moran's henchmen up against the wall and machine-gunned them. It seems that they thought Moran was one of them.

One of the corpses was that of Dr Reinhardt Schwimmer, an optician who appears to have got a kick out of hanging around with gangsters. The men in uniform then escorted their non-uniformed colleagues out of the garage as if they were being arrested.

When the police arrived, top Moran gunman Frank Gusenberg was still alive. Although he knew he was going to die, he refused to talk. But there was little doubt about who was responsible. 'Only Capone kills like that,' Moran declared.

At first the police were afraid that they might be implicated. After all, uniformed men had been seen at the garage. But they quickly found the dismembered remains of the Cadillac that had been used by the gunmen.

It was being stored in a burnt-out garage belonging to friends of Capone. 'Machine Gun' Jack McGurn was the first to be arrested. He had earlier been machine-gunned by Frank Gusenberg and had vowed revenge. McGurn claimed to have been with his [*Cont. p.85*]

'Bugs' Moran

Antonino Joseph 'Tony' Accardo AKA Big Tuna, Joe Batters

JOE BATTERS

Tony Accardo came to fame as Al 'Scarface' Capone's enforcer. Capone was impressed when he watched Accardo kill two would-be traitors with a baseball bat, saying: 'But this kid's a real Joe Batters.' However, Accardo was also respected for his intelligence. It was said that he had 'more brains before breakfast than Al Capone had all day'. In a criminal career that lasted over 70 years, he never did any time in jail.

Accardo's parents were from Sicily, emigrating to the United States the year before he was born. He grew up on Chicago's West Side. Dropping out of school at 14, he became a delivery boy for a florist, then a clerk in a grocery store. These were the only two legitimate jobs he had in his lifetime.

His first arrest – for a motor vehicle violation – came in 1922. The following year, he was fined $200 for disorderly conduct in a pool hall where gangsters hung out. Two more convictions for disorderly conduct brought him to the attention of Al Capone, then well on his way to becoming Chicago's crime czar.

Accardo joined the Circus Café Gang, whose members included 'Screwy' Claude Maddox, Anthony 'Tough Tony' Capezio and Vincenzo DeMora, aka 'Machine Gun' Jack McGurn. The gang became allied to Capone's Chicago Crime Syndicate.

After delivering moonshine from the home

stills in Little Sicily to the speakeasies around Chicago, Accardo quickly graduated to pick-pocketing, mugging, auto theft, burglary, assault and armed robbery, and was arrested several times.

CAPONE'S HITMAN

DeMora graduated to Capone's inner circle as a hitman and when Capone sought to expand his crew he recommended Accardo, who quickly showed his usefulness by saving Capone's life. When an assassination attempt was made by the North Side Mob, Accardo pulled Capone down and shielded him with his body. As a result, he became his personal bodyguard.

In later years, Accardo boasted of participating in the St Valentine's Day Massacre, where seven members of Bugs Moran's North Side Gang were wiped out. Although he was never officially tied to the murders, he was seen in the lobby of the Lexington Hotel on Michigan Avenue – Capone's headquarters – with a machine gun. Accardo was arrested soon afterwards, but no one was ever charged. He certainly carried out other hits for Capone.

When two of the other gunmen, Giovanni Scalise and Alberto Anselmi, tried to take over, Capone invited them to a formal dinner with other gangsters. After the speeches, Accardo sadistically beat them to death with a baseball bat. This was the occasion on which he earned his sporting soubriquet.

PLAYING THE SLOTS

When Capone went to jail for income-tax evasion in 1931, Accardo was given his own gang that helped run gambling in Chicago and Florida. He quickly rose to number seven in the Chicago Crime Commission's 'public enemy' list.

Paul 'the Waiter' Ricca took over the Chicago Outfit in 1943, naming his friend Tony Accardo as his underboss. Together they ran the mob until Ricca's death in 1972, expanding their operations to Texas, Arizona, Nevada, Colorado and California, as well as Florida, Cuba and the Bahamas. They also pulled out of areas such as labour racketeering, which were attracting too much attention from the authorities. Instead the Outfit moved into slot machines, which appeared in petrol stations, restaurants and bars in the area controlled by the Outfit, as well as in the casinos in Las Vegas.

SINATRA'S CONTRIBUTION

In 1946, Accardo headed the Outfit's delegation to the meeting of the Commission called by Meyer Lansky in Havana. They took over the top four floors of the Hotel Nacional. Lucky Luciano was there. Delegates paid tribute with envelopes stuffed with cash, totalling $200,000, which Luciano said he would invest in the Nacional's casino. Frank

Sinatra flew in to Cuba with Accardo, it is said, carrying a suitcase containing a million dollars for Luciano.

In 1957, Accardo was at the historic Mafia summit at Apalachin, upstate New York, to divide up the operations of Albert Anastasia following his assassination. It was held on the country estate of Joseph 'Joe the Barber' Barbara. However, the police noticed a large number of expensive cars with out-of-state licence plates turning up and so they staged a raid. Accardo and Sam Giancana fled through the woods. Giancana later complained that he tore up a $1,200 suit on some barbed wire and ruined a new pair of shoes.

For some time in the late 1950s and early 1960s, Giancana handled the day-to-day running of the Outfit. He had begun his career in the mob as Accardo's driver and they had been arrested together for questioning in a kidnapping case. But his connection with John F. Kennedy gave him too high a profile to be boss, so Ricca and Accardo stepped in and deposed him.

KEEPING HIS HAND IN

Even while Giancana was in charge, Accardo still kept his hand in as an enforcer. He was thought to have been responsible for the killing of William 'Action' Jackson, a juice man or debt collector for the mob, who had possibly become an FBI informant. Jackson was stripped naked and beaten with a baseball bat and then he was hung by his rectum from a meat hook. His knees were broken, a cattle prod was applied to his genitals and his body was punctured with ice-picks. Then he was left for three days before he died.

When Ricca died, Accardo brought in his buddy Joe Aiuppa, who had been boss of the rackets in Cicero. Meanwhile Accardo began to spend more time with his wife Clarice, a Polish-American former chorus girl, in their 22-room mansion – which boasted two bowling alleys, an indoor swimming pool, a pipe organ, a tub carved from a single piece of Mexican onyx and gold-plated bathroom fittings said to be worth half-a-million dollars.

'A cattle prod was applied to his genitals and his body was punctured with ice-picks'

CHAMPAGNE LIFESTYLE

The Internal Revenue Service investigated Accardo and in 1960 he was convicted of tax evasion, specifically for deducting $3,994 as operating expenses for his sports car, a red Mercedes-Benz 300SL. Accardo claimed to have used the car in the course of his employment as a salesman for a Chicago beer company. The jury found this hard to believe and convicted him. He was fined $15,000, and sentenced to six years in prison. The

Singer and actor Frank Sinatra (second from left) with Carlo Gambino (second from right) at a gathering in September 1976

conviction was overturned on appeal.

Accardo did little to hide his personal wealth. He had lavish parties at his palatial home, with fountains gushing champagne and violinists mingling with the guests. He also enjoyed country sports. A phalanx of Cadillacs would take Accardo and his cronies out to South Dakota, where they would shoot pheasants with machine guns. And he got his nickname 'Big Tuna' for a 400-pound fish he caught.

Accardo also liked indoor sports; it could make him vulnerable. Once he was taken for $1,000 by a pool hustler who wedged the table and tweaked his game accordingly. When the trick was spotted,

Accardo blamed himself for being such an easy dupe. 'Let the bum go,' he ordered. 'He cheated me fair and square.'

Accardo appeared before US Senate committees three times, carrying a cane with a tuna-fish handle. During his testimony, he invoked the Fifth Amendment, which protected citizens against self-incrimination, 172 times – including in answer to the question: 'Have you any scruples against killing?' He continued to deny any involvement in organized crime, while admitting that he knew leading figures in the Mafia. The only time he admitted breaking the law was years before when he had gambled.

Tony Accardo's daughter, Linda, at her wedding to Michael Palermo in 1961: the wedding was such a lavish affair that one investigator later wrote if you were an Outfit guy and didn't get an invitation, you had a problem

WRONG HOUSE BURGLED

In January 1977, while Accardo was away, his home was broken into by some foolhardy burglars. When Accardo was told, he ordered Tony Spilotro, Aiuppa's most savage enforcer, to handle the case. The word got out and thieves and cat burglars fled the city, fearing they may be mistaken for the culprits. It took some time for Spilotro's men to crack the case, but this only made things worse because Accardo's temper continued to escalate.

Then a year after the break-in, Cook County began to reverberate with what they called 'trunk music'. The first burglar was found shot dead, another had been castrated and a third had had his face burned off with an acetylene torch. In each case, the coup de grace had been delivered with a bullet to the head or a slashed throat. For good measure, two of the executioners had also been killed. There were no further break-ins at Accardo's property.

Accardo died at the age of 86 of natural causes, a rare thing for a crime boss. He now lies in a mausoleum at the Queen of Heaven Cemetery in the Chicago suburb of Hillside, Illinois.

Under investigation for labour racketeering, Accardo takes the oath before the Senate Government Affairs Committee

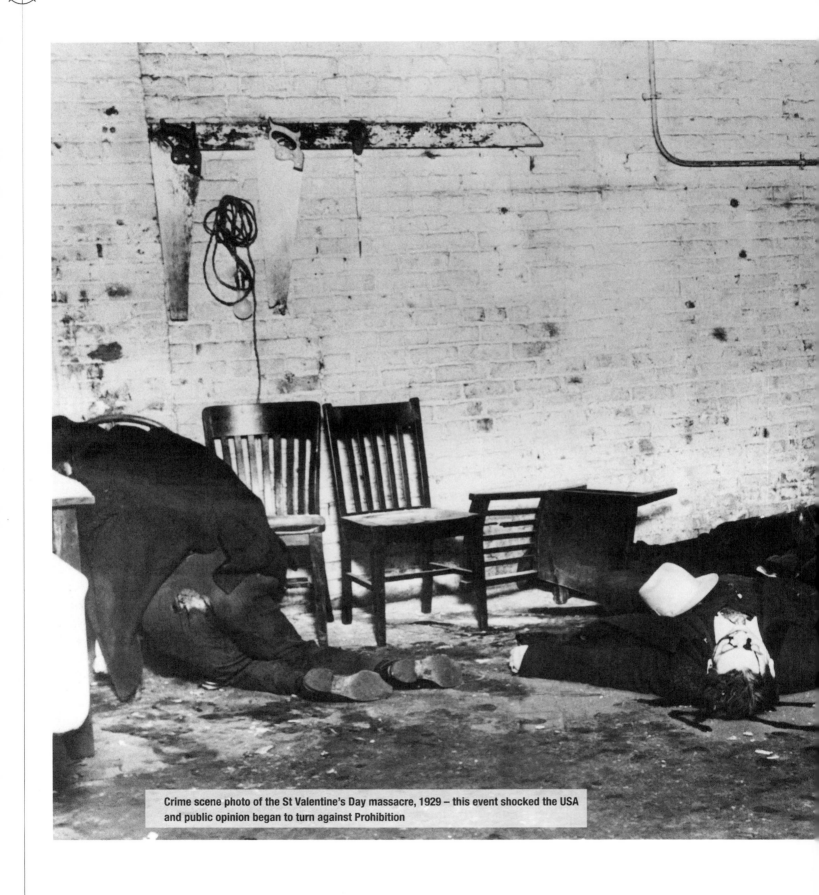

Crime scene photo of the St Valentine's Day massacre, 1929 – this event shocked the USA and public opinion began to turn against Prohibition

girlfriend at the time, but the prosecutor did not believe him. He was then charged with perjury, but he quickly married his girlfriend so she could not be made to testify against him.

Giovanni Scalise and a young trigger man named Tony Accardo were also picked up, but there was no evidence against them.

No one was ever charged with the St Valentine's Day massacre and the case remains officially unsolved.

Capone himself was questioned in Florida by the Dade County solicitor. Afterwards he held a party for the celebrities who were there to watch the world title fight. When he was asked who he thought was responsible, Capone suggested 'Bugs' Moran.

With his power greatly reduced, Moran was no longer a threat to Capone. His enforcers could not compete with Capone's tough guys, Anselmi and Scalise. The two thugs simply walked into any speakeasy that did not buy its beer from Capone and then smashed up the barrels. But the pair of Sicilians had ambitions of their own – they wanted to take over in Chicago. To that end they plotted with Joe Giunta, the head of the *Unione Siciliana*. But Capone had eyes everywhere. He and Frank Rio faked a falling-out and when Anselmi and Scalise tried to convince Rio to support them, he reported back to his boss. Capone then arranged a big party in the back room of a restaurant in Hammond, Indiana to which he invited Anselmi, Scalise and Giunta.

After dinner, Capone made a speech praising his honoured guests. Then someone handed him a baseball bat and he said: 'I understand you want my job. Well, here it is.' And he began beating them savagely. They were then shot several times and their bodies were dumped in a local park.

In March 1929, Herbert Hoover became president. He was determined to crack down on gangsters so he turned to the Treasury's Special Intelligence Unit, who sent their top investigator, Frank Wilson, to find out why Capone had not paid any taxes.

TAXING CIRCUMSTANCES

Capone had never filed a tax return. This was not illegal unless you earned more than $50,000 a year. As Capone's name did not appear on any business records or bank accounts, his income was hard to prove. Indeed, right up until 1927 professional criminals believed that they were not liable to taxation, because declaring their earnings from illegal activities would be tantamount to self-incrimination – which would be a violation of their rights under the Fifth Amendment. Bootlegger Manley Sullivan argued this in front of the Supreme Court, who decided that the Fifth Amendment had not been passed in order to guarantee criminals freedom from taxation.

Armed with this ruling, Wilson and his investigators went after other bootleggers. Soon they were closing in on Capone. Jake Guzik, Capone's underworld accountant, was jailed for five years and his brother, Sam 'Big Belly' Guzik, went down for three years,

along with Capone's underboss, Frank 'The Enforcer' Nitti. Capone's brother Ralph was also jailed for three years after banking $8 million under a false name.

Al Capone did not have a bank account and he did not sign cheques or own any assets – on paper at least – but it was possible to show that he lived a lavish lifestyle. He spent $1,500 a week on hotel bills and $39,000 a year on telephone calls, while over $7,000 a year was spent on handmade clothing. Then there was the $26,000 he had spent on furnishings for his Miami home. Some of those who ran his gambling operations in Cicero were also persuaded to speak up. In the end, Capone was charged with non-payment of tax on $1 million between 1925 and 1929.

Capone's lawyers made a deal with the prosecution. He would plead guilty if he did not go to jail for more than two-and-a-half years. The judge threw this deal out. Capone's henchmen then bribed the jury, but another jury was sworn in at the last moment. In court, Capone tried to play the part of Robin Hood, but this was the Depression and the jurors were appalled by his extravagance. He had spent $50,000 on improvements to his Miami home, $8,000 on diamond belt buckles like the one he had given to Jake Lingle and $135 on handmade shirts with a special pistol pouch. The foreman on his Florida estate testified that Capone paid him $550 a month – more than Capone himself claimed to be earning.

In an attempt to rescue the situation, his lawyers produced bookmakers who confirmed that Capone had lost $327,000 betting on horse races. But this only made the situation worse. It showed that Capone must have had the money in the first place and could afford to throw it away recklessly. Capone was convicted, fined $50,000 and sentenced to 11 years' imprisonment – the heaviest sentence ever imposed for tax evasion. After an appeal failed, he was moved from the county jail to the Federal Penitentiary in Atlanta. In August 1933, he became a founder inmate of Alcatraz in San Francisco Bay. After Alcatraz he was transferred twice before ending up in the Lewisburg Penitentiary in Pennsylvania. By the time he was released from Lewisburg in November 1939, he was suffering from tertiary syphilis. He lived for another seven years in his Florida home, while his brain slowly decayed.

When Capone was sentenced, Judge Herbert Wilkerson said: 'This is the beginning of the end of gangs as Chicago has known them for the last ten years.' But he was mistaken.

By the time Prohibition was repealed in 1933, the bootleggers had made so much money that they had diversified into gambling, prostitution and a range of legitimate businesses.

And their bars and clubs were no less popular because they were legal. Flashy, high-profile Al Capone might have taken a fall but the mafiosi who were modestly dressed and liked to stay in the background continued to thrive.

Al Capone, pictured in court during his trial in Chicago, 1931

UNIONE SICILIANA

The *Unione Siciliana* was founded as a benevolent society for the Sicilian immigrants who settled in Illinois in the 1890s. There were rumours that it had been infiltrated by Ignazio 'Lupo the Wolf' Saietta in the 1910s, but it had opposed the Black Hand gangs in Chicago so that seems unlikely. Around 1919 it was taken over by Mafia boss Antonio D'Andrea, who had been convicted of counterfeiting in 1903. Officials began asking for tributes, or protection money, from members, threatening retribution if they did not pay up. Then in 1921 D'Andrea was shot and fatally wounded. Mike Merlo was on holiday in Italy at the time, but he quickly returned to take over the *Unione*. According to early *pentito* Nick Gentile, the first thing Merlo did was order the murder of D'Andrea's assassin.

When Merlo died Angelo Genna became president, but he was killed in the following year. Genna's fate was shared by several of his successors. Samuzzo Amatuna followed him later that same year. He was allegedly murdered by O'Banion's lieutenant, Vincent Drucci. And then it was Tony Lombardo's turn. Formerly Al Capone's *consigliere*, he was appointed by the Mafia bosses. However, he annoyed a lot of people by attempting to reform the society too quickly. One of the things he did was rename it as the Italo-American National Union. According to Gentile, Joe Masseria gave Al Capone permission to eliminate the troublesome president.

Lombardo's bodyguard, Pasqualino 'Patsy' Lolordo, was the next person to occupy the job – but not for long. He was assassinated by Lombardo's underboss Joe Aiello, who was in turn machine-gunned by Capone's Chicago Outfit.

Antonio D'Andrea's nephew Phil D'Andrea then became president while serving under Capone's successor Frank Nitti. D'Andrea lived to tell the tale, but by then the *Unione* was in decline. It eventually became part of the Italian Sons and Daughters of America (ISDA).

Alcohol trafficker Frank 'The Enforcer' Nitti, treasurer for Al Capone, being 'booked' by Chief Inspector Pat Roche. The fastidious Nitti had fingers in many pies, including the *Unione Siciliana*

A crowd gathers outside the home of the murdered head of *Unione Siciliana*, Joseph Aiello, on Kolmer Avenue, Chicago

ELIOT NESS AND THE UNTOUCHABLES

Bureau of Prohibition agent Eliot Ness

While Frank Wilson and the Internal Revenue Service got to work on the tax front, the Bureau of Prohibition set up a special squad to raid Capone's breweries, stills and speakeasies, using information gleaned from an extensive wire-tap operation.

It was headed by Eliot Ness, a law graduate with a background of retail credit investigation in the Chicago area. His brother-in-law, an agent with the Bureau of Investigation – the forerunner of the FBI – recommended him for the job.

The job paid less than $3,000 a year and Ness had no illusions about the inevitable dangers.

'After all, if you don't like action and

A 'fair haul' by the liquor squad, Washington DC, 1922

excitement, you don't go into police work,' he said. 'And, what the hell, I figured, nobody lives forever!'

Finding reliable men in the Chicago area where Mob money had corrupted key government officials was difficult. Ness explained what he was looking for.

'I ticked off the general qualities I desired, single, no older than thirty, both the mental and physical stamina to work long hours and the courage and ability to use fist or gun and special investigative techniques. I needed a good telephone man, one who could tap a wire with speed and precision. I needed men who were excellent drivers, for much of our success would depend upon how expertly they could trail the Mob's cars and trucks... and fresh faces – from other divisions – who were not known to the Chicago mobsters.'

The squad initially comprised 50 men, most of them in their twenties.

It was then slimmed down to 15, then 11 and finally just nine. They were as follows:

• **Marty Lahart**, an Irish sports and fitness enthusiast

• **Sam Seager**, a former guard on Sing Sing's death row

• **Barney Cloonan**, a large, muscular, black-haired Irishman

• **Lyle Chapman**, former Colgate University football player

• **Tom Friel**, a former Pennsylvania state trooper

• **Joe Leeson,** a genius when it came to tailing automobiles

• **Paul Robsky**, a short, ordinary-looking man, who brought telephone expertise and extraordinary courage to the job

• **Mike King**, an unobtrusive-looking man with a special talent for absorbing and analyzing facts

• **Bill Gardner**, a former professional football player of Native American descent

Lt. O.T. Davis, Sergt. J.D. McQuade, George Fowler of the IRS and H.G. Bauer with the largest still ever found in the US capital, 1922

Their first task was to travel to Chicago Heights and close down 18 stills in a single night. Each man was given one or more stills to target. The regular Prohibition agents going in with them were only informed at the last moment and were given no opportunity to get to a telephone.

All the raids would kick off simultaneously at 9.30 at night, in the hope that they could make a clean sweep before the news got around.

Ness himself had chosen to target the Cozy Corners Saloon, which was at the centre of the Chicago Heights operation. It was also a supply centre for other cities in the Midwest. Leading the raid, Ness burst in through the front door carrying a sawn-off shotgun. 'Everybody keep his place! This is a federal raid!' he yelled. That night all 18 stills were shut down and 52 people were jailed.

Another consignment of moonshine falls into the hands of the authorities

Next Ness targeted Capone's breweries, the lifeblood of his operation. After locating a fully operational brewery, Ness smashed through the wooden door with an axe – only to find a steel door behind it. It took several shots to smash the lock. Once inside, his men found two trucks half-loaded with barrels, but there was no one in sight. Everyone had escaped through the roof. Nevertheless Ness's men confiscated the trucks, 140 barrels of beer and 19 1,500-gallon vats capable of producing 100 barrels of beer a day.

But Ness wanted arrests, so he acquired scaling ladders so that his men could climb directly on to the roofs of the breweries. The ladders were mounted on a ten-ton flatbed truck with a reinforced steel bumper, which enabled it to smash through brewery doors.

Ness's men located another brewery on South Cicero Avenue. However, word of the early raid had spread and the guard had been doubled. This time Ness went to the Prohibition Bureau for help. His last raid had been conducted without their participation, so they were unco-operative. The head of the Chicago Prohibition Bureau said he could only spare 'a mousy little man with thick, horn-rimmed glasses', according to Ness. A former department store clerk, he had no experience and had only got the job as a political favour.

At five o'clock in the morning, the former clerk found himself jammed between Ness and another burly agent in the front of the truck as it rammed through the doors of the brewery. Other agents were already waiting at the back of the property and on the roof. Capone's associate Frank Conta and his top brewer Steve Svododa were among those apprehended and Capone was down another 100 barrels a day. The diminutive Prohibition agent then quit.

Within the first six months, Ness boasted that his team had seized breweries worth over one million dollars. Capone was

Supervised by New York City deputy police commissioner John A. Leach, agents pour seized liquor into the sewers

hurting, but he figured that eliminating the members of a team set up by the president might bring even more trouble down on his head. Instead, Ness was offered $2,000 to turn a blind eye, while two other agents had an envelope full of money thrown through the window of their car. They chased after the man who had thrown it and threw the money back at him. Ness seized upon this as an opportunity for publicity. Newspapers ran the story coast-to-coast and one of them dubbed his men 'The Untouchables'.

Capone responded by having Ness's men tailed and the team's telephones tapped. But when it came to telephone tapping Ness was a jump ahead. It was an easy task to climb the telegraph pole opposite Ralph Capone's headquarters in the Montmartre Café and listen to his conversations. Ness learned enough to close down a newly reopened brewery. Frustrated, Capone ordered Ness's assassination.

Capone went on to make several unsuccessful attempts on Ness's life. On one occasion Ness had just walked his long-term girlfriend Edna Staley to her front door when he realized that the neighbourhood was suspiciously quiet. After he returned to his car, a bullet shattered the windscreen. He drew his gun and chased after his would-be assassin, but he disappeared into the night. Capone tried again by ordering one of his henchmen to drive his car at Ness and knock him down, but Ness dived to safety between two parked cars.

However, the Outfit did manage to murder Ness's friend and former assistant Frank Basile. Ness responded by gathering 45 shiny new trucks together. He then barged into the Lexington Hotel, called Capone on the house phone and told him to look out of his window.

As he did so, Ness's convoy slowly rumbled by the house.

Even a seasoned gangster like Capone must have blinked at the sight. Then Ness closed down Capone's new brewery, which was producing 20,000 gallons of liquor a day. Capone's response was swift. Ness found a bundle of dynamite under the bonnet of his car – it was wired to detonate when he pressed the starter.

When government accountant Frank Wilson brought 22 charges of tax evasion against Capone, Ness added 5,000 violations of the Volstead Act. However, the income tax case took precedence over the Prohibition charges, which were never brought to court.

When Capone was taken off to Atlanta, Ness boarded the train to check that the compartment was secure. Capone took off his coat and lit a cigar.

'I'm on my way to do eleven years,' he said. 'I've got to do it, that's all. I'm not sore at anybody. Some people are lucky. I wasn't. There was too much overhead in my business anyhow, paying off all the time and replacing trucks and breweries. They ought to make it legitimate.'

'If it was legitimate, you certainly wouldn't want anything to do with it,' said Ness.

After the repeal of Prohibition, Ness became head of the alcohol tax unit of the Treasury. He went on to become head of public safety in Cleveland, where he took on the local Mafia in the person of 'Big' Angelo Lonardo, 'Little' Angelo Scirrca, Moe Dalitz, John and George Angersola, and Charles Polizzi. However, his time there was marred by his failure to catch the Cleveland Torso Murderer, aka the Mad Butcher of Kingsbury Run, who killed and

dismembered at least 12 victims.

Ness finally married Edna Staley, but he later divorced her. He then became a social drinker, which might have contributed to a car accident in 1942. During the Second World War, he was director of the Division of Social Protection of the Federal Security Agency which aimed to cut down on the amount of venereal disease being spread among military personnel by prostitutes. After the war, he went into private business. His memoirs, *The Untouchables,* were published a month after his death in 1957.

Government accountant Frank Wilson, who brought 22 charges of tax evasion against Capone

Chapter 4

THE CASTELLAMMARESE WAR

The Mafia–Camorra War between the Sicilian Morello crime family and the Neapolitan Camorra had effectively wiped out the influence of the Neapolitans in New York.

But the Morellos were not the only significant Mafia family in town. In 1902, Nicolo 'Cola' Schiro arrived in America from Castellammare del Golfo – a small port 25 miles west of Palermo with a strong criminal tradition. Between 1905 and 1910 the Castellammarese in Brooklyn formed themselves into a gang.

A second Mafia family in Brooklyn was formed by Alfredo 'Al Mineo' Manfredi, who was from Palermo.

In 1906, another Palermitano, Salvatore 'Toto' D'Aquila, turned up on the police blotter. First of all, he challenged the Morellos in East Harlem, attracting defectors from the other Mafia gangs. These included Giuseppe Fontana, who had been convicted for the Notarbartolo murder, and Giuseppe Fanaro, who was arrested on the night of the Barrel Murder in 1903 – though the charges against him were dropped because of lack of evidence. With Giuseppe Morello in jail, D'Aquila declared himself 'boss of bosses'. As such, he was able to summon the New York mafiosi to meetings and he could control who joined the four families. However, in 1913 D'Aquila relaxed his grip by taking a holiday back in Sicily. The Morellos and the Mineos quickly seized the opportunity to take their revenge against the defectors and Fontana and Fanaro were gunned down.

D'Aquila treated this episode as a skirmish, rather than a declaration of war, so he let the Morellos take the lead in the Mafia–Camorra War. This robbed them of key figures such as Nicolo Terranova, who was murdered by the Navy Street gang in 1916. However, things changed when Giuseppe Morello and 'Lupo the Wolf' were released in 1920. After being accorded a rapturous welcome back in East Harlem, they formed an association with Umberto 'Rocco' Valenti, a former Navy Street gangster who had taken over the burgeoning Little Italy in the East Village.

'In 1913, D'Aquila relaxed his grip by taking a holiday back in Sicily. The Morellos and the Mineos quickly seized the opportunity to take their revenge against the defectors'

Valenti was reputedly one of the best gunmen in New York. D'Aquila saw this alliance as a challenge to his 'boss of bosses' status. He called a meeting, denounced the new syndicate as a threat to the established order and sentenced those concerned to death.

Morello, Lupo and Valenti fled back to Sicily, where they got Nicola 'Zu Cola' Gentile to intercede for them. Gentile used his influence to get another Mafia meeting called in New York, where the death sentences

NICOLA GENTILE

'Nick' Gentile was born in the small village of Siculiana on the south coast of Sicily in 1885. When he arrived in New York in 1903 he quickly went to work with the Black Hand. He then moved to Kansas City, where he formed a gang that made a living by theft and extortion. Although he was arrested several times, he generally kept on the move, working in Detroit, Houston and New Orleans. When he got to Pittsburgh in 1915, he was surprised to discover that the Camorra was stronger than the Mafia in the city. Finding this situation intolerable, he recruited his own gang and set about assassinating the Camorra leaders, forcing the survivors to the negotiating table. Then he had his inept capo shot and shipped back to Sicily in a luxurious coffin.

During his stay in Chicago in 1919, he got to know Antonio D'Andrea, the first head of the *Unione Siciliana*. He then travelled to Cleveland, where he survived a murder attempt by local boss Joseph Lonardo in 1920. At that point he fled back to New York to seek the protection of Vincent Mangano, head of the Mangano family (now known as the Gambino family), and Umberto Valenti, who had defected from the Navy Street gang to the Morellos. Then he returned to Sicily, where he became known as 'Zu Cola', or 'Uncle Cola'.

In a bid to take over the Morello family he aligned himself with Umberto Valenti and Salvatore Mauro against Joe Lonardo and Salvatore 'Toto' D'Aquila, who had declared himself 'boss of bosses'. While in Sicily he was visited by Giuseppe Morello, who had just been released from prison and hoped to make peace with D'Aquila. But when Gentile returned to New York, he found that Giuseppe 'Joe the Boss' Masseria had taken over the Morello gang. Ever the diplomat, Gentile became a Masseria ally.

During the Castellammarese War, Gentile acted as negotiator between Masseria and Salvatore Maranzano. When the war was over, he became an aide to Charles 'Lucky' Luciano and ran drugs between Texas and New York. Arrested in 1937, he skipped bail and returned to Sicily where he was welcomed back into his local Mafia clan. Like other mafiosi, he took advantage of the rise in the status of the Mafia following its role in the Allied invasion of the island in 1943. Later, he became an important canvasser for the Christian Democrat party. When Luciano was deported to Italy the two men teamed up again, dealing in drugs with other Mafia contacts.

Then in the early 1960s he did the unthinkable. With the aid of journalist Felice Chilante, he wrote his memoirs. His book became an important tool for the American authorities in their fight against organized crime. A contract was taken out on Gentile for breaking the *omertà*, but it was never filled. Gentile was left to live out a lonely old age, surviving on charity at the end.

were retracted. However, the settlement left Morello and Valenti at each other's throats.

Back in New York, Prohibition had set off a vicious turf war. On 8 May 1922, Vincenzo Terranova was gunned down from a car as he stood outside an ice-cream parlour on East 116th Street. He had been a key figure in the city because he was married to Bernardina Reina, daughter of the Reina family who ran the ice racket – few people had refrigerators, so ice was delivered. Terranova's bootlegging partner, Diamond Joe Viserti, had already been killed and then it was the turn of Vincenzo Salemi, husband of Lucia Terranova, to be murdered.

MASSERIA, 'BOSS OF BOSSES'

The rising star of the Mafia was another associate of the Morello family, Giuseppe Masseria, who was from Marsala, less than 30 miles from Castellammare. By 1920 he was considered to be subordinate only to D'Aquila. He was short, fat and slovenly, though well-dressed, and he had a reputation for ruthlessness. After several failed attempts on his life he became known as 'the man who can dodge bullets'. On 9 August 1922 he had just walked out of his apartment on Second Avenue when he was shot at by two gunmen. After chasing him into a store they kept on shooting until they ran out of bullets, then they made their getaway on the running boards of a waiting car. The driver ploughed straight through the crowd that had formed. Masseria escaped unscathed, though there were two bullet holes in the straw hat that had remained on his head throughout the incident. Valenti was thought to have been responsible, possibly working on the orders of D'Aquila.

Realizing that he could not resume his position as New York's effective 'boss of bosses', Giuseppe Morello became Masseria's *consigliere* and chief strategist. Masseria and Morello then invited Valenti to a meeting at a restaurant on Twelfth Street, but when Valenti arrived he was met by three of Masseria's gunmen. In the ensuing shoot-out, a street cleaner and an 8-year-old girl were wounded. Valenti tried to escape by jumping on to the running board of a taxi, but it is thought that he was shot down and killed by 'Lucky' Luciano. Joe Masseria then took over the Morello family, with Giuseppe Morello as his number two.

The Mafia then confined itself to making money out of Prohibition, which presented an easy option. Masseria still coveted the top job, so on 10 October 1928 D'Aquila was gunned down as he left his doctor's office. D'Aquila had played the part of a self-effacing mafioso so well that his death only made page 20 of *The New York Times*, where he was described as a 'cheese importer'. However, a careful observer might have been alerted by the fact that an eyewitness suddenly had an attack of amnesia.

Masseria was now 'Joe the Boss' and a 'boss of bosses' unlike any who had gone before him. He demanded a piece of every [Cont. p.104]

Joseph Valachi taking the oath on the witness stand

Senator John McClellan (standing) during the preliminary investigation of the case by the Senate committee

JOSEPH 'JOE CARGO' VALACHI

Born in New York in 1903, Valachi had been arrested five times before being sent to Sing Sing. When he was released in 1925, he made the mistake of joining an Irish gang. His former gang, who were Italians, objected and then went to Ciro Terranova for arbitration. As far as Valachi knew, a settlement had been reached. He was back in Sing Sing when fellow burglar Frank LaPluma was shot while sitting on the lavatory one morning. Valachi could not understand why this had happened until another prisoner told him that the deal Terranova had brokered had taken the form of a death sentence. First LaPluma had died and now it was the turn of Valachi. Soon after, Valachi was stabbed by another prisoner. The knife wound ran under his heart and around to his back and required 38 stitches.

When he got out, Valachi became a driver for the Mob. Then the Castellammarese War gave him a chance to advance his criminal career. Siding with Maranzano, he rented an apartment in Pelham Parkway, overlooking a flat belonging to Steven Ferrigno, one of Masseria's lieutenants. It was from there that Ferrigno and Al Mineo, who had also joined Masseria, were shot and killed by a team led by hitman Bastiano Domingo. But even though Masseria was with them he escaped unscathed once again.

As a reward for his participation in the incident, Valachi was 'made', becoming a full member of the American Cosa Nostra even though he was not Sicilian by origin.

After the Castellammarese War he ran a numbers racket, an illegal 'horse room', slot machines and a loan-sharking operation. In the Second World War he made around $200,000 from selling gasoline on the black market but in 1960 he was convicted for selling drugs. He was sent to the Atlanta Federal Penitentiary, where he shared a cell with Vito Genovese. Convinced that Genovese was going to have him killed, Valachi got jumpy.

So much so that when another prisoner innocently spoke to him, Valachi beat him to death with a length of iron pipe. He thought the dead man was Genovese's hitman. Now he really was facing a death sentence – from the authorities. In an attempt to save his life, he broke the *omertà* and became the first man to admit to membership of the Cosa Nostra – until then its existence had only been a rumour. In 1963, he testified before Senator John L. McClellan's committee on organized crime. His testimony was so detailed that the McClellan hearings became known as the Valachi hearings. Although the United States Department of Justice banned the publication of Valachi's memoirs, they were used by journalist Peter Maas as the basis of his 1968 book, *The Valachi Papers*. In 1972 the book was made into a movie of the same name, starring Charles Bronson as Valachi.

Valachi died of a heart attack at La Tuna Federal Correctional Institution in Texas in 1971.

> *'Convinced Genovese was going to have him killed, Valachi got jumpy. He beat another prisoner to death with a length of iron pipe'*

racket that existed and it was suicide to refuse.

When Gaetano 'Tommy' Reina opposed him he was gunned down. The strongest opposition came from the Castellammarese in Brooklyn under Nicolo 'Cola' Schiro, but it was Detroit Mafia boss Gaspare Milazzo who paid the price, when Morello ordered his assassination.

Then Morello persuaded Milazzo's closest ally, Joe Aiello of Chicago, to plot against Al Capone. Aiello's dangerous game ended when he was machine-gunned down in the street.

In an attempt to intimidate Schiro, Masseria demanded a tribute of $10,000. He got it. Then he sent gunmen to shoot wealthy bootlegger Vito Bonventre, the only Castellammarese rich enough to finance a war. Schiro then went into hiding and was never heard of again. His place was taken by Salvatore Maranzano, who was again from Castellammare. He had trained to be a priest but he had renounced his vows so that he could take revenge when rustlers stole the family's cattle. His mother was the daughter of a powerful don and so he soon became a 'made man'. The fact that his wife was also a boss's daughter gave him an even stronger Mafia connection. He was sent to New York, possibly by Don Vito Cascio Ferro, to take control of the Schiro family. Maranzano was an educated man who spoke seven languages and he was fanatical about Julius Caesar. In his house in Brooklyn, an entire room was devoted to the great Roman leader.

When Maranzano met Morello in Sicily he agreed to a meeting with Masseria, but it soon became clear to Maranzano that he would have to fight Masseria. He divided the Schiro family into squads and dispersed them, so that only he and the trusted squad leaders knew where they were. Then he used a network of informants, mainly Italian cab drivers, who would raise the alarm if any of Masseria's men entered Brooklyn. Masseria and his bodyguards were constantly ferried between safe houses in the Bronx, Yonkers and Long Island, using armoured cars and convoys. Maranzano took no chances. He carried a Colt, a Luger and a machine gun, along with a knife strapped to his back, and he paid inordinate attention to detail. He even filled his own shotgun cartridges every night before he went to bed.

Maranzano recruited as many gunmen as he could. He preferred people from Castellammare, but he was so short of manpower that he took anyone he could get. Even Joe Valachi, a small-time burglar of Neapolitan extraction, found himself initiated into the Schiro family. But Maranzano's best recruit was Bastiano Domingo, usually known as 'Buster from Chicago'. His father had been blown in half by a shotgun and his mother had been terribly disfigured by a car bomb. Because he looked like a college boy, he could follow Masseria's men unnoticed, though Joe Bonanno said he was a 'virtuoso' with a machine gun. So Buster was sent to kill Morello. On 15 August 1930, he and another man turned up at Morello's second-floor loan-sharking office on East 116th Street. Blithely assuming that Maranzano was on the run, Morello had no guards on the door. He was discussing building contracts with Gaspare Pollaro and his nephew Joseph Perrano when the gunmen burst in, firing wildly. Hit twice, Perrano tried to escape out of the window, but he fell to his death. Morello stumbled into another room with at least four bullets in him before falling down dead. Pollaro lived just long enough to tell the police what had happened.

However, Charlie 'Lucky' Luciano told a different story. He said that Albert Anastasia and Frank Scalise had attacked Morello on his orders. It was his first move to take over the Morello family – and the whole of New York. Masseria responded to Morello's murder by sending Al Mineo to machine-gun Joe Aiello, Maranzano's ally in Chicago. However, it was Capone who was blamed for the crime, mainly because he was seen as one of Masseria's allies.

With Morello dead, the Reina family began to co-operate secretly with Maranzano. They were joined by defectors from the Mineo family, though Masseria managed to replace Morello with Al Mineo himself. But Mineo was not cunning like 'Clutch Hand' Morello. The only strategy now was to find Maranzano and kill him.

JOE'S FAREWELL LUNCH

After Mineo had been gunned down his place was taken by Charles 'Lucky' Luciano. But Luciano had misgivings about Masseria. In 1929, they had fallen out over a consignment of whiskey worth nearly a million dollars. First of all, they had made an agreement that the whiskey was Luciano's and then they had shaken hands on the deal. At that point, Luciano reminded Masseria that the Sicilian code of the handshake could not be broken. But Masseria then changed his mind. He claimed that the whiskey was his and said: 'I break the handshake.'

'Luciano reminded Masseria the Sicilian code of the handshake could not be broken. But Masseria claimed the whiskey was his and said: "I break the handshake"'

Afterwards, Luciano got together with Benjamin 'Bugsy' Siegel, Joe Adonis, Meyer Lansky, Vito Genovese and Johnny Torrio, who had returned to the United States in the previous year for a council of war. It was then that Lansky suggested that they should 'eliminate the two roadblocks' – Maranzano and Masseria – and make Luciano the 'boss of bosses'.

Luciano had fallen out with Masseria and he was no friend of Maranzano's either. A few days after his confrontation with Masseria, Luciano met his friend Tommy Lucchese in a Turkish bath on upper Broadway and agreed to meet Maranzano. The meeting would take place on Staten Island, a neutral territory controlled by Joe Profaci, a Maranzano lieutenant but a friend of Luciano's from childhood. Luciano agreed to go alone.

'I figured that in spite of everything, Maranzano wanted me with him bad enough so he'd live up to his word,' said Luciano.

Luciano agreed to switch sides. But Maranzano put a condition on the alliance – Luciano would have to kill Masseria. However, under Mafia rules Luciano could not expect to succeed his boss if he killed him. He could take only a secondary role in the new hierarchy. More likely, he would be murdered in revenge.

After Luciano had refused to murder Masseria he was knocked unconscious. When he came to he was hanging by his wrists from a beam. Although the men that surrounded him were masked, he could see that one of them was Maranzano. When Luciano again refused to kill Masseria, they started beating him with clubs and belts and burning him with cigarette butts. In the end he passed out, but when he came to the torture began again. Maranzano made it clear that if Luciano did not agree to kill Masseria he would die. Somehow Luciano found

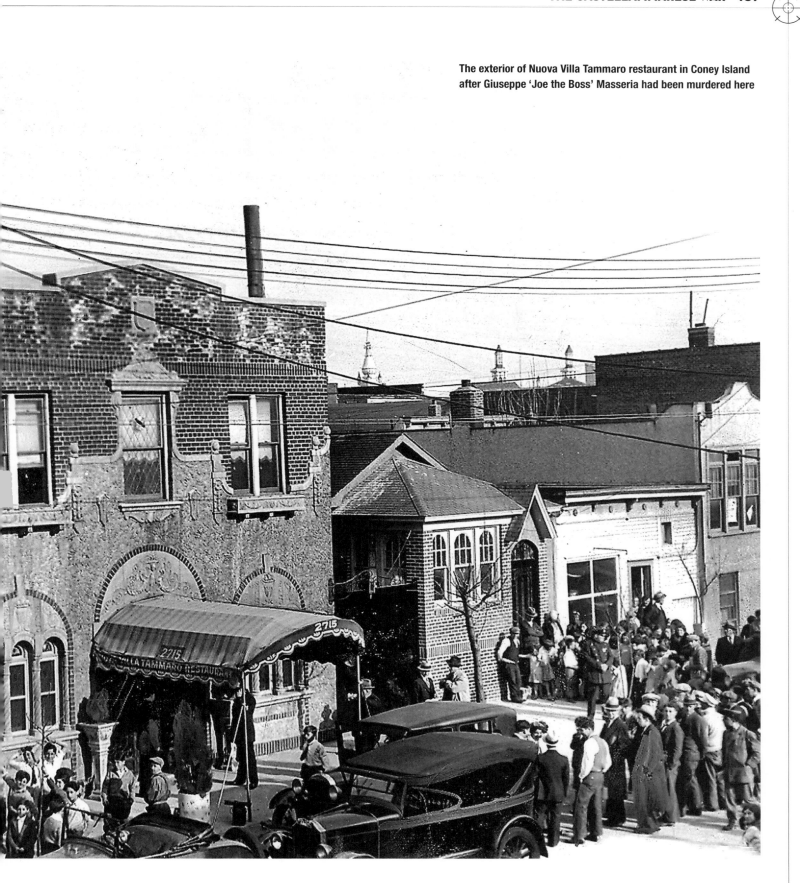

The exterior of Nuova Villa Tammaro restaurant in Coney Island after Giuseppe 'Joe the Boss' Masseria had been murdered here

enough strength to lash out with his feet, catching Maranzano in the groin. Furious, Maranzano grabbed a knife and slashed Luciano's face, severing the muscles that covered his right cheekbone. Luciano would bear the scars for the rest of his life. Maranzano also slashed Luciano's chest, but when an underling pulled out a gun he told the man not to shoot him.

'Let him live,' said Maranzano. 'He'll do what has to be done or we will see him again.'

They cut him down, bundled him into a car and threw him out on to the road, some distance away. A police car patrolling the area found him and took him to hospital. Luciano refused to talk, so rumours circulated that he had survived a 'one-way ride'. He had been 'lucky' to live, said Meyer Lansky. The epithet stuck. All 'Lucky' Luciano would ever say was: 'I'll take care of this in my own way.'

Lansky said it would be easy for Luciano to get rid of Masseria and Maranzano. All he had to do was figure out a way of getting them to kill each other. But Luciano bided his time. In early 1931, Maranzano let it be known that no reprisals would be taken against Masseria's men once 'Joe the Boss' was dead.

Another meeting with Maranzano was arranged, this time outside the lions' cage at the Bronx Zoo. Luciano was accompanied by Tommy Lucchese, Joe Adonis and 'Bugsy' Siegel. Maranzano took Joe Bonanno and Joe Profaci along.

Maranzano addressed Luciano as 'bambino', but Luciano made it clear that the old way of doing things was finished.

'My father's the only one who calls me *bambino*,' he said.

Maranzano was offended, but he promised to drop what Luciano called that 'exclusive Sicilian crap'. He would let Luciano and his Italian and Jewish friends get on with their business unmolested, once Masseria was dead. For his part, Luciano agreed to forget about the scars on his face. Maranzano embraced him.

'Whether you like it or not, Salvatore Lucania, you are my *bambino*,' he said.

On the morning of 15 April 1931 Luciano went to Masseria's office on Second Avenue in Manhattan. The two men then sat down and planned the murder of Maranzano's key lieutenants. Masseria was smiling and laughing, said Luciano, 'like he could just taste Maranzano's blood out of a gold cup'. Then he leapt from his chair and did a little dance like the one Luciano had seen Hitler do on a newsreel after the defeat of

> *'Luciano agreed to forget about the scars on his face. Maranzano embraced him.'Whether you like it or not, Salvatore Lucania, you are my* bambino,*' he said'*

France – 'Two fruitcakes in search of a brain,' he remarked.

It was a sunny day and Luciano suggested that they drive out to Coney Island for a leisurely lunch. They went to the Nuova Villa Tammaro, where the owner Gerardo Scarpato showed them to a corner table. 'Joe the Boss', a notorious glutton, gorged himself on antipasto, spaghetti with red clam sauce, lobster Fra Diavolo and a quart of Chianti. The meal took three hours and by the time he had finished the rest of the customers had left. Luciano then suggested a game of *klob*, a Hungarian card game that Masseria had learned from Frank Costello. Scarpato brought a deck of cards and then went for a walk on the beach. Masseria was on his second bottle of wine.

After one hand of *klob*, Luciano excused himself and went to the men's room. At that moment, the front door opened. Vito Genovese, Joe Adonis, Albert Anastasia and 'Bugsy' Siegel burst in and emptied their pistols into Masseria. The getaway driver, Ciro Terranova, was so shaken that he could not get the car into gear, so Siegel pushed him aside and drove off at speed.

Luciano then emerged from the lavatory and quietly called the police. When they arrived, he told them that he had no idea why anyone would want to kill Joe.

THE RISE AND FALL OF MARANZANO

Maranzano, the winner of the Castellammarese War, called a meeting of the Cosa Nostra in a big hall on Washington Avenue in the Bronx. Four or five hundred mafiosi turned up. Maranzano, still a shadowy figure, was introduced by Joe Profaci. He then made a speech explaining why Masseria had been eliminated. Things were going to be different, he said. In the new set-up, he was going to be the '*capo di tutti capi*' – the 'boss of all bosses'. The New York Mafia was going to be divided up into new families. Each would have a boss and an underboss and beneath them there would be lieutenants, or *capo régimes*. Soldiers would then be assigned to each lieutenant.

Maranzano then spelt out the rules. The Cosa Nostra came before anything else. The penalty for talking about it – or sleeping with another member's wife – was death. They were not even allowed to talk to their own wives about the Cosa Nostra, on pain of death. And mafiosi must obey orders from their bosses and lieutenants or die.

Members were not allowed to lay hands on

'Maranzano then spelt out the rules. The Cosa Nostra came before anything else. The penalty for talking about it – or sleeping with another member's wife – was death'

Giuseppe Masseria

Oppostie: **The body of Salvatore Maranzano after he was murdered in his office on the ninth floor of the Helmsley Building**

chief of staff, Joe Bonanno, as bosses of their respective mobs. Vincent 'The Executioner' Mangano would be head of the Gambino family, while Tom Gagliano, who had originally been appointed by Masseria, would remain head of the Reina family. Vito Genovese would be underboss of the Luciano family, Albert Anastasia would become underboss of the Mangano family, and Tommy Lucchese would be appointed underboss of what now became the Gagliano family. Some of those who had been in the Schiro family under Maranzano would remain with him as a palace guard. The others would join the Gagliano family.

A huge banquet was then held in Maranzano's honour. Mafiosi across America were obliged to buy tickets. Even Al Capone sent $6,000. As guests arrived, they threw their contribution on to a table. 'I never saw such a pile of money in my life,' said Joe Valachi.

Maranzano worked out of the offices of a real estate company in the Grand Central Building at 46th Street and Park Avenue. In September 1931, he told his men not to come into the office carrying guns because he was expecting a police raid. But soon afterwards he was warning his sidekicks that they would have to 'go on the mattress again'. That is, another war was about to break out, so they would have to move from apartment to apartment, sleeping on mattresses. Maranzano had decided that he had to get rid of Luciano and Genovese. Costello, Adonis, Capone and Willie Moretti from Fort Lee, New Jersey would also have to go, along with Dutch Schultz, who was not

another member in anger and disputes were to be decided by hearings. Maranzano insisted that the war was now over. There was to be no more ill-feeling. They must forgive and forget.

'If your own brother was killed, don't try to find out who did it to get even,' said Maranzano. 'If you do, you pay with your life.'

These rules were adopted by other Mafia families across the United States.

Maranzano also set up New York's Five Families, naming Luciano, Profaci and his own

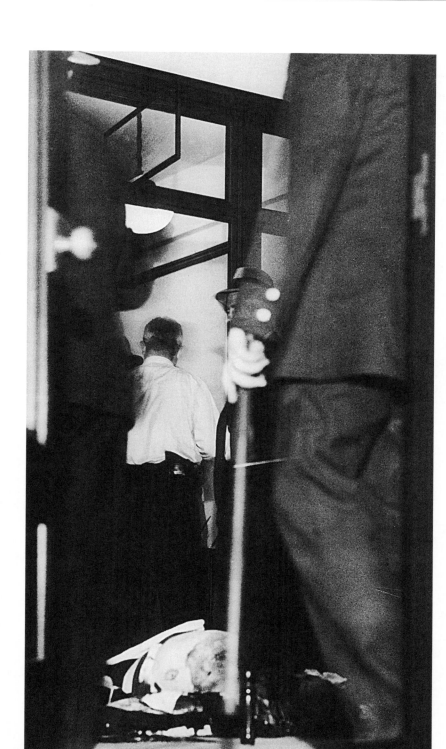

part of the Cosa Nostra. Maranzano hired Irish gunman Vincent Coll to kill Luciano, paying him $25,000 in advance. There would be another $25,000 when the job was done. Coll was known as the 'Mad Dog' after killing a child and wounding several others during a failed attempt to kidnap one of Dutch Schultz's lieutenants.

On 10 September 1931, Maranzano invited Luciano to his main office on the ninth floor of the Helmsley Building. The plan was that Coll would turn up shortly afterwards and kill him. But Luciano had received a tip-off. He sent two assassins dressed as policemen along to the office – probably Lansky's hitman Red Levine and Schultz's lieutenant Abraham 'Bo' Weinberg – along with Tommy Lucchese. They shot and stabbed Maranzano to death. As they were making their escape they bumped into Coll who fled, thinking they were real police officers.

It was not the only killing that day – as many as 60 mafiosi were gunned down. Luciano claimed to have organized it all, but it seems that the younger Americanized gangsters, the 'Young Turks', simply seized the opportunity to rid themselves of the 'Moustache Petes' – the older Sicilian immigrants, who were more interested in continuing the traditions and vendettas they had brought from the old country than making money.

Five months later, Coll was machine-gunned in a telephone booth. It was thought that Owney Madden, bootlegger and owner of the Cotton Club, had kept him talking long enough for the killers to catch up with him.

THE RISE OF THE YOUNG TURKS

Born Salvatore Lucania in the village of Lercara Friddi, Sicily, in 1896, 'Lucky' Luciano's family emigrated to the United States when he was 9 years old, settling on the Lower East Side of Manhattan. By the age of 10, he was already involved in mugging, shoplifting, burglary and extortion. When he was at school he tried to extort protection money from some of the Jewish boys. One of those boys was Maier Suchowljansky. Born in Grodno, then part of Russia, in 1902, Suchowljansky moved to New York with his family in 1911 and then anglicized his name to Meyer Lansky. Luciano and Lansky became firm friends, along with Lansky's younger sidekick – who was Benjamin 'Bugsy' Siegel.

Below: **'Bugsy' Siegel**

Above: **Meyer Lansky**

Meyer Lansky, 'Bugsy' Siegel, Frank Costello, Joe Adonis and Vito Genovese. Together they began robbing banks, pawn shops and moneylenders on the Lower East Side. When America entered the First World War, Lucania was old enough to be called up, but he had no intention of serving. It was not because he was afraid of fighting. He just knew that his life with the gang would be over if he joined the military. Instead he contrived to catch gonorrhoea, though later on he said that if he had known how painful the cure was he would have gone to the trenches.

When the National Prohibition Act was passed in 1919, the Lucania gang went into the bootlegging business. The operation was financed by veteran gangster Johnny 'The Fox' Torrio and Arnold Rothstein, whose mythic reputation included the unfounded claim that he had fixed the 1919 World Series. Both Masseria and Maranzano wanted a share of Lucania's bootlegging business, but Lucania disliked Brooklyn, Maranzano's territory, so he sided with Masseria, becoming his chief lieutenant. In that role he directed bootlegging, prostitution, the distribution of narcotics and other rackets.

After regularly failing to attend school, Lucania was sent to a reformatory for truants in Brooklyn. On his release, he got a job as a delivery boy for a milliner, his only legitimate job. However, in 1916 he was caught carrying heroin concealed under the hat bands and was sentenced to a year in jail. While he was inside he thought it better to change his name to Charlie because 'Sal', the diminutive of Salvatore, invited homosexual interest. When he was released, he formed a gang with

In 1928, he was arrested for robbery under the alias 'Luciano'. The police found it easier to pronounce than Lucania, so he adopted the name. However, in order to steer clear of the law he quit front-line crime and confined himself to strategy. He was a strict disciplinarian. Under him, failure was not an option. Those who disappointed 'got their fingers broke or their knuckles cracked or maybe had their heads busted'.

Luciano fell out with Masseria and Maranzano in the following year. He was recuperating in his suite in the Barbizon Hotel when Wall Street crashed. Lansky quickly alerted him to what an opportunity this presented. The gangsters were flush with cash and could buy up legitimate businesses for a song. Costello pointed out that they were also indispensable to the politicians and the police. In fact, New York Police Commissioner Grover Whalen had called him to borrow the $30,000 he needed to cover the

shares he had bought on margin. It was then that Lansky suggested that they should get rid of Masseria and Maranzano and take over. But Luciano was too busy to do anything about it. He realized that the crash would mean the end of Prohibition, so he was preparing to go into the legal whiskey business when the day came. Meanwhile, the profits on loan-sharking and gambling soared. Luciano went into a nationwide betting syndicate whose national wire service brought the racing results to every bookmaking parlour.

When Masseria discovered that Reina was in secret negotiations with Maranzano, he told Luciano he must prevent Reina from defecting. Luciano called Adonis, Costello,

FBI photo of 'Lucky' Luciano

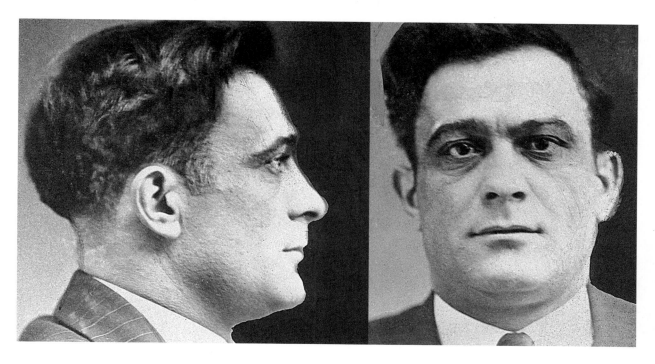

**Mobster Vito
Genovese**

Genovese, Siegel and Lucchese to a meeting on a fishing boat off Oyster Bay, Long Island. It was a cold and snowy night in January. Lansky was unable to attend because his wife was having a difficult labour. When she gave birth to a crippled child she saw it as a judgement from God. Lansky had a breakdown.

Lucchese brought the news that Masseria intended to murder Profaci and Bonanno in the hope that it would keep Reina in line. Luciano realized that he was being set up. Masseria was going to make it look as if Luciano was the one who had attacked Profaci and Bonanno, so Maranzano would come after him.

Siegel suggested they turn the tables on Masseria by killing Reina and making it look as if Masseria had ordered it. Accordingly, Vito Genovese blew Reina's head off with a

shotgun outside his home on 26 February 1930. Masseria confirmed the impression that he had been responsible by calling in Reina's top lieutenants – Gaetano 'Tom' Gagliano, Tommy Lucchese and Dominick 'The Gap' Petrilli – and telling them he was installing one of his own men, Joe Pinzolo, as their new boss. They complained to Luciano, who gave them the go-ahead to eliminate Pinzolo. Then they reopened negotiations with Maranzano.

Luciano made up his mind about what he was going to do. He confided in Albert Anastasia, who hugged him. According to Luciano, it was Anastasia who insisted they kill Giuseppe Morello first – 'because this guy can smell a bullet before it leaves the gun'. That done, Masseria and Maranzano were next. And then the 'Young Turks' took over.

Chapter 5

THE COMMISSION

'Lucky' Luciano managed to convince the heads of the other families that the power-mad Maranzano had been planning to kill him for no reason. In such circumstances, eradicating him was within the rules. Even Joe Bonanno, Maranzano's protégé, saw the need for his elimination. Although he had lived in New York for six years, Maranzano spoke little English and understood nothing of the street slang of the younger hoodlums.

'Maranzano was old-world Sicilian in temperament and style,' said Bonanno. 'But he didn't live in Sicily any more.'

Luciano was now *de facto* 'boss of bosses'. But he was not an old-style authoritarian like Masseria and Maranzano – he did not want a piece of everyone's pie. He was astute enough to realize that if there was peace everyone would make money. Bonanno agreed with him and the two of them then held a conclave with Gagliano, Mangano and Profaci. Before the end of 1931, they all travelled to Chicago for a national convention with Al Capone and the leaders of 20 other Mafia factions around the country. They accepted Maranzano's blueprint for how the families should be run. The *omertà* would remain a guiding principle. But Luciano insisted that as well as a *sotto capo* (underboss) each family should also have a *consigliere*

Left: **Chicago in the 1930s**

'Before the end of 1931, they all travelled to Chicago for a national convention with Al Capone and 20 other Mafia leaders'

(counsellor), who could resolve disputes within the family and sort out problems with other gangs. Membership would be open to anyone of southern Italian descent, not just those of Sicilian parentage, though both parents had to be Italian.

Although Meyer Lansky attended meetings with Luciano, he could not join in the discussions. The Bonanno family, however, clung to the old rule that all members should be Sicilian.

The number of 'made men' in each family was fixed. New members could only replace those who were dead. Indeed, membership of the Cosa Nostra was a lifetime commitment.

'The only way out is in a box,' said Luciano.

But that was only codifying the existing position. Luciano's innovation was the introduction of the Commission. Originally, it was to be called the 'Commission for Peace', but that was too difficult for the younger Americanized mafiosi to say in Italian or Sicilian. The Commission was to be the American Mafia's national board of directors. There would be members from each of New York's Five Families, plus one from Chicago and one from Buffalo, where Bonanno's cousin Stefano Magaddino, another migrant from Castellammare del Golfo, was an important figure. There was provision for other families to join if required. Luciano was influential, of course, but he did not formally want to take the position of *capo di tutti capi* because he realized that it would only lead to more bloodshed.

The Mafia no longer referred to itself by that name. In New York it was 'La Cosa Nostra'; in Chicago it was 'the Outfit' or 'the Syndicate'; in Buffalo it was 'the Arm'; and in New England it was 'the Office'. Mafiosi were spoken of as 'made men' or being 'connected'.

The national convention ended with a party at the Blackstone Hotel, where Al Capone laid on a flock of prostitutes. Plans were made for a similar convention to be held every five years. Meanwhile there was another meeting in the Franconia Hotel in New York, where Jewish gangsters agreed to throw in their lot with the Italians and form a national crime syndicate. The rules laid down by Lucky Luciano in 1931 paved the way for 30 years of peace. In that time, the only major mafioso to serve significant time in jail for racketeering was Luciano himself.

THE FIVE FAMILIES TAKE OVER

When Prohibition was repealed in 1933, New York's Five Families were so wealthy that they had taken over all the rackets from the Irish and Jewish gangs. The biggest and most famous of the Jewish leaders, Arnold Rothstein, had been shot in 1928.

It took him two days to die, but he refused to say who was responsible. 'You stick to your trade, I'll stick to mine,' he told a detective.

Stefano Magaddino

The leading Irish gangster, Owney Madden, wisely took the hint and retired to Hot Springs, Arkansas in 1933, where he ran the city's gambling operation. In Chicago, the remnants of the Irish gangs simply became the hired hands of the Italians.

Assisted by Meyer Lansky, Luciano took over the garment industry. It had

Arnold Rothstein was murdered in the Park Central Hotel in 1928. It took him two days to die, during which time he refused to divulge who the perpetrators were

previously been ruled by Jewish gangsters who had controlled both the unions and the management since a series of strikes in the 1920s. Bonanno ran a number of legitimate businesses as fronts, including a funeral parlour which specialized in double-decker coffins. Bona fide clients occupied the upper half while inconvenient corpses were stowed in the lower compartment. The families also ran the wholesale markets in Manhattan and Brooklyn, together with trucking and construction companies, restaurants and hotels. Tommy Lucchese even managed to take over the kosher chicken market, which was worth $50 million a year. These operations always made money because the Mafia took over the labour unions, so competitors were driven out of business or crippled by strikes. Owning legitimate businesses also meant that New York bosses would not be arrested for tax evasion. They had learned from Al Capone's mistakes. Such fronts were useful in other ways. Joe Colombo ran a real estate company, so his associates could always say that they had gone to see him to rent an apartment or get a mortgage.

Everything was going swimmingly until a grand jury demanded an investigation into racketeering and Thomas E. Dewey, a 33-year-old former US attorney from Michigan, was appointed special prosecutor in 1935. His job was made much easier by the newly passed Joinder Law – making it possible to prosecute several criminals under a single indictment – and wire tapping. Dutch Schultz was the first criminal on Dewey's list.

Schultz was born to a family of German-Jewish immigrants. His original name was Arthur Flegenheimer, but he took the name Schultz from a trucking company he once worked for. Schultz took control of beer distribution in the Bronx during Prohibition. As he extended his territory into Harlem, he came into conflict with the Irish-American gangster Jack 'Legs' Diamond. While Diamond was dining with his mistress in her suite at the Hotel Monticello, the room was sprayed with gunfire. Diamond was hit five times. When he recovered, he moved out to Catskill where his car was shot up in another assassination attempt. He was machine-gunned again near Cairo, New York. Then on December 1931, after a party celebrating his acquittal on kidnapping charges, Diamond was shot three times in the back of the head. Schultz was one of the many suspects.

He was also thought to have been responsible for the murder of Vincent Coll, who made the mistake of asking for a cut from the rackets he was involved in, rather than the regular salary that Schultz paid him. Schultz's lawyer, J. Richard 'Dixie' Davis, said that Schultz killed 'just as casually as if he were picking his teeth'. On one occasion, Schultz pulled out a gun, stuck it in the mouth of a lieutenant he suspected of stealing from him and pulled the trigger. Afterwards he apologized to Davis, who had witnessed the murder. On another occasion, he ordered Bo Weinberg's legs to be set in cement before he was dropped, still living, into the Hudson.

> *'Schultz was thought responsible for the murder of Vincent Coll, who made the mistake of asking for a cut… Schultz's lawyer said he killed "just as casually as if he were picking his teeth"'*

After Prohibition, Schultz took over the numbers racket (an illegal lottery) in Harlem, employing accountant and arithmetical genius Otto 'Abbadabba' Berman to manipulate the odds. After gaining control of the restaurant unions, he extorted money from the terrified owners. By the mid-1930s, Schultz was grossing over $20 million a year.

When the federal prosecutors charged him

Thomas Edmund Dewey – Schultz started planning his assassination

with tax evasion, he made sure that the trial was moved to Malone, in rural New York, where he bribed the entire town. Outraged at Schultz's acquittal, New York Mayor Fiorello La Guardia gave instructions to arrest him on sight if he returned to the city, which forced Schultz to relocate to Newark.

When Dewey assembled a new grand jury to investigate Schultz's avoidance of the law, Schultz tried to ingratiate himself with the Mafia bosses by converting to Roman Catholicism. He also began plotting Dewey's assassination. Albert Anastasia was hired to kill Dewey when the prosecutor made a

'Dutch' Schultz

call to his office from his usual drug store phone booth. An alarmed Anastasia told Luciano, who called an emergency meeting of the Commission. Killing a man like Dewey would make the Mob the focus of attention. Consequently, it was decided that Schultz was too dangerous, so he had to go.

Anastasia hired two professional Jewish hitmen, who murdered Schultz in the men's room of the Palace Chop House and Tavern in downtown Newark, along with his bodyguards and Berman, his accountant. Luciano then took over the numbers game in Harlem, as well as Schultz's restaurant racket. Schultz's murder was one of the few Mafia hits that anyone was convicted for. In 1941 Murder Inc. hitman Charlie 'The Bug' Workman was jailed for killing Schultz and his henchmen. He served 23 years. The other gunman, Emmanuel 'Mendy' Weiss, went to the electric chair for the murder of Joseph Rosen.

NOT SO LUCKY LUCIANO

With Schultz dead Dewey went after Luciano, who was unknown to the public because he preferred to stay out of the limelight. But Luciano was well known to Dewey. He and his *consigliere* Frank Costello were close associates of a number of leading figures in Tammany Hall, New York's corrupt Democratic establishment. Unfortunately for them, Dewey was a Republican. He also believed that Luciano's stated occupation as a gambler could not fund his ritzy lifestyle. At that time, he had a private plane and was living in a three-roomed suite in the Waldorf-Astoria, which was costing him $7,600 a year.

However, Luciano kept no written records and he was wary about what he said on the phone. Then Dewey got lucky. Eunice Carter, the only woman on his staff, was making investigations for the Women's Court when she came across a chain of 300 brothels across Manhattan and Brooklyn, which employed 2,000 working girls and made $12 million a year. When she dug further she discovered that it was being run by David 'Little Davie' Betillo, a man who had often been seen in Luciano's company. In January 1936 Dewey's men raided 80 whorehouses, arresting hundreds of pimps, madams and hookers – three of whom claimed direct knowledge of Luciano's involvement in the business.

With Dewey closing in, Luciano flew out to Hot Springs, Arkansas, then a sanctuary for Owney Madden and other gangsters. Dewey drew up an extradition order on 90 counts of 'aiding and abetting compulsory prostitution' – then known as white-slaving. Luciano was jailed in Arkansas, but within four hours he was freed on $5,000 bail provided by Hot Springs' chief detective. Dewey was not to

> *'Luciano had a private plane and was living in a three-roomed suite in the Waldorf-Astoria costing him $7,600 a year'*

June 1936: 'Lucky' Luciano (2nd from right) is led from a New York courtroom by a posse of detectives to start a sentence of 30–50 years

be thwarted though. With the aid of a squad of state troopers, his men simply kidnapped Luciano and took him back to New York.

Using the new Joinder Law, Luciano and his 12 co-defendants were brought to trial in May and June 1936. Luciano was billed as the 'czar of organized crime' and head of the 'Combine', as the brothel chain was known.

In court, a prostitute claimed to have had sex several times with Luciano in the Waldorf-Astoria. Furthermore, she said she had overheard him ordering a brothel to be wrecked, in order to penalize a recalcitrant madam. Heroin addict 'Cokey Flo' Brown said she had been at meetings with Luciano where he discussed putting madams on a regular salary, rather than a slice of the takings. He also talked about franchising his whorehouses, like the A&P interstate supermarket chain. A waiter and a chambermaid from the Waldorf-Astoria also said they had seen him with co-defendants against whom there was harder evidence.

When he was called to the stand, Luciano maintained that he was a gambler and a bookmaker, who would not demean himself by becoming involved in prostitution – except as a client. However, Dewey was in possession of Luciano's telephone records, which showed that the phone in his suite had been used to call a number of his co-defendants, along with Al Capone and numerous other notorious gangsters. He claimed that he did not even know some of them.

Dewey also had copies of Luciano's tax returns from 1929 to 1935, in which he maintained that he enjoyed a maximum annual income of $22,500. Yet Luciano was unable to explain how he could live like a king. He was further discredited when it was revealed that in 1923 he had avoided a drugs bust conviction by informing on another dealer. The Mafia boss had even failed to observe the *omertà*.

Luciano was convicted on all counts and sentenced to between 30 and 50 years in jail. In the following year his appeal failed, even though the three main witnesses had recanted. Dewey supplied evidence that the retractions had been obtained by coercion. The verdict made Dewey a national hero and he was elected district attorney of Manhattan in 1937.

Luciano was sent to the Clinton State Penitentiary in Dannemora, less than 20 miles from the Canadian border. It was one of the toughest prisons in the system, but Luciano did not suffer too much. His co-defendant 'Little Davie' Betillo served as his personal chef and valet and he spent most of his time playing cards and strolling around the place 'like he was the warden', as one guard remarked.

The mobster continued to run things from his cell. When Dewey ran for governor of New York State in 1942, as a stepping stone for his presidential bid in 1944, Luciano offered to ensure his success, provided Dewey pardoned him when he was elected. However, Luciano's lawyer, Moses Polakoff, saw a flaw in this strategy. If Dewey pardoned Luciano he would probably be impeached, thereby ruining any chance he had of becoming president. Luciano needed to give Dewey a legitimate reason for releasing him.

'OPERATION UNDERWORLD'

Luciano had read in the newspapers that the United States Navy was worried by the number of Italian immigrants working in the docks in New York. America was at war with Italy, so the Italians had divided loyalties. Strikes in the docks hindered the war effort, vital supplies were being stolen and merchant ships were being sunk off the east coast, possibly because of tip-offs from dock workers. However, the Mafia controlled the International Longshoremen's Association. If Luciano could ensure the security of the docks, releasing him could be seen as a patriotic gesture. What he needed was a front-page story that would bring home to the public the ever-present danger of sabotage.

On 7 December 1941 – the day the Japanese attacked Pearl Harbor – the American authorities seized the French luxury liner SS *Normandie*, which was tied up in New York harbour. They planned to convert it into a troop ship. But Albert Anastasia had other plans. On 9 February 1942 he set fire to the *Normandie*, which succeeded in putting waterfront security on the front page.

In order to avoid prosecution for the murder of fellow racketeer Ferdinand Boccia, Vito Genovese had fled back to Italy in 1937, where he became a close friend of dictator Benito Mussolini. Frank Costello was now acting head of the Luciano family. At his prompting, union bosses and other leading figures in the Italian community pledged their allegiance. They let it be known that even Italian and Sicilian gangsters were patriotic Americans who would rally to the flag. Encouraged by this show of support the Navy set up 'Operation Underworld', a government-approved plan that made organized crime part of the war effort.

> *'Lanza ran the Fulton Street fish market. No one had a stall there without Lanza's say-so. Every boat that landed fish there paid him $100 and every truck that hauled fish away paid another $50'*

A young reserve officer named Lieutenant Charles R. Haffenden was put in charge of the operation. Dewey's office put him in touch with Luciano loyaltist Joseph 'Socks' Lanza, who ran the Fulton Street fish market.

No one had a stall there without Lanza's say-so. Every boat that landed fish there paid him $100 and every truck that hauled fish away paid another $50. He exercised such tight control, through murder and intimidation, that he could even run the fish market from his prison cell in Flint, Michigan, when he was imprisoned there for conspiracy in the 1930s.

Tom Dewey on the campaign trail

telephone call from Frank Costello. However, Luciano refused to meet anyone from the government unless he was moved to a better jail. Dewey's office duly got him moved to Sing Sing State Prison, just 25 miles north of New York City.

'It was like goin' from Siberia to civilization,' said Luciano. 'I got a very nice cell all to myself, a clean one with hot and cold running water. I even had decent toilet paper for the first time in six years. A little thing like that can mean a helluva lot when you're shut up in jail.'

When he arrived at Sing Sing Luciano went to the lawyers' room, where Lansky had laid out a spread of all of his favourite food from New York delicatessens. Haffenden had to wait until Luciano had finished eating before he would discuss business. Then Haffenden asked Luciano if he would be willing to use his influence to help the government.

'Why are you fellas so sure that I can handle what you need while I'm locked up in the can?' asked Luciano.

Haffenden said that he had it on 'very good authority' that anything Luciano said would be acted on where it counted. Luciano then agreed to help. While Haffenden

Wary of being seen talking to a man in uniform, Lanza agreed to meet Haffenden outside Grant's Tomb on Riverside Drive and 122nd Street. He agreed to supply the Navy with union cards so that its agents could work in the fish market, but any assistance in the docks or along the rest of the waterfront would need to come from Luciano, he said. After an initial meeting with Lansky in a hotel dining room on West 58th Street, overlooking Central Park, Luciano was called to the warden's office at Dannemora. There he took a 'confidential'

went off to convey the news to his boss at Naval Intelligence, Luciano tackled the representative from Dewey's office.

'I repeated my promise that Dewey would get all our support and we would deliver Manhattan, or come damn close, in November, which would mean he'd be a shoo-in,' said Luciano. 'Then, as soon as he got into office, he hadda make me a hero. The only difference would be, a hero gets a medal, but I'd get parole.'

If not, Luciano would smear him in the newspapers, claiming that Dewey had persuaded witnesses to perjure themselves at Luciano's trial. He had tried this tactic before at his appeal, but with Dewey running for president the Democrat newspapers would print all the dirt on him they could get. While Dewey's man consulted his boss, Luciano, Lansky and Costello discussed cornering the market in meat and gasoline now that rationing had been introduced.

The best that Dewey could offer Luciano was to have him deported back to Italy once the war was over. For his part, Luciano agreed to pay Dewey $90,000 – $25,000 straight away to his 'secret campaign fund' and the remaining $65,000 to be delivered in cash, in small bills, when he boarded the boat. When Luciano later checked he discovered that the $90,000 never appeared in Dewey's books or tax returns, nor did it appear in his campaign funds. It had simply been pocketed.

As good as his word, Luciano stopped strikes and sabotage in the docks and information obtained from Operation Underworld led to the capture of eight German agents who landed from a U-boat in June 1942.

With Luciano's help, Dewey was elected governor in 1942, serving three consecutive terms.

He won the Republican nomination for the presidency twice, but then went on to lose to the incumbent Franklin D. Roosevelt in 1944 and Harry S. Truman in 1948.

His defeat at the hands of Truman was entirely unexpected. The *Chicago Daily Tribune* even printed the headline 'DEWEY DEFEATS TRUMAN', before the true result became known.

After the war, Governor Dewey granted Luciano executive clemency and he was deported in 1946.

While Luciano duly gave Dewey the $65,000 he had promised, Lansky gave Luciano a going-away present of his own – a suitcase containing $1 million. They later got together in Cuba, where they ran drugs into the United States. Luciano died in Naples in 1962. His body was returned to New York to be buried in the family vault in St John Cemetery, Queens.

Lansky fled to Israel in 1970, in order to avoid prosecution for tax evasion, but he returned and was eventually acquitted. In 1979 the House of Representatives Assassinations Committee linked Lansky to Jack Ruby, the nightclub owner who killed John F. Kennedy's assassin, Lee Harvey Oswald. Lansky died in 1983 and is buried in an Orthodox Jewish cemetery in Miami.

FRANK COSTELLO

Born Francesco Castiglia in Calabria in 1891, he emigrated to the United States at the age of 4. The steerage section of the ship was so overcrowded that he had to sleep in a large cooking pot. He grew up in East Harlem and led the 104th Street gang. Although he was arrested twice for robbing women, alibis provided by family and friends got him acquitted. In 1915, he went to prison for ten months for carrying a concealed weapon. After that he never carried a gun, he said, preferring to get what he wanted with his head rather than with violence.

When he was released he changed his name to Costello and joined Masseria's gang alongside 'Lucky' Luciano. Backed by Arnold Rothstein he became a bootlegger, running expensive Scotch from Canada. After the deaths of Masseria and Maranzano, he became Luciano's *consigliere* and the Mob's link to Tammany Hall, later using his position to influence the election of judges and politicians. With the incarceration of Luciano he became acting boss of the Luciano family, winning the resentment of Vito Genovese, who thought the position was rightfully his. The situation was resolved when Genovese fled to Italy to escape a murder charge in 1937.

Costello had prepared for the end of Prohibition by upgrading his gambling operations. One of his most successful innovations was to allow smaller bookmakers to lay off their bets — for a price — if they faced huge losses when a large number of their customers had picked a potential winner. He also became 'King of the Slots', with 25,000 one-armed bandits grossing him over $500,000 a day. When New York Mayor Fiorello La Guardia pledged to rid the city of slot machines, he moved his operation to Louisiana. He also had interests in Las Vegas.

At one point, Costello underwent psychoanalysis, but when his analyst advised him to turn his back on the Mafia and spend more time with his cultured friends, he gave up the analyst instead.

In 1951 he was jailed for 18 months for contempt after refusing to answer questions put by a United States Senate committee headed by Estes Kefauver, which was investigating organized crime. When Genovese returned from Italy he disputed Costello's acting leadership of the Luciano family and Costello was shot in the head by a Genovese gunman — allegedly Vincente 'The Chin' Gigante — in a hotel lobby. He survived, but was returned to jail for contempt of a grand jury. Gigante was charged with the shooting, but Costello refused to identify him and he was acquitted.

After the murder of Albert Anastasia, Genovese took over the Luciano family. Costello took his revenge by plotting with Luciano, Lansky and Carlo Gambino to frame Genovese, Gigante and future Bonanno crime family boss Carmine Galante on drugs charges. Despite his career as a bootlegger, Costello was a supporter of the Salvation Army. In 1949, he held a fund-raising dinner for them at the Copacabana nightclub, inviting prominent mafiosi as well as the judges, politicians and city officials that owed their positions to him.

During his retirement Costello remained the 'Prime Minister of the Underworld', dispensing advice and influence from his penthouse in the Waldorf-Astoria. He died of a heart attack in a Manhattan hospital in 1973, aged 82. When Carmine Galante was paroled in 1973, he took his revenge by blowing the doors off Costello's mausoleum in St Michael's Cemetery in Queens. Five years later, Galante was gunned down by three men with shotguns in Joe and Mary's Italian-American restaurant in the Bushwick section of Brooklyn.

Costello emigrated to the USA at the age of 4 in a ship so overcrowded that he had to sleep in a cooking pot

MURDER, INC.

The Mafia's enforcement arm, Murder, Inc., was the brainchild of Louis Buchalter – more commonly known as 'Lepke', from the Yiddish diminutive 'Lepkeleh' or 'Little Louis'. He was born on the Lower East Side in 1897. While his three brothers went on to become a rabbi, dentist and pharmacist, Lepke became a mugger, shoplifter and burglar, serving two prison terms before he was 22.

By 1927 he was leading a predominately Jewish gang called the Gorilla Boys, who were engaged in extortion and labour racketeering. Their murderous record was so well known that in 1935 Albert Anastasia awarded the contract on Dutch Schultz to Lepke's outfit.

Expanding into Brooklyn, Lepke hired a gang of young killers, the Brownsville gang, to handle his rackets in the garment industry. The gang also undertook further contract killings for Anastasia. Anastasia persuaded Costello and the Commission that they should relay orders through him to Lepke, who would send the 'Boys from Brooklyn' to kill anyone the Mafia wanted eliminated. The Italians who ordered the killings would have an

Louis Lepke handcuffed to FBI chief J Edgar Hoover in a publicity shot for the latter

Louis Lepke (left) with Emanuel 'Mendy' Weiss, Phillip 'Little Farvel' Cohen (both shielding their faces) and Louis Capone in a Kings County courtroom during jury selection

alibi, while the Jews who carried them out would not be connected to the victims.

By the late 1930s, Lepke had around 250 tough guys administering different rackets and distributing heroin. He also ran a team of around 12 specialist killers, who were dubbed 'Murder, Inc.' by Harry Freeman, a reporter on the *New York World-Telegram*. They included the pious Samuel 'Red'

Levine who would not commit murder on the Sabbath and Harry 'Pittsburg Phil' Strauss, who stabbed a waiter in the eye with a fork when the restaurant's service was slow. They operated out of the back room of Midnight Rose's, a sweet shop in Brownsville.

Anastasia, who relished the suffering of his victims, sometimes used to participate in the killings, taking with him a corps of hand-picked Italian assassins, including Vito 'Chicken Head' Gurino – who practised by shooting the heads off chickens.

Those who had offended the Mob were not simply executed. Their corpses were also arranged according to the Mafia's own language of symbolism. A canary or a rodent would be placed in the mouth of a victim who was a 'squealer' or a 'rat'; witnesses would have their eyes shot out or removed; those who had stolen from the organization would have money inserted in their mouths or up their anuses; and a man who had fooled around with another man's wife, girlfriend or relative would be castrated and his penis would be jammed into his mouth. To avoid detection, the Boys from Brooklyn developed the technique of pushing an ice pick into the victim's ear, so the pathologist performing the autopsy would think they had died of a brain haemorrhage. However, men of honour were shot in the face, so they could see their death coming.

When Lepke discovered that Dewey was pursuing him because of the estimated $5 million to $10 million a year he was extorting from businesses in Brooklyn and Manhattan, he went into hiding. Before he did so he gave Anastasia a list of witnesses he wanted disposed of before Dewey got to them. At least seven of them were killed. The federal authorities were also on Lepke's tail – this time because of drug offences. At that point the Commission decided that Lepke had become a liability. Instead of killing him, however, they arranged for him to give himself up to FBI chief J. Edgar Hoover, using newspaper columnist and broadcaster Walter Winchell as a go-between. Anastasia convinced Lepke that he would only face a federal narcotics charge. However, no deal had been done with Dewey. Lepke was handed a 14-year sentence for drug misdemeanours and a further 30 years for extortion.

During the investigation, Lepke's involvement with Murder, Inc. came to light. One member, Abraham 'Kid Twist' Reles – so called for his deft method of strangulation – had been arrested for homicide in 1940. To save his neck, he agreed to testify against Lepke. However, three days before he was due to take the stand, Reles fell from his hotel bedroom window and was killed – in spite of 24-hour police protection. The press called him 'The canary that could sing but not fly'. Nevertheless, in 1944 Lepke went to the electric chair for the murder of Brooklyn candy store owner Joseph Rosen.

Italian-American Mafia boss Albert Anastasia smiling in a park. Italy, 1940s

THE LORD HIGH EXECUTIONER

The eldest son of a railroad worker, Umberto Anastasio began calling himself Albert Anastasia after his first arrest – 'to save the family from disgrace', his brother Anthony said. With three of his nine brothers he began working on board freighters after his father died in the First World War. They jumped ship in New York in 1919.

Anastasia set up his own bootlegging

Game over: gunned down in a Coney Island restaurant, Joe Masseria clutches the ace of spades – the death card

operation under the wing of Brooklyn gang boss Joe Adonis. He murdered at least five people in disputes over territory. In 1920 he killed Joe Torino in a quarrel over the right to unload ships with valuable cargoes, stabbing and strangling him in front of witnesses. He was convicted and sentenced to death.

After 18 months on Death Row in Sing Sing he won a new trial. Some of the previous witnesses had mysteriously vanished and others had reversed their original testimony, allowing Anastasia to walk free. But in 1923 he was sent away for another two years for carrying a gun. He was then taken on as Joe Adonis' enforcer, becoming known as 'The Lord High Executioner', 'The Mad Hatter' or simply 'Big Al'.

Anastasia used strong-arm tactics to take control of the International Longshoremen's Association. This brought him into contact with Giuseppe 'Joe the Boss' Masseria, the most powerful boss in Brooklyn. Masseria's top aides were Frank Costello and 'Lucky' Luciano, who worked with Vito Genovese, Meyer Lansky and 'Bugsy' Siegel.

OUT WITH THE OLD

During the Castellammarese War, Anastasia joined the other young turks to rid organized crime of the old-style 'Moustache Petes'. The war ended when Luciano lured Masseria out to lunch in a restaurant on Coney Island. When

Meyer Lansky, known as the 'mob's accountant', developed an international gambling empire

This was extraordinarily eloquent for Anastasia. Short and thickset, he was normally a man of few words and his Italian was scarcely better than his English. He had left school at 11.

MURDER, INCORPORATED

To prevent the infighting that had caused the Castellammarese War, the National Crime Syndicate, also known as the Commission, was set up. It was realized that this would need some 'muscle', so Murder, Incorporated was set up under the command of Louis 'Lepke' Buchalter and Anastasia, now underboss in the Mangano crime family. Over the next ten years, this gang of hitmen carried out some five hundred murders for 'business reasons'.

Luciano went to the bathroom, Anastasia, Genovese, Siegel and Joe Adonis came rushing in, guns blazing, killing Masseria.

When Luciano had first told him of the plan, Anastasia hugged him and said: 'Charlie, I have been waiting for this day for at least eight years. You're gonna be on top, if I have to kill everybody for you. With you there, that's the only way we can have any peace and make the real money.'

Its team of celebrated killers included Harry 'Pittsburgh Phil' Strauss, Frank 'the Dasher' Abbandando, 'Buggsy' Goldstein, Harry 'Happy' Maione – known for his permanent scowl – and Vito 'Chicken Head' Gurino, who practised by shooting the heads off chickens. Anastasia was also active. In 1932, he was indicted on charges of murdering a man with an ice-pick, but the case was dropped due to lack of witnesses. The following year, he was accused of murdering a man in a laundry, but again no witness could be found.

It was Anastasia who came up with the new vocabulary of 'contracts', 'hits' and 'marks'. Although the traditional Sicilian mafiosi were suspicious of his close association with Jewish gangsters, he was present at the first meeting of the national criminal cartel in Atlantic City in 1929. The event was hosted by the town's boss, Nucky Johnson. Also present were Capone, Luciano, Adonis, Torrio and Costello. They had all turned up to meet Moses Annenberg, who was setting up a national wire service for bookmakers, financed by Meyer Lansky.

Anastasia had earned the reputation of cold-blooded killer. When Dutch Schultz asked for Dewey to be killed, Anastasia staked out Dewey's apartment, posing as a loving father with a child. He reported that the special prosecutor was lightly guarded and could easily be eliminated.

Murder, Inc. came to an end when one of its top lieutenants, Abe 'Kid Twist' Reles, was arrested for a number of murders and turned state's evidence. His testimony led to the arrest, trial and execution of lieutenants Louis Capone and Mendy Weiss, along with Pittsburgh Phil Strauss, Happy Maione, Dasher Abbandando, Buggsy Goldstein and Louis Buchalter, who was already in jail for narcotic trafficking and extortion.

Reles' testimony was also used to build a case against Anastasia. Although Anastasia was fiercely loyal to Lepke, it was he who persuaded Lepke to turn himself in, a move that ultimately led to Lepke's execution. It is thought that Anastasia put him up to it because he was jealous of the power Lepke was accruing.

ANASTASIA'S WAR EFFORT

In 1942 Anastasia helped Luciano secure the waterfront for the war effort, thereby obtaining a pardon for Luciano. Fearing that he might be implicated in the murder of Reles, who had mysteriously fallen from his hotel window, he then joined the army, but when his unit was posted overseas Anastasia bribed his way into a post in a transportation centre in Town Gap, Pennsylvania. He rose to the rank of technical sergeant and put it about that he had performed heroic deeds. He paraded around Brooklyn wearing his uniform after the war. Dangling from his chest was a row of medals he had bought from a pawn shop. But whether or not he had been a hero, his military service earned him United States citizenship.

HEAD OF THE FAMILY

Anastasia eremained underboss of the Mangano crime family, but frequently argued with the boss, Vincent Mangano. For 20 years he remained loyal. But in 1951 he formed a compact with Frank Costello, head of the Genovese family. Vincent Mangano then disappeared and has never been found. The same day, the body of his brother, Philip, was found shot to death in a swampy area near Sheepshead Bay. While he never admitted to the murders, Anastasia took over the family with the approval of the Commission.

After the war Anastasia bought into a dress factory and purchased a house overlooking the Hudson River in Fort Lee, New Jersey. He lived there with his wife and son behind a chain fence, guarded by a 'chauffeur' and

'Anastasia said: "Hit the guy . . . I can't stand squealers"'

watchdogs. He also bought a house in Italy for his aged mother and sister.

Both in front of the US Senate Special Committee to Investigate Crime in 1951 and the State Crime Commission in 1952, Anastasia refused to say how he made a living, on the grounds of self-incrimination. He refused to tell them anything else either. In 1952, the federal government began deportation proceedings against him on the grounds that he had lied on his naturalization papers and had used fraud to obtain a 'certificate of arrival' from the Immigration and Naturalization Service. He had also said that he had never been arrested and had only used one name, Umberto Anastasio, neither

of which was true. It was also alleged that for many years he had taken part in activities he knew to be prohibited by state and federal laws. But the courts ruled against the government and the case was dropped in 1956.

DODGING THE ASSASSINS

Several attempts had already been made on his life. When underboss Willie Moretti was killed in a restaurant in Cliffside Park, New Jersey, in October 1951, Anastasia was supposed to be with him. A few weeks later Anastasia was at a party in Newark, celebrating the acquittal of associate Benedicto Macri on a murder charge, when he had to flee out of the back door as gunmen came in through the front.

Meanwhile, Anastasia developed a greater passion for murder than ever. After watching a young Brooklyn salesman named Arnold Schuster on television, talking of his part in the arrest of America's most prolific bank robber Willie Sutton, Anastasia said: 'Hit the guy . . . I can't stand squealers.'

In March 1952 Schuster was shot outside his own home, twice in the groin and once in each eye. Anastasia had now violated the founding rule of Murder, Inc., first outlined by Bugsy Siegel: 'We only kill each other.'

In 1954 he was indicted on two counts of income tax evasion. The first trial ended with a hung jury. Before the retrial, the body of Vincent Macri, Benedicto Macri's brother, was found stuffed in the boot of a car in the

On 12 May 1936, Charles 'Lucky' Luciano (right) attempts to cover his face with a handkerchief while being transferred to a prison van. In 1998, Time magazine characterized Luciano as one of the foremost criminal masterminds of the 20th century

Plain clothes detectives examine the barber shop of the Park Sheraton Hotel, New York, where the body of Albert Anastasia lies partially covered

Bronx. A few days later, Benedicto himself was found floating in the Passaic River. Another key witness was Charles Lee, a New Jersey plumbing contractor who had received $8,700 for work he had done on Anastasia's home. He and his wife went missing from their blood-splattered home in Miami, Florida. The government case now in tatters, Anastasia accepted a plea bargain and spent just one year in a federal penitentiary.

VISIT TO BARBER'S CUT SHORT

At the time, Vito Genovese was trying to take over the Luciano family, but Anastasia supported his rival, Frank Costello. Normally Meyer Lansky would also have supported Costello, but Anastasia was trying to muscle in on his gambling operation in Cuba. Consequently, Anastasia had to go.

On the morning of 25 October 1957, Anastasia entered the barber's shop of the Park Sheraton Hotel. His bodyguard Anthony Coppola parked the car in the underground car park, then took a stroll. While Anastasia relaxed in the barber's chair, two masked men raced in. The shop's owner was told: 'Keep your mouth shut if you don't want your head blown off.'

Pushing the barber out of the way, they opened fire. The first volley brought Anastasia to his feet, but he did not turn towards his killers. Instead he lunged at their reflection in the mirror. Grabbing for the glass shelving in front of the mirror, he brought it crashing to the floor. There were two more shots – one in the back of the head.

Anastasia was not afforded the lavish funeral normally given to a crime boss. There were just 12 mourners. No Mass was said for him, though his brother Salvatore, a Catholic priest, had visited the cemetery earlier and blessed the grave. Anastasia's obituaries in the newspapers said that he had been responsible for at least 63 murders.

THE MAFIA VERSUS MUSSOLINI

Benito Mussolini founded his *Partito Nazionale Fascista* in Milan in 1919. It came to power fighting the labour movement and the socialists in the industrial north. While Mussolini was popular in Sicily, Fascism had no strong roots in the south, so in May 1924 'Il Duce' visited Sicily for the first time. Travelling through the small town of Piana dei Greci, the mayor, mafioso Don Ciccio Cuccia, took a disparaging look at Mussolini's elite bodyguard and said: 'What do you need these men for? There's nothing to worry about as long as you are with me. I'm the one who gives the orders around here.' Indeed, when King Vittorio Emanuele had visited the island a few years earlier, Don Ciccio had skilfully manoeuvred him into Piana dei Greci's Greek Orthodox church, where the head of state unexpectedly became the godfather to the Mafia Don's new son.

'Perhaps it was as well Don Ciccio did not listen for he would have heard Mussolini declaring war on the Mafia'

When Mussolini failed to show Don Ciccio the respect he considered his due, he sabotaged Mussolini's speech by emptying the town square of everyone except for a handful of beggars, boot-blacks, village idiots and lottery ticket sellers. It is thought that Don Ciccio did not even listen to the speech. Perhaps it was just as well, for he would have heard Mussolini declaring war on the Mafia. Back in Rome, Mussolini repeated the call to arms in the Fascist parliament, telling his followers in the south: 'I have the power to solve... even the problem of Italy's Mezzogiorno [Southern Italy]. It is my most fervent aspiration to do so.'

By that time, Don Ciccio was already in prison, serving a lengthy sentence.

CESARE MORI

The man Mussolini chose to take on the Mafia was Cesare Mori. It was an odd choice. Mori was a conservative monarchist who had been an enemy of Fascism while he was police chief in Rome and prefect of Bologna, where Blackshirts had surrounded the prefecture and urinated on the walls. However, during the First World War he had pursued the gangs of brigands who had taken to the hills in Sicily, rather than be drafted into the army. He then became a hero by capturing Paolo Grisalfi, a prominent bandit.

In 1925, Mori was appointed prefect of Palermo. Mussolini called him his 'Iron Prefect' and the locals called him the 'Man with Hair on his Heart'. When Mori returned to the island he found that the Mafia had prospered, so he began his campaign against them with a series of mass arrests. First of all he rounded up the elegantly dressed young men who drove ostentatiously along the city's most fashionable streets, on the grounds that their money must have been obtained dishonestly.

Left: **'Il Duce'**

Cesare Mori was prefect of police in Mussolini's all-out war against the Mafia

He then moved out into the villages of the mountainous Madonie region.

On 1 January 1926, Mori sent his men to besiege the village of Gangi, a notorious gangster's stronghold. Built into the side of a hill, many of the houses had exits on two different levels, making it easy to escape if the building was raided. The houses also had false walls and hideouts constructed in the attic or under the floor.

Mori swamped the area with *carabinieri*, leaving the mafiosi no choice but to give themselves up. The first man to do so was Gaetono Ferrarello, the so-called 'King of the Madonie', who had been on the run for over 30 years.

He emerged from hiding on the morning of 2 January. Then he walked to the house of Baron Li Destri on the central square and surrendered himself to Questore Crimi, the man Mori had sent to head the operation. According to the newspapers, Ferrarello flung his walking stick on the table and said slowly: 'My heart trembles. This is the first time I have found myself in the presence of the law. I am giving myself up to restore peace and tranquillity to these tormented people.' After shaking hands with the local police and officials, he was led away. A few days later he was dead, having flung himself down a stairwell in the jail.

Mori was not just out to capture the mafiosi – he wanted to humiliate them. 'I wanted to give the population tangible proof of the cowardice of criminals,' he wrote in his memoirs upon which the 1977 film *Il Prefetto di ferro* was based.

The police were told to enter the houses of wanted men at night, when they were asleep. Their cattle were slaughtered and the meat was sold at cut price to local merchants. If the men could not be found, their wives and children were taken hostage. Driven by their fierce sense of honour, the mafiosi quickly surrendered.

Next Mori went after Don Vito Cascio Ferro. Making a speech in Don Vito's territory, Mori announced: 'My name is Mori and I will make people die' – '*morire*' means 'to die' in Italian.

When he was arrested, Don Vito's godson asked the local landowner to intervene, only to be told: 'Times have changed.' In 1926 alone there were 5,000 arrests in the province of Palermo, which created a mountain of paperwork. Mori left Sicily in 1929, claiming that the Mafia had been eradicated. He was wrong, even though 11,000 men were now behind bars. However, the Mafia had been dealt a serious, almost life-threatening, blow.

According to Antonio Calderone, a mafioso from Catania who in 1986 became a *pentito* (informer):

'Many were sent to prison island, just from one day to the next... they gave mafiosi five years of internal exile without trial, the maximum. And when those five years were over they issued a decree and gave them five more... After the war the Mafia hardly

Mafia suspects securely handcuffed and behind bars, 1928

existed any more. The Sicilian families had all been broken up. The Mafia was like a plant they don't grow any more. My uncle Luigi, who had been a boss, an authority, was reduced to stealing to earn a crust.'

'GENERAL MAFIA'

But the war eventually provided the Mafia with an opportunity. On the night of 9 July 1943, the first of 160,000 Allied troops began landing on the southwest beaches of Sicily. While the British and the Canadians fought their way up the east coast against stiff opposition, the Americans had been given what seemed to be an even tougher assignment. They had to fight their way across the mountainous central region. The key point in the German–Italian defensive line was Mount Cammarata, just west of the towns of Villalba and Mussomeli, which dominated the two roads the Americans must pass down to reach Palermo. It was held by a mixed brigade of motorized artillery, anti-aircraft guns and 88mm anti-tank guns, plus a squadron of German panzers, including the latest Tiger tanks. The mountain caves and craggy outcrops had been used as a redoubt against invaders since Roman times. In command of the defence force was Lieutenant-Colonel Salemi. He did not believe that he could hold back the American advance because he had little air cover. However, he was confident that he could at least delay the Americans and make them pay a very high price.

On 14 July 1943 a small American army plane flew low over Villalba.

It trailed a yellow banner with a large, black 'L' on it and it dropped a nylon bag containing a big yellow handkerchief that bore the same initial 'L'. This fell near the house of the village priest, Monsignor Giovanni Vizzini, who was the brother of the local Mafia boss. It was picked up by Private Raniero Nuzzolese, a soldier from Bari on the mainland. He handed it to Lance-Corporal Angelo Riccioli, commander of the *carabinieri* stationed in Villalba.

The plane returned the following day and dropped another bag near the home of the priest's brother. This time it had the words *'Zu Calò* – 'Uncle Calò' written on it. The bag was picked up by Carmelo Bartolomeo, a servant in the Vizzini household, who delivered it to Don Calogero Vizzini (Don Calò), the intended recipient.

Don Calò was one of the most powerful Mafia bosses in Sicily – some said he was the *capo di tutti capi,* though no such formal post existed in Sicily at the time. Born in 1877, he had begun his career providing protection for peasants who wanted to get their grain safely to the Mafia-controlled mills. During the First World War he made a fortune by dealing in the black market and

> **'On 14 July 1943 a small American army plane flew low over Villalba. It trailed a yellow banner with a large, black "L" on it'**

taking over the land of absentee landlords. He escaped prosecution several times due to his influential friends. In all, Don Calò's criminal dossier is thought to have included 39 murders, 6 attempted murders, 13 acts of private violence, 36 robberies, 37 thefts and 63 incidents of extortion.

During the Mori crackdown he was kept under house arrest for his outspoken opposition to Mussolini and in 1931 he was exiled to the mainland. The whole town turned out to greet him on his return in 1937.

When Don Calò opened the bag, he found another yellow silk handkerchief with the letter 'L' on it. Silk handkerchiefs had long been used as a means of identification among mafiosi. In 1922, a lowly member of the Mafia in Villalba named Lottò had committed a murder for which he had not asked permission. He was in breach of all Mafia etiquette. The killing had been ill-planned and he had made no effort to conceal the crime. Arrest and conviction would inevitably follow.

But Don Calò would have suffered a certain 'loss of respect' if he had left a 'man of honour' to his fate, so Lottò was declared insane. He was then taken to the asylum at Barcellona Pozzo di Gotto, near Messina, an institution conveniently under the control of the Mafia. Soon after he arrived there Lottò was declared dead. After being

Don Calogero Vizzini, one of the most powerful Mafia bosses in Sicily last century – some said he was the *capo di tutti capi*

carried out of the asylum in a well-ventilated coffin, he was then given false documents and sent to New York. He carried a yellow silk handkerchief with the initial 'C' for Calò on it, so that he could identify himself when he got there. So when Don Calò received a yellow silk handkerchief, he knew he was being asked for help. The letter 'L' stood for 'Luciano'. Although he had left Sicily at the age of 9, Luciano was well known there, if only by reputation. Vito Genovese had written to Luciano to inform him of this fact, so the American authorities were also aware of how influential Luciano was.

That evening, a young man named Mangiapane set off for Mussomeli with a letter. It read:

> 'Turi, the farm bailiff, will go to the fair at Cerda with the calves on Thursday, the 20th. I will leave on the same day with the cows, ox-carts and the bull. Get faggots for making the cheese, and provide folds for the sheep. Tell the other bailiffs to get ready. I'll see to the rennet.'

Turi was the Mafia boss in Polizzi Generosa, 13 miles to the northeast of Villalba. 'Calves' were the American motorized divisions, which he would lead to Cerda above the key road that ran from Palermo to Messina; 'cows' were troops; 'ox-carts' were tanks; and the 'bull' was the commander-in-chief. The letter was addressed to 'Zu Peppi'– Giuseppe Genco Russo, the Mafia boss of Mussomeli, who would one day succeed Don Calò as Sicily's most prominent gangster. On the following day, Mangiapane returned with a reply from Zu Peppi, who wrote that Liddu, his bailiff, had got the faggots ready.

Three days later, with the American front line still 30 miles from Villalba, a lone jeep made a dash across enemy territory. It was carrying two soldiers and a civilian and it flew a yellow pennant with a black 'L' on it. Not far from the town it ran into the Italian rearguard. One of the American soldiers was hit. He toppled out on to the road as the jeep made a screeching U-turn and headed off in the opposite direction.

A villager soon found out that the dead soldier had been carrying another nylon bag addressed to Don Calò. Again it was swiftly delivered to the addressee.

That afternoon, three American tanks rolled into Villalba. A yellow pennant with an 'L' on it was flying from the radio aerial of the first tank. An American officer emerged from the turret and asked the locals to fetch Don Calò. He spoke with a Sicilian accent that had been mellowed by years in America.

In due course, Don Calò shambled across town wearing a short-sleeved shirt. A pair of braces held his trousers up over his large round belly and his hat was pulled down so far that it almost covered his tortoise-shell spectacles. The Americans were surprised by the dishevelled appearance of the rotund 66-year-old, but in Sicily it was not done for a

Mafia boss to show off. Without a word, Don Calò pulled out the identifying handkerchief. He then clambered up on to the lead tank with the help of his nephew, Domiano Lumia, who had returned from the United States shortly before the outbreak of war. Mangiapane was told to return to Mussomeli and tell Zu Peppi that the Americans had reached Villalba. Then Don Calò was carried off behind the Allied lines, where the GIs referred to him as 'General Mafia'.

That evening, Colonel Salemi still controlled the roads from his position on the heights of Mount Cammarata, but two-thirds of his men were missing at roll-call on the following morning. During the night, the Italian troops had been visited by groups of local men, who had 'persuaded' them to abandon their positions and avoid needless bloodshed. They were given civilian clothes so they could return to their families. Others were warned that it was not just Allied forces they faced. People who knew the terrain better than they did might take advantage of the darkness to grab them and hand them over as prisoners to the Americans. Resistance was pointless – and dangerous. Later that day, Colonel Salemi was himself seized by the Mafia in Mussomeli and held in the town hall. Meanwhile, a body of Moroccan troops under the command of General Juin

'Two-thirds of Salemi's men were missing at roll-call... local men had "persuaded" them to avoid needless bloodshed'

had halted at the village of Raffi. At four o'clock that afternoon Juin got a message from the Mussomeli Mafia, which told him that it was now safe to advance. The battle for Cammarata was over without a shot being fired.

Don Calò spent six days with the Americans. While Turi the Mafia boss accompanied the Allied column up the road to Cerda, Don Calò travelled with the other claw of the pincer, which encircled the troops in Palermo province and cut off Trapani. When the columns met up at Cerda, Don Calò went home, his job done. Many historians dismiss this story as apocryphal, but it is widely believed by the inhabitants of Villalba and it was recorded by Michele Pantaleone, a journalist and one-time political rival of Don Calò.

When he returned to Villalba, the Fascist mayor was deposed and Don Calò took his place, supported by the American occupying force. Michele Pantaleone was made his deputy. At Don Calò's inauguration, supporters cried: 'Long live the Mafia! Long live crime! Long live Don Calò!' The Americans granted him permission to carry firearms in case he had any more trouble with the Fascists and the *carabinieri* barracks in the town was named after him. One of his first acts as mayor was to have the records of his previous crimes expunged. [*Cont. p. 154*]

VITO GENOVESE

Born in Rosiglino near Naples in 1897, Don Vito emigrated to New York in 1913. In the 1930s he was Luciano's underboss, with headquarters in Manhattan's Little Italy, where he specialized in narcotics. Despite his fearsome reputation as a killer he was only imprisoned once, when he was 20 years old. He was jailed for 60 days on a gun charge. When his first wife died he fell in love with his married cousin, Anna Vernotico, and it is said that he had her husband strangled so he could marry her. However, he could not bring himself to order her killing when she later informed on him.

During the Castellammarese War, he killed both Gaetano Reina and Masseria and was rewarded by being made underboss of the Luciano family. However, when Luciano went to jail he was passed over for the top job. In 1934, Genovese and Ferdinand 'The Shadow' Boccia set up a crooked card game in order to sting a rich Italian businessman Boccia had introduced to Genovese. Not one to share, Genovese hired Willie Gallo and Ernest 'The Hawk' Rupolo to kill Boccia when he asked for his cut.

When Boccia's body was pulled from the Hudson three years later, Genovese feared he might be linked to the killing, so he tried to have Gallo shot. When Gallo realized the situation he went to the police and implicated Rupolo and Genovese. Rupolo was jailed for 20 years while Genovese fled to Italy with a suitcase containing $750,000. Periodically, Anna would take another $50,000 or $100,000 given to her by Genovese's brother Michael, who ran the Genovese rackets while Vito was away. While he was in Italy Genovese made large donations to the Fascist Party. He also organized the murder of Carlo Tresca, the editor of an anti-Fascist Italian-language newspaper in New York, as a favour to

> '*When Boccia's body was pulled from the Hudson, Genovese feared he might be linked, so he tried to have Gallo shot*'

Mussolini. His reward was the title of Commendatore.

During the Allied invasion of Italy Genovese became an interpreter and liaison officer with the American occupation forces. He also ran the black market. When the military government cracked down on illegal trading Genovese was arrested and sent back to the United States to face murder charges. However, a key witness was murdered – poisoned, in fact – while he was in protective custody, so Genovese walked free.

He rejoined the Luciano family, but his position as underboss had been taken by the feared New Jersey racketeer 'Willie' Moretti and he was busted down to *capo*. To take his revenge, he ordered the murder of Moretti, Costello and Anastasia. Costello survived but he relinquished control of the family, leaving Genovese as 'boss of bosses'.

In 1959, he was sentenced to 15 years in jail for the smuggling and distribution of heroin, though it is thought that the chief prosecution witness against him was lying. He continued to run the family while he was inside, ordering killings from his cells in Atlanta and Leavenworth. He was still locked up when he died of a heart attack in 1969.

Vito Genovese is handcuffed as he leaves Federal Court to start a 15-year sentence, 1960

WORKING WITH THE ALLIES

Before the invasion of Sicily began the Mafia supplied maps and helped smuggle Allied agents in and out of the country. When the invasion was under way they conducted sabotage behind the lines. Charles Poletti, the governor of Sicily for the six months of the occupation, had slipped into Palermo under Mafia protection long before the landings. His driver and interpreter was Vito Genovese.

> ## '"That conniving louse was selling American goods to his own people, things that'd save their lives or keep them from starving"'

'We had no problems at all with the Mafia,' said Poletti. 'Nobody ever heard of it. While we were there, nobody heard of it. Nobody ever talked about it.'

Luciano described Poletti, once briefly governor of New York, as 'one of our good friends'. He was less generous when it came to the black market operation that Genovese ran with Don Calò's nephew, Domiano Lumia.

'He made more than a million dollars in untraceable cash in almost no time,' said Luciano. 'That conniving louse was selling American goods to his own Italian people, things that'd save their lives or keep them from starving. He made a fortune out of penicillin, cigarettes, sugar, olive oil, flour, you name it... Maybe if I had it to do again, I would've arranged for Poletti's troops to line

General G. Castellano shakes hands with Dwight D. Eisenhower during the signing of armistice papers

Vito up against a wall and shoot him.'

But Mafia black marketeering was popular. People were at least getting the things they needed to survive. A warehouse containing ration books was looted and at least 25,000 extra books were in circulation. And when the Allies tried to commandeer all of the grain on the island the farmers were unco-operative. They preferred the black market prices that were paid by the Mafia.

As the Allies advanced the mafiosi were freed from the prisons, because they were anti-Fascists. They were regularly installed as mayors and given other political positions, thanks to the OSS – the Office of Strategic Services, the forerunner of the CIA. Even the mayor of Palermo, Lucio Tasca Bordonato, was a member of the Mafia, according to Nick Gentile, in spite of the fact that he had been nominated by the Allies. Not only were the mafiosi anti-Fascists, they were also opposed to the Communists who formed the backbone of the guerrilla force that had taken to the hills to fight Mussolini. The last thing the American government wanted was a Communist takeover in the countries they had liberated, so that was another reason why the mafiosi were so popular with the Allies.

Joseph Russon, the Corleone-born head of the OSS bureau in Palermo, had meetings with Don Calò and Palermo lawyer Vito

'Mafia leaders held a number of secret meetings to end the crime wave. As a result the bodies of eight men were found'

Guarrasi, whose home was used for a meeting of the Mafia bosses of the three western provinces. Guarrasi was the right-hand man of General Giuseppe Castellano, the man who negotiated the armistice between Italy and the Allies in September 1943. Castellano also met Don Calò and other Mafia leaders on several occasions, along with Sicilian Separatists such as the Tasca brothers, who were also mafiosi.

An OSS report called *The Mafia Leadership Fighting Crime* described how the Mafia were using summary justice to suppress banditism in the countryside.

It recorded how at the beginning of March Mafia leaders in Palermo had held a number of secret meetings to bring an end to the crime wave. As a result the bodies of eight men were found outside Mussomeli. They had been strangled and shot numerous times and their bodies had been burnt.

A further 14 known criminals were killed over the following three weeks. It was just like old times. According to Don Calò:

'Some elements have already been eliminated but one hundred more must also fall. We were thought of as a penal colony. The Prefect Mori and his agents are responsible for the moral, political and economic decay of Sicily. But today, the Americans can

see that the island is the jewel of the Mediterranean.'

Meanwhile the civil authorities stood by and did nothing. The report concluded:

'The carabinieri and other public safety agencies were openly favourable to the Mafia leadership's interest in enforcing respect of the law and were avoiding any investigation into the killings of wanted criminals.'

The vendetta had returned with a vengeance. As mayor of Villalba, Don Calò allowed the Communists to hold a rally there. It had been arranged by Michele Pantaleone, who had recently refused to marry Don Calò's niece, Raimondo. An unwise move, because the crops on his family estates had been destroyed and he had just managed to escape an assassination attempt.

The guest speaker was regional Communist leader Girolamo Li Causi, who had spent some years in jail under Mussolini and had led the resistance against the Nazis in Milan. He gave a rousing speech about the oppression of the workers and the peasants, which incensed Don Calò. Then he made a direct reference to Don Calò himself, declaring that the peasants had been deceived. Don Calò shouted out: 'It's a lie.'

At that point gunfire broke out and a grenade was thrown by Don Calò's nephew. Li Causi was injured and dragged to safety by Pantaleone. In all, 14 people were wounded.

Don Calò and his cohorts were arrested soon after the incident, but the court proceedings dragged on for 14 years. Thanks to various amnesties, pardons and remissions, few of the accused served more than a couple of months in jail. Don Calò and his nephew were convicted of wounding Li Causi and were sentenced to five years' imprisonment. However, Don Calò simply disappeared and would not return until he was granted conditional freedom pending an appeal. The sentence was confirmed in 1954 but he was freed on the grounds of his age, even though the judge admitted there were indications that he was 'head of the Mafia'. The prosecution did not stop Don Calò setting up a sweet factory in Palermo with 'Lucky' Luciano, thought to be a front for heroin trafficking.

On 10 July 1954, 76-year-old Calogero Vizzini died of natural causes at his home in Villalba.

The town was plunged into mourning for eight days and thousands of peasants, politicians, priests and mafiosi turned out for his funeral. On the church door hung an elegy written by his brother, the priest:

'He showed with his words and deeds that his Mafia was not criminal.'

Nevertheless, the illiterate Don Calò was said to have left over a billion lire. Although Don Calò usually avoided talking about the Mafia, he once told a journalist: 'When I die, the Mafia dies.'

Like Cesare Mori, he was wrong.

The glamorous
Salvatore Giuliano
with a lady on
horseback

SALVATORE GIULIANO AND SICILIAN SEPARATISM

At the end of the Second World War many Sicilians wanted their island to be independent of the Italian government in Rome. The movement, which was supported by the Mafia, was called Sicilian Separatism.

Lucio Tasca Bordonato, the mafioso who had been nominated as mayor of Palermo by the Allies, was a Separatist, as was Don Calogero Vizzini (Don Calò). In September 1945, Don Calò attended a secret meeting of Separatist leaders where they decided to mount an armed insurrection. One of those present at the meeting was Bordonato's son. But the most charismatic Separatist was Salvatore Giuliano. He was even aided by James Jesus Angleton, head of Secret Counterintelligence (SCI) and later the CIA, because of his anti-Communist stance.

Born in 1922 in Montelepre in the hills ten miles west of Palermo, Giuliano was about to be called up into the Italian army when the Allies invaded. He then became a black-marketeer. His life changed when he shot a *carabiniere* dead after he had been caught with a sack of grain. Injured in the exchange of fire, Giuliano was helped by his family, who were jailed for sheltering him.

He helped them to escape from the jail in Monreale, along with a number of other prisoners who became the core of his gang.

They funded their lifestyle by means of robbery and kidnapping. When the *carabinieri* came after them they were met with machine-gun fire.

Thanks to Giuliano's fierce good looks and his habit of giving interviews to newspapers and taking foreign mistresses, he managed to cultivate a glamorous international image. It was also said that he robbed the rich and gave to the poor, which led to the Sicilian peasants – and *Time* magazine – comparing him to Robin Hood. However, he ruthlessly murdered anyone he suspected of betrayal. During his career he is thought to have killed 430 people, though many of them died in shoot-outs with the authorities. He also worked hand in hand with the Mafia, who negotiated the ransom for his kidnap victims. In fact, he is thought to have actually been initiated into the Mafia. *Pentito* Tommaso Buscetta maintained that Giuliano was presented to him as 'the same thing' – that is, a fellow mafioso.

In early 1945, Giuliano met other Separatist leaders and asked to be paid ten million lire for joining their cause. He settled for one million and the rank of colonel in the armed wing, on the understanding that he would be given a pardon and a post in the new administration if the Separatists won. In fact, Giuliano had another agenda. With the help of a journalist he wrote a letter to President Truman, in which he requested him to annex Sicily. His father had lived in the United States for 18 years and he hoped to escape there and start a new life.

Giuliano then attacked government and police targets in the name of the Separatist movement, funding his activities with ever more lucrative endeavours, such as holding up the Palermo–Trapani train. In January 1946, as many as 1,000 Separatists took on the police and the *carabinieri* at Montedoro. Though the authorities could not crush the 'King of Montelepre', the Separatists' insurrection collapsed when they suffered a crushing defeat in the 1946 elections. Things were no better when Sicily went to the ballot box in 1947. The Communists and the Socialists united in a People's Bloc and won an impressive 30 per cent of the vote, while the Christian Democrats came in with 21 per cent. The Separatists took a slightly bigger share of the vote than they had done in 1946, but it was hardly the result that Giuliano had hoped for – or needed.

Things were different in Montelepre, where the Separatists had gained 1,521 votes against the Communists' 70, but it was not enough to prevent Giuliano from committing his most heartless crime.

A week later, one of Giuliano's gang reported that another bandit had turned up with a letter for Giuliano. He read the letter, then burnt it. Afterwards he said: 'The hour has come… We have to go into action against the Communists.' The target was Portella della Ginestra and the date was May Day. The peasants would be celebrating a leftist festival that had been banned under Mussolini.

On that fateful day the people of Piana degli Albanesi (formerly known as Piana dei Greci) – 2,739 of whom had voted for the People's Bloc against 13 for the Separatists – gathered in the valley of Portella della Ginestra to celebrate May Day and their electoral victory. But just as a leader of the People's Bloc rose to speak, the crowd was raked with machine-gun fire from the surrounding hills. Eleven people were killed, including four children, and 33 were injured, including one little girl who had her jaw shot off.

Giuliano wrote an open letter taking responsibility for the massacre but claiming that he only wanted his men to fire over the heads of the crowd. The deaths and injuries had been a mistake, particularly where children had been involved. 'Do you think I have a stone instead of a heart?' he asked. Any number of letters could not have placated the outraged populace, particularly as Giuliano went on to attack institutions such as Communist Party offices, killing even more innocent people.

There were rumours that the letter Giuliano had received contained orders from the 'high' Mafia, perhaps even Christian Democrat minister Bernardo Mattarella. Born and brought up in Castellammare del Golfo, Mattarella was one of those who greeted Joe Bonanno when he returned to Sicily for a holiday in 1957.

The Communist Girolamo Li Causi, who had gone on to become a senator, blamed the Mafia for the Portella della Ginestra massacre and called on Giuliano to name names. Giuliano refused, because he had to observe the *omertà*. Having lost popular support, he now depended on the protection of the Mafia. Li Causi then warned Giuliano that the minister of the interior, Mario Scelba, a Sicilian from Caltagirone, wanted him dead. Giuliano claimed that this was because: 'I can make sure he is brought to account for actions

'As a leader of the People's Bloc rose to speak, the crowd was raked with machine-gun fire from the surrounding hills. Eleven people were killed, including four children, and 33 were injured'

that, if revealed, would destroy his political career and bring an end to his life.'

There was now a bounty of three million lire on Giuliano's head. Nevertheless, he goaded the police with letters, even leaving one with the tip in a Palermo restaurant. On 14 August 1949, Giuliano's men exploded mines under a *carabinieri* convoy at Bellolampo, killed seven and wounding eleven. This propelled the

Italian government into action. A special force – the *Corpe delle Forze per la Repressione del Banditismo in Sicilia* – was formed under the leadership of Colonel Ugo Luca and an extra 1,000 troops were sent to western Sicily. The Mafia did not welcome this sort of attention. By the end of 1949, many of Giuliano's men had either been killed or captured and taken to Viterbo on the mainland to stand trial. In early 1950, Giuliano decided it was time to flee. He left his base in the mountains around Montelepre and made his way 60 miles (96 km) south to the town of Castelvetrano, where there was an airstrip. From there, he was to fly to Tunis, then on to the United States.

On 5 July 1950 Giuliano was found dead in the courtyard of a house in Castelvetrano. His body was riddled with machine-gun bullets. The official version was that he had been killed in a shoot-out with the *carabinieri*. This was quickly discounted. Giuliano's cousin, Gaspare Pisciotta, who was also his lieutenant, later admitted to the murder. He had fallen out with Giuliano over attempts to rescue those standing trial in Viterbo and had contacted Colonel Ugo Luca, the leader of the troops. On 5 July 1950 Pisciotta shot Giuliano in the head. A carload of *carabinieri* sat waiting as Pisciotta murdered his kinsman. They then dragged his body outside and shot bullets into it so they could take credit.

But the water is murkier than that. Shortly before the killing, an unescorted Colonel

Luca was seen leaving his HQ in Palermo. He was on his way to see 'Three-fingers Frank' Coppola, who had taken control in Partinico after being deported from the USA. Pisciotta claimed that he had been promised a pardon and a reward, but two days after Giuliano's death he turned up at police headquarters, begging to be arrested.

The police happily obliged and he was sent to Viterbo, where he was sentenced to life imprisonment for his part in the Portella della Ginestra massacre. He was poisoned with strychnine while he was incarcerated in Ucciardone prison in Palermo. The truth about the massacre at Portella della Ginestra and the murder of Salvatore Giuliano would now never be known.

Curiously, the plaque at the site of the Portella della Ginestra massacre does not mention Giuliano at all. Instead, it reads:

> *'On May 1, 1947, here on the rock of Barbato, celebrating the working class festival and the victory of April 20, people of Piana degli Albanesi, San Giuseppe Jato and San Cipirello, men, women, and children, fell under the ferocious barbarity of the bullets of the Mafia and the landed barons, who mowed down innocent victims in order to put an end to the struggle of the peasants for liberation from the servitude of feudalism...'*

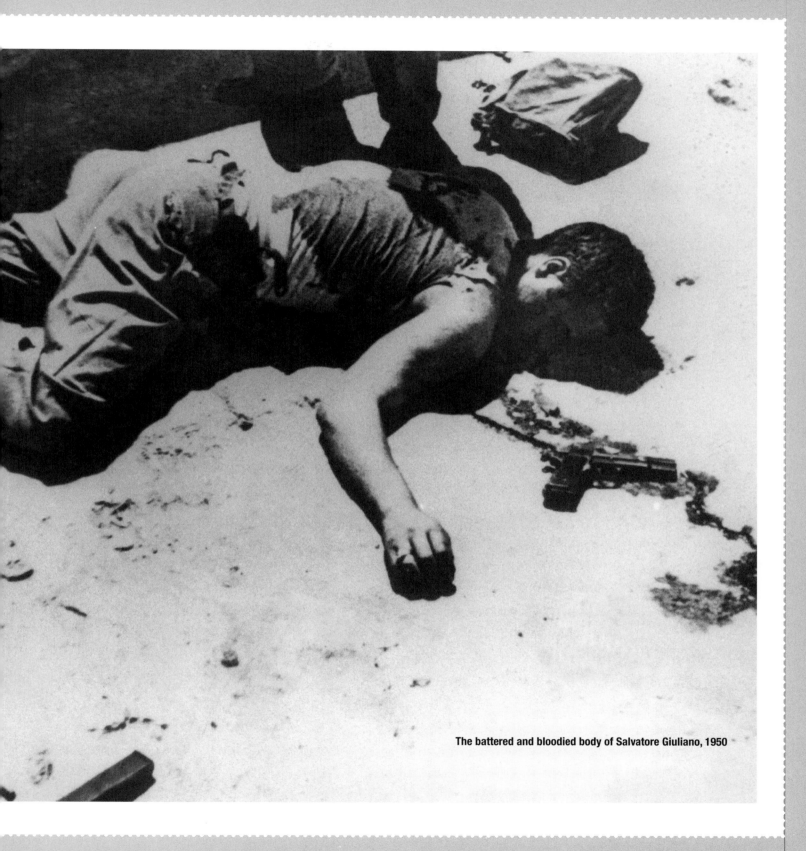

The battered and bloodied body of Salvatore Giuliano, 1950

GIUSEPPE BONANNO

Born in Castellammare del Golfo in Sicily in 1905, Giuseppe Bonanno emigrated to the United States with his parents when he was 1 year old. The family settled in Brooklyn. However, when Joe was 6 years old the family returned to Sicily. Orphaned at the age of 15, he enrolled in the nautical college in Palermo, but was expelled for anti-Fascist activities. During Mussolini's crackdown on the Mafia a warrant was issued for Bonanno's arrest, so he was forced to flee.

After returning to America illegally via Cuba, he went to work for Al Capone as a bootlegger and a hijacker. Back in Brooklyn, he went to work for the local Mafia boss Nicolo Schiro and he soon rose in the ranks. At the beginning of the Castellammarese War, Bonanno transferred his allegiance to Salvatore Maranzano. However, he sympathized with the American-born 'Young Turks' under 'Lucky' Luciano, realizing that the day of the 'Moustache Petes' — the Sicilian-born old-timers — was fast drawing to a close. When the war was over and Maranzano was dead, Bonanno was awarded what was left of Maranzano's crime family, together with a gambling and loan-sharking empire that stretched from Haiti to Montreal.

Fearing the investigations that had led to the arrests of Luciano and Lepke, Bonanno fled back to Sicily in 1938. He returned to become a naturalized United States citizen in 1945, marrying the sister of crime boss Frank Labruzzo. In 1953 he bought a luxury home in Tucson, Arizona and announced that he was going into semi-retirement. In fact, he spent the next ten years consolidating his position. With Vito Genovese in jail, Bonanno figured he could take over the Five Families. In 1964, he ordered his enforcer, Joe Magliocco, to wipe out the top American Mafia bosses, including Tommy Lucchese, head of the Mafia in Manhattan and New Jersey; Carlo Gambino, family boss in Brooklyn; Steve Magaddino, Bonanno's cousin, who ran Buffalo; and Frank DiSimone, head of the family in Los Angeles.

Overweight and suffering from high blood pressure, Magliocco passed on the assignment to Joe Colombo. Figuring that he had nothing to gain from the war that was likely to ensue, Colombo told Lucchese and Gambino about the plot. Bonanno and Magliocco were ordered to appear before the Commission, but only Magliocco obeyed. He was fined $50,000 and forced to retire but he died soon afterwards, possibly poisoned by Bonanno.

In the early 1960s Bonanno handed over his crime empire, estimated to be worth over $2 billion a year, to his son Salvatore ('Bill') to run, making him *consigliere*.

Bill was married to Joe Profaci's niece. This did not go down very well with his ambitious underboss Gaspar DiGregorio, who had been the best man at Bonanno's wedding and was religious godfather to Bill. Shortly afterwards, in 1964, Bonanno was kidnapped by Steve Magaddino, who held him at his retreat in the Catskills.

While Bonanno was away the Bonanno family split into two factions. One contingent was led by Bonanno's son Bill, while the other group fell in behind DiGregorio. This was dubbed the 'Banana split'. After a time the Commission appointed DiGregorio as the family's boss. Naturally, Bill Bonanno was incensed by the decision and the family was soon torn apart by conflict. When

Giuseppe Bonanno smiling his enigmatic smile

DiGregorio called a peace conference, Bill suggested that they meet at his grand-uncle's house on Troutman Street in Brooklyn. However, as Bill's party approached the house they were greeted with gunfire. More than twenty shots were fired and the police found seven handguns on the pavement. Miraculously, no one was hurt.

Bonanno then issued a threat from his Tucson mansion – next time one of his men got hit, he would take out one of the *capi*. As good as his word, he had Calogero Lo Cicero, a Colombo *capo*, machine-gunned as he sat by the soda fountain in a New York drugstore. In all, around 20 gangsters died in the Bananas War. Bonanno then had a heart attack, after which he made peace again. His family were allowed to keep some of their rackets, provided the killing stopped.

By this time the Commission had become dissatisfied with DiGregorio, so they appointed Paul Sciacca in his place. Sciacca was also given a seat on the Commission. Bonanno responded by ordering three of Sciacca's top men to be machine-gunned in a Brooklyn restaurant. Bonanno's loyal chauffeur, Sam Perone, was killed in retaliation.

The fighting finally came to an end in 1968, when Bonanno announced his retirement. In 1983 he wrote a self-serving autobiography called *A Man of Honor*. This led to further investigations into the existence of the Commission. But Bonanno refused to answer questions in front of a grand jury and was jailed for contempt. He was released after a year, due to ill health.

The last of the mafiosi to survive Fascism and the Mafia wars in New York, he died of heart failure at the age of 97 in 2002. Bonanno is thought to be the model for Don Vito Corleono in Mario Puzo's novel *The Godfather*.

Chapter 7

THE TEACHER

Ninetta Bagarella was born into a Mafia family. From 1963 to 1968, her father Salvatore Bagarella had lived in exile in northern Italy because of his involvement with the Mafia. Her eldest brother Giuseppe was also sent into exile and was murdered in prison in 1972. The next eldest, Calogero, was a childhood friend of Bernardo Provenzano and Salvatore 'Totò' Riina.

At the age of 12, Totò Riina effectively became head of the family while his father Giovanni Riina was emptying the explosives from a wartime shell, so he could sell the metal casing as scrap. The shell slipped from Giovanni's grasp and exploded, killing him and one of his sons, seven-year-old Francesco, and wounding another son, Gaetano. Only Totò was left unhurt.

YOUNG MAFIA RECRUIT

Unrestrained by the firm hand of a father, Totò soon turned his back on the life of a peasant and hung about in the piazza of Corleone, telling his friends that he was not going to die poor. He and Provenzano were recruited by Luciano Leggio, hitman for the local doctor and *capomafia* Michele Navarra. The three of them did a brisk trade in stealing cattle and selling the butchered meat. They would greet each other with a kiss on the cheek, a typical Mafia gesture. Riina was warned off joining the Mafia by a local policeman, Provenzano by an older brother. It did no good.

In May 1949, after the procession of the crucified Christ in Corleone, Riina and his friends got into a fight with Domenico Di Matteo using sticks and knuckle-dusters. Ten days later there was another fight outside town.

Right: **From the 1960s onwards, the town of Corleone became infamous for Mafia activities**

Left: **Antonietta Riina, née Bagarella, the teacher who joined the Mafia**

This time it ended with gunfire. Riina loosed off half-a-dozen shots with an automatic. One shot fatally wounded Di Matteo and Riina himself was wounded. He was arrested in his hospital bed.

In court, in chains, he spoke abusively to the judge and was sentenced to 12 years. He served only six.

TRADITIONAL COURTSHIP

The year after Riina's release, he was invited to stay for dinner at the home of his friend Calogero Bagarella. Calogero's sister, 13-year-old Ninetta, served at table. Although at 26 Totò was twice her age, he was instantly smitten with her pretty oval face, black eyes and long black hair, which she wore in a ponytail.

For Riina, her family background could not have been better – by then a third brother had joined the Mafia. What's more, Calogero was in love with Riina's sister. But Ninetta was something special. While Riina was barely literate, Ninetta was an avid reader, improving her mind by poring over books from the school library. She sat in the front row in class and studied Latin and Greek. A model pupil, she saw education as a way of escaping poverty and she was determined to get a proper job when she grew up.

She also consumed novels to give herself a broader perspective. The ones she picked usually concerned the plight of the oppressed and poor and their struggle against their oppressors.

'What I read in those books,' she said, 'was life in Corleone.'

She was also fascinated by Machiavelli – 'because his principle, the end justifies the means, was applied to the letter by the local police,' she said.

Despite this intellectual rift between them, Riina wooed Ninetta in the traditional way. Every morning he would wait in the narrow alleyway where she lived and follow her to school. On the way, not a word was spoken.

'For years I followed her with my eyes, for years I never gave her a moment's rest,' he said, 'until she decided to marry me.'

DEADLY FEUD

Meanwhile a feud had broken out between Leggio and Navarra, who had vetoed a lucrative construction project Leggio was involved in. Leggio then put the squeeze on one of Navarra's lieutenants. Navarra arranged an ambush and Leggio was wounded in the arm. Honour had been satisfied, or so Navarra thought. He was wrong.

On 2 August 1958, Navarra was being driven home from Lercara Friddi, birthplace of 'Lucky' Luciano, by a doctor who had no Mafia associations. Navarra was unarmed and had no bodyguard. They were ambushed by Leggio, Provenzano and Riina, who had abandoned the traditional *lupara*, or sawn-off shotgun, in favour of Al Capone-style sub-machine guns and automatic pistols. They fired 124 bullets into the car; 92 of them hit Navarra.

A Mafia victim, 1966; part of a long history of violence in Sicily

A month later, they made peace overtures to Navarra loyalists and Riina was sent alone and unarmed to a Mafia meeting.

'Who's dead is dead,' he said. 'The dear departed has gone away. Let us think of the living.'

Solemnly he crossed himself. Before there was an answer, Provenzano and another man appeared and opened fire with sawn-off shotguns. One of Navarra's men was shot in the face. The others fled.

In the ensuing chase through the streets of Corleone, a two-year-old girl was wounded by a stray bullet. Provenzano was hit in the head and left for dead. Two women were injured, along with an eight-year-old girl. But when the police arrived, no one had seen anything. Interviewed in his hospital bed, Provenzano claimed to have been on his way to the cinema when he collapsed unconscious.

'I have no idea what happened,' he said.

SILENT WAR

War broke out and Riina quickly became one of Leggio's most trusted killers, never hesitating to cut down Navarra loyalists and any inconvenient witnesses. The final shot was always to the mouth, to warn anyone who knew anything to remain silent. The *omertà*, or code of silence, was absolute. A journalist asked a weeping mother walking behind a coffin: 'Who was killed?' She replied: 'Why, is somebody dead?'

Some 50 people were murdered and there were a further 22 murder attempts. At first, victims were shot down in the streets, shops and bars, or in their homes. Then came the *lupara bianca* or 'white shotgun'. People simply disappeared, their bodies thrown down ravines, dissolved in lime or burnt on giant grills over open fires.

Provenzano was wounded trying to ambush Navarra lieutenant Francesco Paolo Streva in the alleyway where Ninetta lived. As he made his escape, a woman emerged to wipe up the trail of blood. Streva was ambushed again four months later. This time he was murdered and left in a ditch, together with his two bodyguards and their guard dog. Leggio and his two lieutenants, Provenzano and Riina, were now in control in Corleone.

But this was not enough for Leggio. He wanted to move into Palermo. The move prompted another Mafia war. It became so ferocious that Leggio and his men had to go into hiding.

In December 1963, Riina was caught in a police roadblock. He found himself in the Ucciardone prison in Palermo, surrounded by incarcerated Palermo dons wearing silk dressing gowns and brandishing silver cigarette holders. They looked down on the Corleonesi – which only fuelled Riina's ambition further.

'When I get out of here,' he said, 'I want to walk on a carpet of 100,000-lire banknotes.'

Six months after Riina's capture, Leggio was arrested. Provenzano was picked up as well. All three refused to co-operate with the authorities and in 1969 they appeared in the dock together in Bari along with another 61 Mafiosi. Due to the intimidation of the jury, they were all acquitted. Riina was only found guilty of stealing a driving licence and was sentenced to six months, time he had already served.

FORMAL ENGAGEMENT

Riina returned to Corleone, where he was rearrested and sentenced to four years' exile. He was granted a few days' liberty to settle his domestic affairs and he used the time to formalize his engagement to Ninetta, who was by now a 26-year-old teacher. While he had been away she had enrolled at Palermo University, to study literature and philosophy. Travelling there by bus every day, she was accompanied by two police officers who suspected she had links to the Mafia. Then two of her brothers shot a cattle breeder who was wooing her sister. One brother was arrested and the other went on the run. Ninetta was forced to give up her studies. Instead, she took a teaching post in a private institute.

Riina took his mother to meet Ninetta's mother. The two women would formally seek 'clarification' – that is, discuss the dowry and make arrangements for where the couple would live. The dowry was small. Riina was not a rich man, but Ninetta's mother was confident that he could make money, provided he stayed out of jail.

Business concluded, drinks were served and Riina gave Ninetta the ring.

'We got engaged in the intimacy of our families,' said Ninetta. 'It's not as if we said to each other "I love you" or "You're the light of my life". We were serious people.'

Riina then went into exile in San Giovanni in Persiceto, near Bologna in northern Italy. He signed in at the police station there, but disappeared a few days later to become a fugitive again.

'People simply disappeared, their bodies thrown down ravines'

Meanwhile, Ninetta's brother Calogero Bagarella joined Provenzano in Leggio's hit squad to take out Michele 'the Cobra' Cavataio in the ongoing Palermo war. Dressed in police uniforms, they shot up Cavataio's headquarters. Calogero Bagarella was shot and fatally wounded. Provenzano was wounded too, but he finished the job with a machine gun. When it jammed, he hit Cavataio's skull with the butt until it caved in. Riina made a brief appearance in public at Calogero's funeral.

Leggio was in poor health, so Riina and Provenzano went to work for the *capomafia* of Cinisi, Gaetano Badalamenti and Stefano 'the Prince' Bontate, another *capo* in Palermo. Riina seized the opportunity to learn as much as he could about the inside workings of the Sicilian Mafia. It stood him in good stead.

When Leggio moved to Milan, Riina became his representative on the Mafia triumvirate, whose other members were Badalamenti

Palermo is the
economic hub
of Sicily and has
therefore been an
important centre
for the Mafia

and Bontate. But Bontate mocked him for being a peasant and tried to get him arrested. Nevertheless Riina took his place on the broader Commission that replaced the triumvirate.

ON TRIAL FOR LOVE

In July 1971, Ninetta Bagarella arrived at the law courts in Palermo. The 27-year-old schoolteacher looked nothing like a Mafia wife. Eschewing austere black clothing, she wore a blue dress with yellow and red flowers printed on it, the hemline above the knee, high-heeled shoes and her diamond engagement ring. She had been accused of being the liaison between the Leggio clan and several fugitives. The police had evidence that she had arranged Leggio's various stays in hospital.

The year before, the police had requested her passport. She sent it to them, together with a letter calling them 'persecutors, tormentors, torturers'. This brought a charge of slander. The police then brought about her dismissal from the school in which she had taught physical education for four years. They now sought to have her exiled to the mainland. She was the first woman they had tried to banish.

Ninetta brought with her a petition drawn up by the archpriest of Corleone, a colleague of Ninetta's at school, and signed by scores of residents. In it, the archpriest said that the Bagarellas were 'an exemplary family dogged by misfortune and the law that does not respect the affairs of the heart and persecutes a schoolteacher just because she is engaged to Salvatore Riina'.

Of Ninetta's 'exemplary family', a father and brother were in exile; another brother was officially a fugitive but had actually been gunned down in a hit two years earlier; and a third brother was Riina's lieutenant.

However, the archpriest said: 'Her mother comes to Mass every morning and takes communion.'

In court, the presiding judge said: 'Miss Bagarella, you know it has been proposed that you be sent into exile.'

In a clear, calm voice, Ninetta replied: 'I don't believe the court wants to send me into exile. If you have a conscience, if you have a heart, you won't do it. Only the women remain in our family. We have to work for ourselves and for our men, father and brothers who have been dogged by misfortune. I am a woman and I am guilty only of loving a man who I esteem and trust. I have always loved Totò Riina. I was 13 and he was 26 when I first fell in love. He has never been out of my heart. That is all I am guilty of, your honour.'

The judge pointed out that Riina was a dangerous criminal who was wanted for numerous murders.

Ninetta dismissed this: 'A pack of lies. Slander. Salvatore is innocent.'

She was then accused of belonging to the Leggio clan.

'I don't even know Leggio,' she said.

For over an hour she parried every

accusation thrown at her. Her lawyer then delivered dozens of testimonials from fellow teachers, pupils and parents.

'The only thing I want is to marry Riina,' she told the court. 'I don't want our relationship to remain platonic. But I have not seen him for such a long time. I know nothing about him. I don't even know if he still loves me.'

The judge denied the petition to send her to the mainland, but ordered that she be put under police surveillance for two-and-a-half years. She was also placed under curfew from 7.30 pm to 7 am.

After the hearing, she was asked by a journalist: 'What is the Mafia?'

'The Mafia is a phenomenon created by the newspapers to sell more newspapers,' she shot back.

Hearing of her testimony, Riina said: 'I don't want any other woman. I only want Ninetta. They don't want me to marry her? Well, I will carry out a massacre.'

MARRIED ON THE RUN

Just one week before the end of her sentence, a policeman visited the Bagarella household after 7.30 pm. Ninetta was not there. The policeman was told that Ninetta had got a job in Germany. In fact, she was with Riina. Now both of them were on the run. Nevertheless

> *'Riina and Ninetta moved into a villa in Palermo. Although she had over a million dollars' worth of jewellery, she could not visit her mother. Her children had to be escorted to school'*

they were married by Mafioso priest Father Agostino Coppola, nephew of Frank 'Three Fingers' Coppola, a leading light of the Gambino family, though the marriage was never registered. The couple spent their honeymoon in Venice. Nine months later, Ninetta gave birth to their first child, a daughter named Concetta, in an exclusive clinic in Palermo. She gave birth to three more children there – Giovanni, Giuseppe and Lucia. She registered them under her own name and neither she nor Riina, who visited, was bothered by the police.

In 1974, Leggio was jailed for the murder of Navarra, and Riina took over the Corleonesi. He sought to dominate the heroin trade and ordered hits on a number of the policemen, judges and prosecutors who tried to stop him. Snooping reporters were unwelcome too. In 1979, Ninetta's brother Leoluca killed Mario Francese, a journalist on the *Giornale di Sicilia*. Then a fresh Mafia war broke out in Sicily.

Riina and Ninetta moved into a villa in Palermo with a damp-proof underground vault to store her furs. Although she had over a million dollars' worth of jewellery, she could not visit her mother. Her children had to be escorted to school and, according to

Leggio is driven away by the Guardia di Finanza

her sisters, she was reprimanded by Riina for standing on the balcony.

BOSS OF BOSSES

In 1983, convicted killer Tommaso Buscetta, who had been on the losing side in the war, became a *pentito*, that is a 'penitent one' who turns state's evidence – the first senior Mafia figure to do so. He revealed that the Mafia was a single organization run by a Commission, or *Cupola*, headed by Riina. To divert resources from the investigation Riina organized a terrorist-style attack, known as the Christmas Massacre, in 1984. A bomb was detonated in a tunnel through the Apennines between Florence and Bologna, killing 17 and injuring 267. Nevertheless, Buscetta's evidence led to the Maxi Trial in 1986, which led to the conviction of 338 Mafiosi. Riina was given a life sentence *in absentia*.

He continued his campaign of murdering rivals to maintain his position as 'boss of bosses', while simultaneously cultivating political connections. When the Maxi Trial convictions were upheld, Riina ordered the assassination of the former mayor of Palermo Salvatore Lima, along with prosecuting magistrates Giovanni Falcone and Paolo Borsellino.

The killing of Falcone and Borsellino led to public outrage. Fearing the wrath of Riina, the acting boss of the San Giuseppe clan, Balduccio Di Maggio, fled Sicily and became a *pentito*. He told the authorities he had a rough idea of where Riina lived. Studying footage of film shot covertly in the area, he spotted Ninetta getting into a car. Next day, Riina was arrested coming out of the same building.

Although Provenzano became titular head of the Corleonesi, it was thought that the faction was run by Ninetta's brother Leoluca until his arrest in 1995. Two years later, Riina's son Giovanni was arrested. Ninetta wrote an open letter to the Rome newspaper *La Repubblica*, saying: 'I've decided to open my heart, which is swollen and overflowing with sadness for the arrest of my son Giovanni. . . . At home we all miss him, our family situation has become hell, we cannot accept that a boy barely 20 years old, with no previous convictions, is first arrested, then questioned for two days and then jailed.'

Ninetta appealed to the mayor of Corleone for help. While intimidated by her presence, there was nothing he could do. In 2001, Giovanni was sentenced to life imprisonment for four murders. The following year, his younger brother Giuseppe was given 14 years for extortion, money laundering and criminal association. Then in 2007 the widow of Paolo Borsellino filed a civil suit for damages against Ninetta and was awarded €3,360,000 compensation.

> '*The widow of Paolo Borsellino filed a civil suit for damages against Ninetta and was awarded €3,360,000*'

Ninetta Bagarella on her daughter's wedding day in 2008

Chapter 8

THE MAFIA WARS

The Greco family is one of the most powerful Mafia families in Sicily. They can trace their origins back to the end of the 19th century, when police chief Ermanno Sangiorgi identified Salvatore Greco as a *capomafia*. Between them, the Grecos ruled the villages of Ciaculli and Croceverde Giardini on the outskirts of Palermo.

The early activities of the Grecos were similar to those of most rural Mafia clans. In 1916, a priest who denounced the Mafia's interference in the administration of Church funds was murdered – it was said by a husband whose wife he had seduced. Five years later, a Greco who had suffered a *sgarro*, or personal affront, killed two shepherds along with their sheep. Then in 1929 a Greco loosed off 20 bullets into an enemy's wine cask, before calmly sitting down to smoke a pipe. Ten years after that, a Greco set fire to the home of a newlywed couple on their wedding night.

WAR OF THE GRECOS

Until 1946 the Grecos were a threat to the local inhabitants, but not to each other. Things changed in 1946, when war broke out between the Greco clans of Ciaculli and Croceverde Giardini. The feud between the Grecos seems to have had its origins in an incident in 1939, when six young men from Croceverde Giardini visited Ciaculli for the Festival of the Crucifix. A fight broke out with the local boys when they brought a pew out of the church to view the parade. On the way home, the Grecos from Croceverde Giardini were confronted by their Ciaculli cousins, who were carrying guns and knives. In the resulting fracas, Giuseppe Greco – the 17-year-old son of Giuseppe 'Piddu the Lieutenant' Greco, *capo* of Croceverde Giardini – was killed and a Ciaculli cousin was wounded. He died four years later in jail.

On 26 August 1946 the boss of the Ciaculli clan – the brother-in-law of 'Piddu the Lieutenant' who was also named Giuseppe Greco – and his brother Pietro were killed with machine guns and grenades. A few months later, two of Piddu the Lieutenant's men were shot down with a *lupara*, the Sicilian short-barrelled shotgun. Two men from the Ciaculli faction then disappeared. Only their clothes were found. An incident like this was known as a *lupara bianca* – a 'white shotgun'.

The feud reached a bloody climax on 17 September 1947 when Antonio Conigliaro, a close friend of Piddu the Lieutenant, was machine-gunned in the main square of Ciaculli. When it was clear that he was not dead, Antonina and Rosalia, the widow and daughter of one of the Ciaculli bosses killed earlier, finished him off with kitchen knives.

> *'The feud reached a climax when Antonio Conigliaro was gunned down in the main square. The widow and daughter of the Ciaculli bosses finished him off with kitchen knives'*

Left: **Old Sicily**

The brother and sister of the victim then opened fire on the women, killing 19-year-old Rosalia and wounding her mother. The victim's brother was then killed by Antonina's 18-year-old son.

Eleven members of the two clans were killed and several others were wounded. It is possible that the vendetta might have only been an excuse for Piddu the Lieutenant to take over the district and its rich citrus business. But with Conigliaro dead, Piddu himself was now in danger. Meanwhile the other Mafia bosses wanted him to end the feud because it was drawing too much attention to them.

He sought the help of Antonio Cottone, the Mafia boss of nearby Villabate. Cottone had recently been deported from the United States and it is thought that he introduced the term 'family' to Mafia organization in Sicily. Formerly, Mafia bands were called *cosca* – plural *cosche* in Italian and *coschi* in Sicilian. *Cosca* is a Sicilian word for a plant such as the artichoke or the thistle, whose spiny, closely-folded leaves seem to symbolize the bond between members of the Mafia. The word *borgata* or 'brugad' took over in the United States at a later date. *Borgata* is the Italian word for a village or, in a town, a slum.

Antonio Cottone had worked with the Profaci brothers in New York. Joe Profaci, who was also from Villabate, was in Sicily at the time so he helped with the peace negotiations. Piddu the Lieutenant made amends by awarding the co-ownership of a citrus fruit

export business and a bus company to two of his orphaned nephews. They were the sons of Giuseppe and Pietro Greco, the first two to die during the Ciaculli war. Both of the nephews were called Salvatore Greco – one was known as 'Ciaschiteddu' ('Little Flask') because of his narrow shoulders and broad hips and the other was called 'L'ingegnere' ('The

TOMMASO BUSCETTA

Born in the slums of Palermo in 1928, Buscetta joined the Mafia in 1945 and became a 'made man' in the Porta Nuova family in the following year. During the crackdown following the First Mafia War Buscetta fled to the United States, where the Gambino family helped him get started in the pizza business.

In 1968 he was tried *in absentia* in Italy for a double murder and was sentenced to life. Two years later he was arrested in New York, but he was released. He then fled to Brazil, where he set up a drug smuggling operation. In 1972, he was arrested again. After being tortured, he was sent back to Italy to start his life

'Buscetta testified in the Maxi Trials that saw the convictions of some 350 mafiosi. In the Pizza Connection Trial, his testimony sent hundreds more to jail. In return he was allowed to live in the US'

sentence. In the Ucciardone prison, he heard that the Cosa Nostra intended to expel him for being flagrantly unfaithful to his first two wives.

After serving eight years, he was let out on day-release. He took the opportunity to return to Brazil, where he escaped the Second Mafia War that caused the deaths of ten of his relatives. After he returned to Italy he tried to commit suicide. When that failed, he asked to talk to Judge Giovanni Falcone. He then turned informant, explaining later: 'Along with the drugs has come more money, but also more greed, more violence, and less honour. Gone are the men of honour whose word you believed in.'

In Italy, he testified in the Maxi Trials that saw the convictions of some 350 mafiosi. In the New York Pizza Connection Trial, his testimony sent hundreds more to jail. He also testified to the Senate Permanent Subcommittee on Investigations. In return, he was allowed to live in the United States under a new identity provided by the Witness Protection Program.

He lived out the rest of his life peacefully in the United States, dying of cancer in New York at the age of 71 in the year 2000.

Mafia boss Tommaso Buscetta tries to remain incognito in a fortified courtroom at Rebibbia jail, Palermo, 1984

Engineer') or 'Totò il lungo' ('Totò the tall'). Piddu's son – another Salvatore Greco, 'The Senator' – then married Cottone's daughter Maria. Meanwhile Piddu the Lieutenant withdrew from active life as a mafioso and moved to Palermo, where he moved in the higher echelons of society, occasionally dining with the cardinal, though his home was still

used as a base for criminal activities.

Peace reigned until January 1955, when the fruit and vegetable wholesale market controlled by Cottone and the Grecos was moved from the Zisa district to Acquasanta on the waterfront, a move that disturbed the fine balance of the Mafia in the district. Acquasanta was controlled by Nicola D'Alessandro and

Gaetano Galatolo, who saw an opportunity to muscle in on the protection rackets that belonged to Cottone and the Grecos. But ambition was followed by bloodshed. First of all, Galatolo was gunned down in the market. His death was followed by 28 other killings that year. Nino Cottone was machine-gunned outside his villa and Francesco Greco, a 'wholesaler dealing in fruit and vegetables', was also killed. On the Acquasanta side Nicola D'Alessandro was slain and a third *capo*, Salvatore Licandro, was pursued all the way to Como, where he was murdered.

At the same time, arguments over the control of irrigation and transport led to fighting in some of the surrounding villages. That year in the province of Palermo 60 people disappeared. The corpses were disposed of in the concrete that was so much a part of the post-war building boom.

While the local Mafia was pursuing activities such as controlling the wholesale markets, smuggling cigarettes and muscling in on the construction business, it was also dealing in heroin. Before Nino Cottone died the Palermo police recorded his conversation with Joe Profaci in New York. The subject was the export of Sicilian oranges. The Brooklyn number called by Cottone was the one that was used by 'Lucky' Luciano, then resident in Naples, and Frank Coppola, who was living in Anzio. They too were talking about high-grade oranges. In 1959, US customs intercepted a crate. It contained 90 hollowed-out wax oranges filled with heroin. According to Nick Gentile, drugs were also hidden inside shipments of cheese, anchovies, olive oil and other Sicilian products.

Aware of the growing problem of drug addiction, the United States Congress rushed through the Narcotic Control Act of 1956. As a result, over 200 major American gangsters were arrested and sentenced to long jail terms. These included three out of five members of the Lucchese family, one in two of the Genoveses, two in five of the Gambinos and one in three of the Colombos and the Bonannos. These would eventually include Joe Bonanno's underboss Carmine Galante, who was sentenced to a term of from 15 to 20 years, while two ranking Luccheses were each handed sentences of 40 years.

> *'That year in the province of Palermo 60 people disappeared. Corpses were disposed of in the concrete that was so much a part of the post-war building boom'*

THE FIRST MAFIA WAR

In October 1957 'Lucky' Luciano held a summit in the Little Red Room off the Sala Wagner in the Grand Hotel Et Des Palmes in the centre of Palermo. It was the room in which Wagner is said to have orchestrated *Parsifal*. Renoir also painted Wagner's portrait in

A cheerful Angelo La Barbera confers with his lawyer during the trial of 152 Mafia members in Catanzaro, Italy, 1967

that same room. The purpose of the meeting was to set the ground rules for renewed co-operation between the Sicilian and the American Mafias. The Grecos attended, along with the Inzerillos, Bontades, Badalamentis and La Barberas, whose delegation included Tommaso Buscetta. Another delegate was Giuseppe Genco Russo, who had succeeded Calogero Don Calò Vizzini as boss of bosses.

Representing the Americans was Joe Bonanno. He would allow nothing but the Sicilian dialect to be spoken in his home and he hired only Sicilians. Bonanno first flew to Rome, where he received the VIP treatment from the Italian minister of foreign trade, Bernardo Mattarella, who was also from Castellammare del Golfo. Because the American Mafia could not continue in the drugs business in the face of the penalties then being handed down, they were prepared to 'rent' out their cities to the Sicilians, who were able to provide fresh faces with no criminal records and no mugshots and fingerprints on file. This suited the Sicilians because there was no demand for drugs in Italy and there was then only a small market in northern Europe.

Luciano spotted the tension between the Sicilian families at the meeting. As Bonanno put it: 'There were too many dogs going after one bone.' So it was agreed that a Commission would be set up, like that in New York, to iron out any difficulties. The first Commission only covered the province of Palermo. Even then there were 15 families – too many to be represented on the Commission, it was decided. The solution was that three families in each district or *mandamento* would pick one of their number to represent them on the Palermo Commission. Each province would then set up its own Commission. It was not until 1975 that a Commission was set up for the whole island.

The first secretary – or head – of the Palermo Commission was Salvatore 'Ciaschiteddu' Greco. This did not help when the First Mafia War broke out between the well-established Grecos and the up-and-coming La Barberas. In 1962, a consignment of heroin was forwarded to New York by Calcedonio Di Pisa, an ally of the Grecos. The shipment had been funded by the Grecos, the La Barberas and Cesare Manzella, who sat on the first Mafia Commission, but when it reached Brooklyn it was found to be underweight. Di Pisa was acquitted by the Commission of any wrongdoing. Nevertheless, on 26 December 1962 he was shot dead outside a kiosk in the Piazza Principe di Camporeale in Palermo. Three men with shotguns and a revolver had carried out the shooting, but when the police

> *'On 26 April 1963, Cesare Manzella, who sided with the Grecos, was blown to pieces by a car bomb. Only a shoe and his broad-brimmed, American-style hat were found at the scene'*

made enquiries no one in the square could recall hearing any shots.

The Grecos suspected Salvatore and Angelo La Barbera, who had contested the Commission's decision. They were part of the 'New Mafia', who ran construction companies, built apartments and dealt in real estate, as well as smuggling cigarettes and heroin. Unlike the 'Old Mafia', who kept a low profile, they lived an Al Capone lifestyle with flashy cars, tailored clothes, beautiful women and frequent trips to Milan and Rome, where they stayed in the best hotels. In January 1963, Salvatore La Barbera disappeared. When his Alfa Romeo Giulietta was found burned out, it was assumed that he was the victim of a 'white shotgun', or mystery disappearance. Buscetta is thought to have been responsible, with the corpse being disposed of in the furnaces of his glass factory. He said the responsibility lay with the Commission.

Angelo La Barbera then disappeared, but he resurfaced two weeks later in Milan, where he held a press conference – unheard of for a mafioso at the time. On 26 April 1963, Cesare Manzella, who sided with the Grecos, was blown to pieces by a car bomb. Only a shoe and his broad-brimmed, American-style hat were found at the scene, though pieces of his body were later found stuck to the lemon trees that grew hundreds of yards from the crater.

On 25 May, La Barbera was shot in Milan, but he survived. He was arrested in his hospital bed. Buscetta admitted to having been given a contract to kill Angelo, but he said that someone else got there first.

The next target was 'Ciaschiteddu' Greco. On 30 June, a car bomb intended for him went off in Ciaculli, killing the seven policemen and army officers who had been sent to defuse it. There was a public outcry. Over the next ten weeks, 1,995 mafiosi were arrested. The Commission was dissolved and many fled into exile. 'Ciaschiteddu' Greco went to Venezuela. Nothing is known of the whereabouts of Salvatore Greco 'The Engineer', though there were rumours that he was also in Venezuela, with his cousin. Others said that he was in Lebanon, where he had continued trafficking in drugs. Even the aged 'Piddu the Lieutenant' was arrested and banished from Sicily in 1966.

1960S SICILIAN MAFIA TRIALS

The first trial started in 1967. Amongst the defendants were Tommaso Buscetta, Giuseppe Genco Russo – known as 'Gina Lollobrigida' for his love of the limelight – and Gaetano Badalamenti, who had taken over as *capomafia* of the *cosca* in Cinisi after the death of Cesare Manzella. They were charged with 'organized delinquency', which was the nearest prosecutors could come to a charge of being a member of the Mafia, which did not become a specific crime until 1982. Joe Bonanno and Carmine Galante were also indicted, but they could not be extradited because the United States did not recognize an 'organized delinquency' charge.

The evidence came from Joseph 'Joe Cargo' Valachi, who became a government witness

in 1962. Appearing in court, Genco Russo presented a petition from 7,000 prominent politicians, priests, bankers, lawyers and businessmen in Mussomeli, who promised to testify on his behalf. His lawyer also promised to publish telegrams from 37 deputies – including one cabinet minister – thanking him for getting them elected. Bernardo

Mattarella denied being one of them. As it was, the evidence was so thin that the defendants walked free. However, in a court in Caltanissetta, Genco Russo was exiled to Lovere, near Bergamo, where he continued to conduct business as usual, spending 125,000 lire a week on telephone calls. Nevertheless, his days were numbered. He was an old-style

Full house as 152 Mafia members are packed into a giant cage in a court in Catanzaro's Aldisio grade school. October 1967

mafioso who, Buscetta complained, would continue conducting his business sitting on the lavatory. A younger generation of mafiosi would soon take charge.

The trial of another 114 suspected mafiosi was moved to Catanzaro on the mainland, in the hope of minimizing the intimidation of witnesses. The defendants were again charged with 'organized delinquency', but also the substantive offences of murder, kidnapping, theft, smuggling and 'public massacre' in respect of the Ciaculli bombing. There were only ten convictions, largely for 'organized delinquency'. However, Buscetta and the two La Barbera brothers were sentenced *in absentia*, though no one was found guilty of the Ciaculli massacre.

Among the 104 defendants who were acquitted was Luciano Leggio. He stood trial again just two months later, this time in Bari, alongside another 63 mafiosi from Corleone. Leggio was a career criminal. After committing his first murder at the age of 20 he was recruited by the Mafia, becoming an enforcer and hitman for Michele Navarra, the local doctor and *capomafia* of Corleone. In March 1948 he and two other men kidnapped trade unionist Placido Rizzotto in broad daylight.

Eighteen months later his two accomplices confessed and then led the police to a 200-foot-deep (60 m) cavern where Rizzotto's remains were found, along with the skeletons of two other men. Rizzotto's mother could only identify his body from his shoes. Despite the testimony of his accomplices, Leggio was freed. However, during his time behind bars he had met 19-year-old Salvatore 'Totò' or 'Shorty' Riina, then serving six years for manslaughter, and the young Bernardo Provenzano, also known as 'The Tractor' because he 'mows people down'. These two killers became known as Leggio's 'beasts'.

Leggio went into cattle rustling and ran up against some of Michele Navarra's men. In June 1958 they shot him as he was walking across a field, though he escaped with a grazed hand.

> *'Navarra was driving home from Lercara Friddi with another doctor when Leggio, Riina and Provenzano ambushed him. They pumped dozens of bullets into the car...'*

His response was ferocious. On 2 August, Navarra was driving home from Lercara Friddi with another doctor – an entirely innocent man – when Leggio, Riina and Provenzano ambushed him. They pumped dozens of bullets into the car, killing both occupants. Leggio then declared himself *capomafia* of Corleone. He spent the next five years hunting down and killing 50 of Navarra's supporters and then he joined the Commission. After the First Mafia War he went to ground, but he was captured in May 1964. He was lodging in a house in Corleone that belonged to the ex-fiancée of Placido Rizzotto, the trade unionist he had killed.

In the third trial, which took place in Bari, all 64 defendants, including Leggio and Riina, were acquitted. Bernardo Provenzano was not even there. Although he had been indicted for murder in 1963, he had somehow escaped the police dragnet and he remained at large until 2006. All of the defendants denied ever hearing of the Mafia, let alone being a member. And the evidence had been tampered with. Pieces of a broken car light had been identified as coming from an Alfa Romeo of the type owned by Leggio, but by the time of the trial they had been replaced with broken lamp parts from a different make of car. And Leggio claimed that he had been framed by a policeman who 'begged

Tony Provenzano arriving at the Bowl-O-Rama for a Teamsters vote count

me repeatedly to pleasure his wife; and I, for moral reasons, refused... Please don't ask me for names, I am a gentleman.'

When the jury retired, they and the judge received an anonymous note:

'To the President of the Court of Assizes of Bari and members of the Jury: You people in Bari have not understood, or rather, you don't want to understand, what Corleone means. You are judging honest gentlemen of Corleone, denounced through caprice by the carabinieri and police. We simply want to warn you that if a single gentleman from Corleone is convicted, you will be blown sky high, you will be wiped out, you will be butchered and so will every member of your family. We think we've been clear. Nobody must be convicted. Otherwise you will be condemned to death – you and your families. A Sicilian proverb says: "A man warned is a man saved." It's up to you. Be wise.'

The judge, Cesare Terranova, himself a Sicilian, appealed against the acquittals, but Leggio and Riina had disappeared. In 1970 they were retried, convicted and sentenced to life *in absentia*. Meanwhile, Leggio had been in a private clinic in Rome for six months. He suffered from Pott's disease, a condition of the spine that meant he had to wear a brace. When the police finally came to arrest him, he had checked out. There were suspicions that he had successfully avoided apprehension thanks to the help of Sicily's attorney general, Pietro Scaglione, who was shot dead in 1971 – by Leggio, it is thought. Leggio was tried twice for Scaglione's murder, but was acquitted for lack of evidence. In 1973 Damiano Caruso was murdered on Leggio's behalf. Leggio blamed him for killing one of his friends years before. When Caruso's girlfriend and 15-year-old daughter went round to see Leggio he raped and strangled them both. A wire-tap brought Leggio to justice in 1974 and he finally began a life sentence for the Navarra slaying.

THE VIALE LAZIO KILLINGS

When Buscetta squealed in 1984, it became clear that the La Barbera brothers were not responsible for starting the First Mafia War at all. The person responsible was Michele Cavataio, the new boss of the Acquasanta *cosca*. He was nicknamed 'The Cobra' because his favourite weapon was the six-shot Colt Cobra revolver. According to Buscetta, Cavataio had ordered Calcedonio Di Pisa's murder, knowing that the La Barberas would be blamed. Other killings and bombings were carried out with the sole intention of fanning the flames of war. It became clear to the other Mafia bosses that Cavataio, not the La Barbera brothers, was to blame for the Ciaculli massacre because Salvatore was already dead and Angelo was out of the picture. Cavataio then took over their *cosca*.

He was arrested in the roundup of July

1963. Despite being tried for five murders at Catanzano, Cavataio was only sentenced to four years in jail, which was immediately suspended. At a meeting in Zürich attended by 'Ciaschiteddu' Greco, who had flown in from Caracas, it was decided to eliminate Cavataio. On 10 December 1969, the two sons of developer Girolamo Moncada – an old friend of Angelo La Barbera, now an associate of Cavataio – pulled up outside their father's office in Viale Lazio, just as four men dressed in police uniforms arrived.

Gaetano Grado, who organized the hit and was on hand to witness it, said that everyone was scared of Cavataio, but the 'soldiers' he had picked were 'veterans'. They had already killed ten people.

The four men bundled the two boys into the office where Cavataio was sitting behind the desk. When Cavataio recognized one of the men he grabbed a revolver and fired, killing Calogero Bagarella, brother-in-law of Totò Riina. The two Moncada brothers took cover – one under the desk and the other in a small back room – but in the ensuing gun battle both men were wounded. Damiano Caruso, a soldier from Giuseppe 'The Tiger' Di Cristina's family in Riesi, was also wounded.

Finally, Provenzano finished the job with a sub-machine gun. By the time the shooting had

'Provenzano finished the job with a sub-machine gun. By the time the shooting had stopped, Cavataio and three of his associates were dead... Some 108 bullets were found at the crime scene'

stopped, Cavataio and three of his associates were dead. Throwing down their guns, the hitmen dragged their wounded accomplice out of the office and bundled him into the boot of an Alfa Romeo.

Then they screeched off into the evening traffic. Some 108 bullets were found at the crime scene, along with a 7.65 Beretta pistol, a 7.63 Mauser pistol, Cavataio's Colt Cobra, a 38A Zanotti shotgun, a 38/49 Beretta machine gun and an MP40 machine pistol. This bloody incident marked the end of six long years of bitter war.

Initially the Moncada brothers were suspected of being part of the plot, so they were arrested. But from his hospital bed, Filippo Moncada began to talk. He described his father's meetings with Cavataio and how he gradually took over the firm. His father was then arrested. Filippo also said that he recognized Francesco Sutera, a soldier in the Santapaola *cosca*, among the assassins. While he was still in prison, threats were scrawled on the yard walls, saying: 'Filippo, withdraw your accusations.' Other prisoners told him: 'Moncada, don't recognize anybody. You'll be safer.' But, though he was a Sicilian, Filippo Moncada had been educated in the north. Sicilian traditions meant nothing to him and the *omertà* began to slip.

Twenty-four men went on trial for the Viale Lazio killings, including Gerlando Alberti, who had been on the run since the Scaglione murder two years earlier. The *carabinieri* had evidence that he was in Palermo at the time of the killings, which was already an offence because he had been exiled to the mainland. He admitted that he had been in Palermo that day, but he claimed that he had spent the night with a married lady. As a man of honour, he could not give her name and would prefer to go to jail rather than disclose any further details. Despite Filippo's evidence, none of the defendants were convicted for the Viale Lazio slayings.

GAETANO BADALAMENTI

During the *Pax Mafiosa* of the 1970s, two more Grecos from Croceverde rose to prominence. They were the sons of Piddu the Lieutenant and like him they also ruled in Ciaculli. Known as 'The Pope', Michele Greco would entertain politicians and bankers at hunting parties on his estate at La Faravelli. In the grounds was a laboratory which processed heroin. With his brother Salvatore Greco – 'The Senator' – and other Mafia families, he controlled the water supply in Palermo, selling water for irrigation in the summer at exorbitant prices. The Grecos also claimed EC subsidies for destroying citrus crops they had never grown, bribing the inspectors to falsify the records. Even so, Michele declared an income of below $20,000 a year – less than the money he received from the EC. He

In Italy, suspicion has often fallen on local *carabinieri* that they are in league with the Mafia. Giuseppe Impastato's brother told a parliamentary inquiry that in Cinisi it was common to see police with the mafiosi

was also an accomplished killer.

In 1974, the Commission had been reformed under Gaetano Badalamenti, who smuggled millions of dollars worth of heroin and cocaine into New York, to be distributed through the Bonanno family's chain of pizza restaurants. One of his first acts as joint Commission leader was to order a hit on a small-time Neapolitan criminal who had once slapped 'Lucky' Luciano at the racecourse. By then Luciano had been dead for eight years. But Badalamenti could report to the Commission in New York that the insult had been avenged. With Stefano Bontade he opposed the Corleonesi, who were represented on the Commission by Salvatore Riina – who in turn was personally plotting to rid the Commission of the Palermo families. As tensions grew, 'Ciaschiteddu' Greco flew in from Venezuela to try and make peace. Nevertheless, Riina and Provenzano killed Giuseppe Calderone and Giuseppe Di Cristina, who had spoken to the *carabinieri* after he realized that the Corleonesi were aiming to take over. Di Cristina was killed on the territory of Salvatore 'Totuccio' Inzerillo as a deliberate insult. Fearing a new Mafia war, Inzerillo had just taken delivery of a bulletproof car.

Before he died, Di Cristina told the authorities that Leggio had created an elite

'Impastato was kidnapped and tortured, and then dumped on a railway track with sticks of dynamite strapped to his body'

14-strong death squad that had infiltrated other Mafia families. They operated out of Rome, Naples and other Italian cities and made their money from kidnapping. According to Di Cristina, Leggio had been behind the 1973 kidnapping of John Paul Getty III, the 17-year-old grandson of the founder of Getty Oil, who paid a ransom of $2.9 million after the victim's ear had been delivered in an envelope.

At the same time the Mafia was under attack by left-wing radical Giuseppe 'Peppino' Impastato, a native of Cinisi, who had been deeply affected by the murder of his uncle Cesare Manzella. After Manzella's death, Gaetano Badalamenti took over as *capomafia* of the *cosca* in Cinisi. Impastato fought back at the Mafia by ridiculing the 'men of honour' on his radio show and in the newspapers. At first he was protected to some degree by the fact that his father was a mafioso, but when his father was run down and killed he lost his immunity. In 1978 he was kidnapped and tortured, and then dumped on a railway track, with sticks of dynamite strapped to his body. His remains were scattered over an area of 300,000 square yards. Friends gathered outside Badalamenti's house, shouting 'Butcher'. Years of agitation led to a parliamentary inquiry being set up in the year 2000. Impastato's brother told the commission that in Cinisi it was common to see the *carabinieri* walking arm-in-arm with the mafiosi. Finally, in 2002, Badalamenti was given a life sentence for ordering the murder of Impastato.

In 1978 Badalamenti was removed from the Commission, even though he was Leggio's godfather. He was replaced by Michele Greco, who sided with the Corleonesi. Next, Badalamenti was expelled from the Cosa Nostra. His cousin, Antonio Badalamenti, took over as head of the Cinisi *cosca* and Gaetano Badalamenti emigrated to Brazil.

THE SLAUGHTER OF THE INZERILLOS

With the war looming, Tommaso Buscetta left Sicily with his young wife and half a million dollars as a going-away present. But Salvatore Inzerillo continued business as usual. Every day over fifty cars would be seen parked outside his villa. They belonged to traffickers, refiners, mules (couriers) and Mafia soldiers. Then leading members of the Inzerillo, Spatola and Gambino families were arrested for heroin trafficking. In protest, Stefano Bontade, the 'prince of Villagrazia', was killed on Riina's orders. Bontade had links to Christian Democrat prime minister Giulio Andreotti. On the way home from his 42nd birthday party, Bontade's car was shot up at a set of traffic lights. The

'Inzerillo's teenage son Giuseppe was murdered after vowing to avenge his father. The arm with which he intended to administer the vengeance was symbolically hacked off'

gunman was thought to be Riina's favourite hitman Giuseppe 'Pino' Greco, a cousin of Michele Greco. 'Pino' Greco was also known as 'Scarpuzzedda' – 'Little Shoe' – because his father was nicknamed 'Scarpa', which is Sicilian for 'shoe'.

In the following month, 'Scarpuzzedda' gunned down Inzerillo in the short walk between his mistress's home and his bulletproof Alfa Romeo. Inzerillo had ordered the killing of prosecuting judge Gaetano Costa, who had signed the 53 arrest warrants against the Spatola–Inzerillo–Gambino heroin-trafficking network, but he had not sought the permission of the Commission first. Inzerillo's teenage son Giuseppe was then murdered after vowing to avenge his father. First of all, the arm with which he intended to administer the vengeance was symbolically hacked off. When Salvatore Inzerillo's brother Santo went to a meeting to discover why members of his family were being killed he was strangled, while another brother, Pietro, was found dead in New Jersey. He had dollar bills stuffed into his mouth and around his genitals.

Over 200 men of the Bontade–Inzerillo clan were killed and their *coschi* were taken over by Corleone loyalists. Others fled across the Atlantic. With the supply of heroin imperilled,

John Gambino came over from New York to find out what was going on. He was told that it was imperative that Buscetta and the others who were fleeing overseas must be tracked down and killed. However, Gambino managed to forge an agreement that the remaining Inzerillos who had fled to the United States could keep their lives, provided that they never returned to Sicily.

TRIAL OF A DEAD MAN

But in Palermo the slaughter continued. The remaining members of Bontade's *cosca* from Santa Maria di Gesù, on the outskirts of Palermo, were invited to a barbecue on Michele Greco's estate. Afterwards, the 11 who had attended were murdered. Salvatore 'Totuccio' Contorno, who had the good sense not to turn up, later escaped another assassination attempt by Pino Greco and his sidekick Giuseppe Lucchese. He then went into hiding. In the attempt to hunt him down, over 35 friends and relatives who might conceivably have given him shelter were gunned down. This was enough to persuade Contorno to become an informer, initially by anonymous letter. However, his arrest for the possession of drugs in Rome, followed by Buscetta's defection, motivated him to break

'Contorno, who had the good sense not to turn up, later escaped another assassination attempt by Pino Greco and his sidekick Giuseppe Lucchese. He then went into hiding'

the *omertà* and talk.

Salvatore Riina began to fear that Pino Greco was becoming too powerful, so in 1982 he played to his arrogance by getting him to murder Filippo Marchese, the boss of the Corsa dei Mille who ran the 'Room of Death' – a small apartment where enemies of the Corleonesi were garrotted. By this time, Greco was not even turning up to meetings of the Commission – he sent his underboss Vincenzo Puccio instead. In order to weaken Greco's position, Riina had eight men massacred in the Piazza Scaffa in the Ciacullo *mandamento*, which showed everyone how little power Greco actually had. Greco still suspected nothing, because he organized and led the group of assassins who murdered Antonino Cassarà, a police investigator who three years earlier had caused the arrest of 163 mafiosi, including Giuseppe Greco and Michele Greco. Then Riina ordered Pioggio Puccio and Giuseppe Lucchese to kill Greco in his own home. At the same time, Riina put out the rumour that Greco had fled to the United States because the police were on his tail. As a result, Greco was tried *in absentia* at the mid-1980s Mafia Maxi Trial. He was sentenced to life imprisonment on 58 counts of murder, although he was already dead.

Ignazio Salvo sits in the courtroom inside the bunker built into the Ucciardone prison in Palermo. He was murdered by the Mafia in 1992, a brutal response to the sentences that were handed out after the Maxi Trial

THE MAFIA IN ITALIAN POLITICS

Following the massacre at Portella della Ginestra (see page 160), Calogero Vizzini (Don Calò) turned against the Separatists and began to cultivate contacts within the Christian Democrats (DC), after being approached by Bernardo Mattarella. During the 1948 elections that made the Christian Democrats the largest party in parliament, Don Calò attended an electoral lunch with

Giuseppe Genco Russo, his successor as Sicily's boss of bosses. The Christian Democrats would hold power in Italy, in various coalitions, for the next 45 years. The Mafia aided them by repeatedly delivering the vote in Sicily, which represents ten per cent of the Italian electorate.

When Amintore Fanfani became leader of the DC in 1954, he gave a new generation of 'Young Turks' *carte blanche* to introduce sweeping reforms in the way the party was run. The young Turk introducing reforms in Sicily was Giovanni Gioia. He ostensibly increased the number of Christian Democrats on the island, though dead people were recruited, along with friends and relatives. This meant that the DC office in Palermo was disproportionately powerful on a national basis. It also gave Gioia and his DC cronies more power within Sicily.

In 1958, with the help of Angelo La Barbera, Salvo Lima became mayor of Palermo and his fellow Christian Democrat, the Corleonisi Vito Ciancimino, was superintendent of public works. Together they began a building boom. Over half of the building permits they issued went to people with no connection to the building trade at all. Art Deco palaces were pulled down and parks were concreted over, while the Mafia took over the developers and ran the contractors. They all made money from government development grants and overcharging for shoddy workmanship. Building works were also used as a way of laundering drugs money. Known as the 'sack of Palermo', this orgy of wanton destruction went on for years.

'Lima was being driven into Palermo when a gunman on a motorcycle pillion shot out the tyres and windscreen of his car. As Lima tried to escape on foot, the motorcyclist returned...'

After being appointed to the Chamber of Deputies in 1968, Lima became a crucial ally of Giulio Andreotti, who became prime minister for the first time in 1972. Tax collecting was contracted out by the government in Italy, so Lima was able to arrange for Nino and Ignazio Salvo to take over the concession in Sicily. The Salvos were mafiosi from the Salemi family in the province of Trapani. Favoured as they were by Lima, the cousins pocketed ten per cent of the take, compared to around three per cent in the rest of Italy. When he was in Sicily, Lima was driven around in the Salvos' bulletproof car. Nino died of cancer in a clinic in Switzerland in 1986 and Ignazio was murdered in 1992, in the aftermath of the Mafia Maxi Trial.

Vito Ciancimino was arrested in 1984 and convicted in 1992 and Lima was killed with ruthless efficiency in the same year. The Mafia felt that he had not tried hard enough to block the convictions in the Mafia Maxi Trial. He was being driven into Palermo from his villa in Mondello, a seaside suburb, when a gunman on a motorcycle pillion shot out the tyres and the windscreen of his car. As Lima tried to escape on foot, the motorcyclist returned. The gunman then shot Lima in the back and finished him off with a bullet in the neck.

Tommaso Buscetta testified that: 'Salvo Lima was, in fact, the politician to whom Cosa Nostra turned most often to resolve problems for the organization whose solution lay in Rome.' He was killed because he had failed to live up to the promises he had made in Palermo, 'because he was the greatest symbol of that part of the political world which, after doing favours for Cosa Nostra in exchange for its votes, was no longer able to protect the interests of the organization at the time of its most important trial'.

POLITICAL FAVOURS

When he died, Lima was busy preparing a grand reception for Andreotti, who was scheduled to start campaigning in Sicily on the following day. Lima's death marked the death of the pact between the Mafia and the Christian Democrats. It had been forged by Bernardo Mattarella and Don Calò back in the days of Salvatore Giuliano. At Lima's funeral, Andreotti defended Sicily and his deceased friend. He had been 'slandered for decades', he said. But Andreotti's connections to the Mafia were becoming all too obvious.

Within a year, Andreotti had been passed over as head of state and had been made a senator for life instead. This gave the prosecutors the opportunity to ask the Italian senate for permission to investigate his connections to the Cosa Nostra. The accusations came thick and fast. In 1995 he was indicted for selling political favours to the Mafia. He was also charged with complicity in the murder of investigative journalist Carmine Pecorelli. Buscetta testified that Gaetano Badalamenti had told him that the murder had been commissioned by the Salvo cousins as a favour to Giulio Andreotti. The one-time prime minister was afraid that Pecorelli was about to publish information concerning the kidnap and murder of former Christian Democrat prime minister Aldo Moro by Red Brigade terrorists in 1978. A revelation like that could have destroyed Andreotti's political career. The murder of Pecorelli was also thought to be linked to the 1982 assassination of *carabiniere* General Carlo Alberto Chiesa, who had been appointed prefect of Palermo by Andreotti.

In 1999, Andreotti, Gaetano Badalamenti and others were acquitted of Pecorelli's murder. Andreotti was also acquitted of involvement with the Cosa Nostra. His dealings with Stefano Bontade, Gaetano Badalamenti, Michele 'The Pope' Greco, Vito Ciancimino, the Salvo cousins and Totò Riina, whom he had greeted with a kiss, had happened too long ago and were outside the statutes of limitation. However, the prosecution appealed and in 2002 Andreotti and Badalamenti were sentenced to 24 years' imprisonment for the murder of Pecorelli. This decision was overturned by the Court of Cassation.

PROPAGANDA DUE OR P2

Carmine Pecorelli, Giulio Andreotti, General Carlo Alberto Chiesa, Salvo Lima and Stefano Bontade were all members of a secret Masonic lodge called Propaganda Due, or P2. A partial list of members was discovered in the home of the lodge's grand master Licio Gelli, during an investigation into illegal currency dealings at the Banco Ambrosiano.

It included 54 members of parliament; 12 generals of the *carabinieri*; 14 judges; the heads of all three secret services; five leading members of the finance police; admirals, generals, journalists and wealthy businessmen; the pretender to the Italian throne; Silvio Berlusconi; and Michele Sindona, a Sicilian financier who had used bribery and fraud to siphon an estimated $30 million out of the Vatican bank and other financial institutions. Sindona was convicted of ordering the murder of Giorgio Ambrosoli, the liquidator of his empire, who compiled a report of over 2,000 pages detailing Sindona's financial misdemeanours. Sentenced to life imprisonment, Sindona had served just two days when he was found dead in his cell after drinking coffee laced with cyanide.

Some of the activities of P2 are shrouded in mystery, but material provided by the security services had been used for blackmail and there was also evidence that P2 was plotting a right-wing coup. Seven million dollars had been deposited in a Swiss bank account belonging to Bettino Craxi, who became Italy's first Socialist prime minister. It had been put there by the head of Banco Ambrosiano, Roberto Calvi, another P2 member. Calvi's connections with the Chicago-born Archbishop Paul Marcinkus at the Vatican bank were so close that he was called 'God's banker'.

Following an investigation in 1978, Calvi was given a four-year sentence and fined $19.8 million for illegally taking 27 million dollars' worth of Italian lire out of the country. There was a further $1.4 billion in 'questionable' loans outstanding to a dummy company that was based in the Bahamas and Latin America and which was owned by the Vatican bank.

On 5 June 1982 Calvi wrote a letter to Pope John Paul II, in which he warned him about the imminent collapse of Banco Ambrosiano and the damage it would do to the Church. Two weeks later, the bank collapsed with debts of some one billion dollars, much of which had gone to Banco Ambrosiano's main shareholder, the Vatican bank. In 1984, the Vatican bank agreed to pay $224 million to the 120 creditors of the defunct Banco Ambrosiano, which was thought to be used by the Mafia to launder drugs money.

Meanwhile, Calvi disappeared from his apartment in Rome on 10 June 1982. He had been released pending appeal. Eight days later, he was found hanging underneath Blackfriars Bridge in London. There were bricks and $10,000 in banknotes in his pockets. An initial inquest in 1982 brought in a verdict of suicide but it was later decided that he had been killed.

Twenty-five years after Calvi's death five defendants – including Sicilian mafioso Giuseppe Calò – were cleared of the murder due to 'insufficient evidence', although 20 months' worth of testimony had already been given. The court did agree, however, that Calvi's death had been murder, not suicide.

As a citizen of the Vatican City, Archbishop Marcinkus could not be charged, while Gelli fled to Switzerland and

Italian banker
Roberto Calvi

was extradited. Escaping from prison by helicopter, he sought refuge on his estates in Uruguay.

Four years later, he was arrested again in Switzerland and was once more extradited, but under the terms of his extradition he could only stand trial on charges relating to the collapse of Banco Ambrosiano. He was later convicted of acting as paymaster to the Fascist terrorists who blew up Bologna train station in 1980, killing 85 people. But he did not serve time. Giuseppe Calò was sentenced to life imprisonment on other Mafia charges and Bettino Craxi fled corruption charges in 1993 to live in his house in Tunis. He never returned to Italy.

Chapter 9

LITTLE DOLL

The wedding of racketeer Pasquale Simonetti and beauty queen Pupetta Maresca in 1955. After a few months, Pasquale was killed

Left: Assunta Maresco, aka *Pupetta*, ('Little Doll')

Assunta Maresca was the only daughter of Camorrista Vincenzo Maresca, whose family, the *Lampetielli* – known for their lightning speed with flick knives and pistols – controlled Castellammare di Stabia, a small town to the south of Naples. Pretty and spoilt, she earned the nickname *Pupetta*, or 'Little Doll'.

She was renowned for her beauty and was jealously guarded by her four brothers, who beat her if she so much as caught a man's eye.

Nevertheless, she entered a beauty contest and became 'Miss Rovegliano'. And when an old-style *guappo*, or Camorra boss, who was ten years her senior – Pasquale Simonetti aka Pascalone 'e Nola (Big Pasquale of Nola) – began courting the buxom 17-year-old, her brothers acquiesced.

When they married in 1955, the whole town turned out. There were five hundred guests at the wedding breakfast. They brought envelopes stuffed with money or jewels for the princess.

In February 1960, among the market workers of Naples, two elegantly dressed men control the trade of pears and oranges. Prior to his death in 1955, the price of fruit and vegetables in Naples had been fixed by Pasquale Simonetti, from his base just outside the city

WIDOWED AND PREGNANT

With her marriage, Pupetta acquired a new status. In the morning, people queued outside her house, bringing gifts of cheese or wine. If a son had been arrested, Simonetti would be asked if he could find a good lawyer. If a girl had been dumped by her boyfriend, could he buy her some furniture to act as a dowry? Simonetti was there as an arbiter. Traditionally he would summon a boy who had seduced and abandoned a local girl and give him a wad of money. 'This is for your wedding or your funeral – you decide,' he would say.

Simonetti made his money from smuggling cigarettes and was reputed to have slapped Lucky Luciano. From Nola, a town ten miles inland from Naples, Simonetti also fixed the price of fruit and vegetables in the city. Another contender was Antonio Esposito, who had ordered a hit on Simonetti.

One day in the marketplace, Simonetti was approached by a man who was called 'the Ship' because of his rolling gait. He went for his gun, but the Ship was too fast for him. After being hit in the stomach Simonetti was taken to hospital, but he told the police nothing. Pupetta rushed to his bedside to find him bleeding heavily.

'I begged him to tell me what had happened,' she said. 'He told me Esposito was behind it. . . That's how I knew who did it.'

Simonetti survived the night, but died the following morning, leaving Pupetta a widow at 20. She was pregnant at the time. Afraid that she might also be on Esposito's hit list, she moved back in with her parents.

'I was frightened in the house on my own,' she said. 'It was like a nightmare, after starting a new life with my handsome prince, to be back living with my mother.'

'I fired the first shot. He was going to kill me'

She told the police that Esposito was responsible, but they did nothing. She had no proof. No one in the market had seen anything apparently, or perhaps they were suffering a convenient lapse of memory. However, if Simonetti's murder went unpunished, it would diminish her status as the widow of an important man.

WOMAN OF HONOUR

Esposito began sending her threatening messages. It seemed that he knew her every move, so she began carrying her husband's gun – a Smith & Wesson .38 – which she had taken from his bedside as a 'memento'.

She was making her daily visit to the cemetery, accompanied by her driver and her 13-year-old brother, when she saw Esposito walking along the road. She stopped the car. Esposito strolled up and said: 'I hear you have been looking for me.'

He reached in the window and chucked her under the chin.

'Here I am,' he said. 'Get out of the car.'

He tried to open the door, but Pupetta reached into her handbag and pulled out Pasquale's gun. Holding it in both hands, she opened fire.

'I fired the first shot,' she admitted. 'He was going to kill me.'

Twenty-nine bullets were found in Esposito's body and Pupetta's brother disappeared.

While awaiting trial, she gave birth to a son, Pasqualino – 'Little Pasquale' – in jail. She wrote reassuringly to her parents: 'Think of me as a girl away at college,' she said. 'Sometimes I laugh and sing.'

While in jail, she was bombarded with proposals of marriage. Inspired by her example, a musician composed a song called '*La Legge d'Onore*' – 'The Law of Honour' – and the newspapers called her 'The Diva of Crime'.

Flowers were showered from the balconies on to the police van carrying her to court. For the first time, microphones were allowed in the courtrooms of Naples Assizes so the crowd could hear what was going on.

While no witnesses could be found for the murder of Simonetti, 85 turned out for Pupetta's trial. She was unrepentant, telling the court: 'I would do it again.' With that, the court erupted with cheers.

Pupetta was found guilty and sentenced to 14 years.

'Prison was a nightmare,' she said. 'It was run by nuns, wizened old hags who were consumed with envy. I was young. I had just got married. I had my lovely silk underwear … they took it away and gave me a rough sack dress to wear, shapeless and several sizes too big. I threw it back at them. "You wear it!" I said.'

She did her best to give the nuns hell, refusing to have her hair cut and demanding to see the governor.

'You can imagine me in the midst of all those old women rotting in jail. There were some young ones too, but they were from Calabria and Sicily – primitive girls.'

Having proved herself to be 'a woman of honour', she inherited her husband's authority. Other prisoners waited on her, bringing her clean bed linen and hot coffee and asking her for favours. She had food brought in for those less fortunate and stuck up for inmates' rights, effectively becoming the boss of the prison and earning the nickname 'Madame Camorra'.

She was allowed to keep her son with her until he was three. Then he was sent to be brought up by her mother. When she was released at the age of 31, her son was a stranger to her.

KILLED BY HIS MOTHER'S LOVER?

A former cellmate introduced Ninetta to handsome Camorrista Umberto Ammaturo, who ran guns from Germany to Libya and cocaine from South America to Italy, via Nigeria. They became lovers and she gave birth to twins. But Ammaturo and Pasqualino did not get on.

The young man wanted to prove himself. He had already pulled a gun on the nephew of a Camorrista known simply as '*O Malommo*' –

'the Bad Man'. And he had let it be known that once he was 18 he was going to kill Gaetano Orlando – the gunman who had killed his father. In January 1974, the day after his 18th birthday, Pasqualino was due to meet Ammaturo on the construction site of Naples' new flyover. He was never seen again.

Pupetta believed that Ammaturo knew something about Pasqualino's disappearance. She asked him about it repeatedly – to the point that he would beat her up for asking. If he had admitted to knowing anything about Pasqualino's death, Pupetta would have killed him. She even approached Judge Italo Ormanni, who was investigating the disappearance, telling him that Ammaturo had killed her son, but she refused to sign a formal complaint. The judge was convinced that Pasqualino's body was in one of the pillars supporting the flyover, but he failed to get permission to knock it down.

Even so, Pupetta did not leave Ammaturo and continued to help him in his criminal activities. When war broke out between Raffaele Cutolo's Nuova Camorra Organizzata and the Nuova Famiglia faction, Pupetta's favourite brother was shot several times. He survived, but was sentenced to four years in prison, where he was again threatened by Cutolo's men.

MEDIA FIGURE

In 1982, Pupetta called a press conference at the Press Club in Naples. 'If Cutolo touches one member of my family, I will have his

Camorra boss
Raffaele Cutolo,
seen here in 2005,
is serving multiple
life sentences for
murder

gunmen killed,' she declared. 'I will kill his lackeys, even the women and babies in their cradles. . . . The whole region is being strangled by an invisible force, seeping through every strata of society. That insidious force is Raffaele Cutolo. He wants to rule at any price – you are either with him or against him. Cutolo wants to become emperor of Naples, and this town is in chains because of him. All these deaths, the rivers of blood which are running through our city as people watch helplessly, all this is caused by one power-crazed madman.'

Cutolo dismissed this as histrionics. 'Pupetta should have more dignity,' he said. 'She has made a complete fool of herself.'

Behind the scenes he started threatening her.

Later that year, Pupetta and Ammaturo were arrested for extortion and the murder of forensic psychiatrist Aldo Semerari, who had helped Ammaturo escape jail by feigning insanity. His severed head was found between his legs. Ammaturo fled to South America leaving Pupetta to face the music alone. She was sentenced to four years. Maintaining her innocence, she claimed that Cutolo had used his contacts in the judiciary to put her away.

'I was tortured by the judges, every day of those four years,' she said. 'The first 14 years were different because I had committed a crime and it was right that I paid for it.

'If Cutolo touches my family, I will have his gunmen killed...even the women and babies in their cradles'

But those four years in prison were terrible because there is no peace for an innocent person in prison.'

Ammaturo was later acquitted on appeal due to lack of evidence. However, when he became a *pentito* in 1993 he admitted to the murder.

After leaving prison, Pupetta retired to Sorrento. In 1988, a film, *Il caso Pupetta Maresca*, was made about her life. The title role was played by Alessandra Mussolini, granddaughter of Benito, the former Italian dictator.

In 2000, Pupetta made the newspapers again when she complained to the police that an employee had run off with the 10 billion lira – $5 million – she had won on Italy's biggest lottery. She said she had dispatched Giovanni Boscaglia, a 67-year-old small-time criminal, to play the numbers they had picked. But when they came up she did not hear from him.

However, Pupetta's contacts in the Neapolitan underworld soon tracked him down. Boscaglia agreed to go to a notary public to hand over the winning ticket and sign a legal agreement that the pair would divide the winnings. But lottery officials said the ticket he handed over was a fake.

Pupetta enjoyed power and wealth and she paid the price. She lost a husband and a son and she endured long spells in jail. But at the age of 80, she does not admit to feeling any regrets.

Chapter 10

THE STRIP AND THE BOARDWALK

The Mafia in America had always been involved in illegal gambling. They even ran the numbers rackets in African-American and Hispanic areas, by laying off the bets of small-time numbers bankers or simply muscling in. As partners they could also offer protection from politicians, policemen, other hoodlums and themselves.

Towards the end of the Prohibition era, Meyer Lansky realized that while the Mob could still make money from illegal gambling, legal gambling would make them even more. At the time, the only state that allowed gambling was Nevada, but it was dusty, inhospitable and hard to get to. So in 1932 Lansky began cultivating Cuban strongman Fulgencio Batista, who took over the government in the following year. Havana was a playground for wealthy Americans, so Lansky offered Batista huge bribes in return for a Mafia monopoly on casinos.

After the Second World War, improved air transport facilities made the island easier for American high rollers to reach. By the 1950s, courtesy of Lansky, every American Mafia family had a piece of the action in Cuba, but in 1959 Fidel Castro marched into Havana and directed his guerrillas to smash up the casinos. The rest were closed down. However, Lansky had already begun gambling operations in the Bahamas and elsewhere in the Caribbean. He also took a share in London's Colony Club, but his representative on the board, Dino

Left; **The Strip, Las Vegas; right: gambling club in Reno, Nevada,** c.1910

Cuban leader Fulgencio Batista in Washington DC, *c.*1935. Batista negotiated lucrative contracts with the US Mafia over drugs, gambling and prostitution in Cuba's capital, Havana

Cellini, was deported along with actor George Raft, who had formerly part-owned a casino in Havana.

Lansky had long realized that political instability in the Caribbean, combined with the strictures of the Gaming Act in Britain, meant that the Mob must build up casino gambling in Nevada, where things were much easier. The 1931 Act legalizing gambling in the state did not prohibit convicted criminals from running casinos, nor did it regulate them. And no authority had been established to oversee the county sheriffs who were assigned to collect the licence money.

Reno was the biggest city in Nevada, with 20 per cent of the state's population. Less than 200 miles (320 km) from San Francisco, it was already the divorce capital of America and a number of legal casinos thrived there. However, Lansky's long-time associate Bugsy Siegel had spotted a better bet – Las Vegas, a sleepy railroad junction little more than 200 miles (320 km) from Los Angeles.

BUGSY'S EARLY YEARS

Born in Williamsburg, Brooklyn, Siegel was the son of a poor Jewish family from Ukraine. He began his criminal career demanding protection money from pushcart vendors. If they did not pay up, he set fire to their merchandise. He then joined Meyer Lansky's gang, stealing cars and running floating craps games. Lansky also hired Siegel out as a hitman.

In 1926, the 20-year-old Siegel was arrested for rape, but Lansky's henchmen told the victim that unless she suddenly developed amnesia they would throw acid in her face, scarring her for life. The Bugs and Meyer Mob then joined forces with Luciano and in 1931 Siegel was one of the gunmen who killed Joe Masseria. He then became part of Murder, Inc. With Abe 'Kid Twist' Reles as his bodyguard, he was sent to co-ordinate syndicate takeovers of local rackets in Miami and Philadelphia. His good looks and natural charm also meant that he was a useful liaison tool in the Mob's dealings with politicians and other VIPs.

As a bootlegger he was arrested on minor charges, though he was involved in the murders of half a dozen rival suppliers.

In retaliation, bootlegger Waxey Gordon sent his top hitman, Francis Anthony Fabrizio, to lower a bomb down the chimney

Bugsy Siegel talks to film star George Raft, 1947

Virginia Hill, *c.*1950: starting as a dancer at the World's Fair in Chicago, she went on to become a gangsters' moll and then hooked up with Bugsy Siegel

of the Bugs and Meyer Mob's headquarters on Grand Street, Manhattan in 1934. Siegel was injured, but when he recovered he tracked Fabrizio down and shot him dead.

Siegel killed several gangsters – including his boyhood friend Abe 'Bo' Weinberg – as a favour to Dutch Schultz. This did not endear him to the underworld. A price was put on his head and for his own protection he was sent to California in 1937. There he hooked up Jack Dragna's gambling dens and bookmakers' parlours to the national wire service. This put

millions in Lansky's pocket, who operated as the cartel's banker.

Siegel was introduced to the Hollywood stars by his childhood friend, George Raft, who based his gangster roles on Joe Adonis and society hostess Countess Dorothy di Frasso. He later used the contacts he had made to extort millions from the Hollywood moguls. The projectionists' union was run by the Mob, so he would turn off the studios' revenue stream unless they paid up.

Although he was married and had many

affairs, Siegel fell in love with Virginia Hill, who was a courier who carried money from the Chicago Outfit to the Swiss banks. Hill had been the lover of numerous mobsters. While she was giving evidence at a Congressional hearing, Senator Charles W. Tobey asked her why this was so. 'I'm the best goddamned lay in the world,' she replied. Together, Siegel and Hill began importing opium and heroin from Mexico, distributing it through syndicate peddlers.

While Siegel had told the IRS that he was a 'sportsman' who made money from legitimate gambling, he still worked as a hitman. In November 1939 Lansky told him to 'take care' of Harry 'Big Greenie' Greenberg, a former member of Murder, Inc. who had fled to the West Coast and was about to turn police informer. With his brother-in-law Whitey Krakower, Siegel shot Greenberg as he sat in his car outside his Hollywood home.

Then when Lansky told him that Krakower was also about to turn informer, Siegel flew to New York and gunned Krakower down in a Brooklyn street.

When another accomplice, Albert 'Allie' Tannenbaum, turned stool pigeon, Siegel was indicted for Greenberg's murder. However, another witness, Abe Reles, did not survive to testify and Siegel was freed. By then he had already spotted the possibilities of Las Vegas.

> *'Lansky told Siegel to "take care" of Harry Greenberg who had fled to the West Coast. Siegel shot Greenberg as he sat in his car'*

FLAMINGO SWAN SONG

First he tried investing in the small downtown casinos that were already there and then he bought a piece of desert seven miles outside the town. It would later be known as 'the Strip'. With $1 million of his own money, he began building the first hotel-casino, the Flamingo – this was his pet name for Virginia Hill – but with overcharging and kickbacks the costs began spiralling out of control. Meanwhile, Siegel was spending time hanging around the Hollywood studios with George Raft, hoping to break into the movies. But no one dared hire him. When one of the contractors overheard Siegel saying that he needed someone 'taken care of' or 'fixed', he blanched, but Siegel quickly reassured him. 'Don't worry, we only kill each other,' he smiled.

In order to finish the hotel he had to borrow $5 million from the syndicate. They soon wanted their money back, however, so Siegel had to open the Flamingo before it was completed. None of his Hollywood acquaintances turned up for the opening, except for George Raft and Jimmy Durante, who was Las Vegas's first star entertainer. But instead of the expected profits, the casino was soon turning in massive losses. The reason was that some of the croupiers, hired from the rival downtown casinos, had been bribed

A coroner's assistant covers the bullet-ridden body of Bugsy Siegel, hit by five of nine bullets fired through a window in Virginia Hill's house, June 1947

to lose money and put him out of business. Siegel's backers saw it a different way. They assumed he was creaming off the profits.

Siegel insisted that what the Flamingo needed to make a profit was publicity. This was an anathema to Luciano and the other old-style Sicilian mafiosi. When they met in Havana in 1947, Luciano called in the loan. Siegel told Luciano to 'go to hell'. He said he would pay the loan off in his own good time. But this cut no ice with Luciano. He told

Lansky: 'Ben must be hit and there will be no arguments.'

Lansky told Siegel's bodyguard, Mickey Cohen, to stick with his boss day and night. He also begged Siegel to make peace with Luciano and pay off at least some of the loan – but Siegel ignored the plea. On the evening of 20 June 1947, Siegel was sitting with gambling buddy Allen Smiley in the home of Virginia Hill – who was conveniently away in Europe at the time – when a bullet from a 30.30 rifle blew his left eye out. It landed 15 feet away on the tiled floor. Another five shots followed. It was a professional hit and Smiley was unhurt.

Hearing of the murder Cohen stormed into the lobby of the Roosevelt Hotel, where the killers were thought to be staying. He then pulled out two .45-calibre automatics. After emptying them into the ceiling he demanded that those responsible meet him outside. When no one but the police turned up, Cohen made off. Virginia Hill did not return in time for Siegel's funeral and George Raft was bedridden with an asthma attack.

THE MOB TAKES OVER

Ironically, the death of Siegel brought Las Vegas the publicity it needed. Punters flocked to the Flamingo. With Siegel out of the way, Lansky put more reliable men in to manage the syndicate's investment. When Moe Sedway and Gus Greenbaum were brought in they quickly turned a profit and within months the Flamingo was out of debt. Sedway continued running the operation until his death in 1952 and Greenbaum went on to run the Riviera for Capone's old enforcer, Tony Accardo. As a syndicate leader in Las Vegas, Greenbaum would later order the deaths of Tony Brancato

The swimming pool at Bugsy Siegel's Flamingo Hotel, Las Vegas, Nevada, 1947

The curtained-off top floor penthouse residence of multi-millionaire recluse, Howard Hughes, at the Desert Inn hotel, one of five casino hotels he owned

and Tony Tombino, as a punishment for robbing a syndicate hotel. But Greenbaum's gambling, womanizing and drug-taking led him to start stealing money himself. He took it directly from the cage, or counting room.

When this was discovered by the Chicago syndicate, Greenbaum and his wife were found in their Phoenix home with their throats slashed. Their killers had been flown in from Miami, which was by then Lansky's base. He rarely visited Las Vegas but he still controlled the syndicate's interests there.

In 1960, Lansky was given a 'finder's fee' of $500,000 from Morris Lansburgh and Sam Cohen when they purchased the Flamingo. He continued to control it while Lansburgh and Cohen skimmed off (failed to declare income to the IRS) some $30 million. In

1971, they were investigated for tax evasion and Lansky was subpoenaed to appear before the grand jury. With estimated holdings of $300 million Lansky feared being indicted for income tax evasion himself, so he fled to Israel and tried to remain there under the Law of Return, which allows any Jew to settle in the country. However, the law does not include those with a criminal past, so two years later he was deported back to the United States. He was convicted for contempt for not obeying the subpoena and was sentenced to one year in jail, but the sentence was overturned on appeal. He was then tried for tax fraud over London's Colony Club, but was acquitted. Lansburgh and Cohen pleaded guilty to tax evasion and were given a token sentence, while further charges against Lansky were dropped. He died in January 1983 in Miami. All of the money he made has disappeared. He was never once convicted of a federal offence and he only spent two months in jail. That was in 1953, when he was sentenced for running a gambling house in Saratoga.

While Lansky controlled the Flamingo and the Thunderbird, he also had a stake in the Sands Hotel with Frank Costello, Joe Adonis and Joseph 'Doc' Stacher, another alumnus of the Bugs and Meyer gang who escaped jail for tax evasion by emigrating to Israel. George Raft had an investment as well and Frank Sinatra was sold a nine per cent share to get him to sing there. In addition to his Sands stake, Costello controlled the Tropicana. The Sahara and the Riviera were owned by Sam Giancana and other members of the Chicago Outfit. They also had a stake in Caesars Palace, along with New England mobster Raymond Patriarca, Vito Genovese's top aide Jerry Catena and Vincent 'Jimmy Blue Eyes' Alo, Lansky's link with the Italian Mob. As comedian Alan King put it, Caesars Palace was not so much Roman as 'more kind of early Sicilian'.

Jimmy Hoffa and the Teamsters also had a $10 million stake in the Palace, with another $40 million on permanent loan around Las Vegas.

The Desert Inn was owned by Lansky's old friend Morris 'Moe' Dalitz and the Cleveland Mob. Once a member of the 'Jewish Navy' that smuggled Canadian whiskey across Lake Erie during Prohibition, Dalitz built the Las Vegas Country Club, Sunrise Hospital and several homes for retarded children. He was a frequent donor to the Las Vegas public library system, as well as to the campaign funds of Nevada senator Paul Laxalt, one of President Ronald Reagan's closest advisers. In 1951, the Senate Committee to Investigate Crime in Interstate Commerce said Dalitz was a leading criminal who had participated in the 'formation of the national crime syndicate'. Then in 1978, California's Organized Crime Control Commission declared that he was 'one of the architects of the skimming process that developed in Las Vegas in the early 1960s'. Yet he has never been arrested or charged with a crime and he is known as 'Mr Las Vegas' in recognition of his efforts to transform Las Vegas into a modern city.

When the Stardust was being built, Dalitz complained that it would take trade away from the Desert Inn – and he was prepared to settle the matter in the old-fashioned way.

But Lansky set up a meeting between Dalitz, New Jersey mobster Abner 'Longy' Zwillman and California gambling-boat operator Tony Cornero, representing the Stardust. A deal was forged giving each of them interlocking interests in each other's hotels.

In 1966, Howard Hughes moved into the ninth floor of the Desert Inn. After losing heavily at the tables, he offered $30 million to buy the place. After that he began buying up other casinos in Las Vegas and Reno. This suited the Mafia owners, because they were being investigated for skimming at the time.

Hughes was convinced that he could raise the profit margin to 20 per cent, but the casinos were still staffed by Mob employees, so the money continued to go to the Mafia.

RUNNING THINGS IN VEGAS

What Hughes did not understand was that the Mob did not just make its money from skimming the casinos. Through the labour unions, it controlled the suppliers who provided the casinos with food, drink and laundry services – everything they needed. Hughes never turned a profit of more than six per cent. The Mob then bought back most of the casinos, mainly through seemingly legitimate front companies.

The hotels and casinos were not just useful to the Mob for the money they earned, they were also a useful way to launder money from drugs, loan-sharking and extortion, and to make pay-offs. Prominent members of the Mafia were given free rooms and entertainment. They were also 'comped' thousands of dollars in free chips, which they then cashed, leaving without even gambling. In Nevada, there was no tax on such 'losses'.

The Mafia also took over debt collection. The targets were inveterate gamblers who paid nothing for their flights, hotel rooms, food and entertainment, provided they gambled, say, $5,000, win or lose. The Mob would buy up the losses of those who did not pay up at 25 cents in the dollar. Then they would track down the debtors and force them to pay off their debts, while interest accrued at

five per cent a week. Debtors would find that they were in the hands of loan sharks for the rest of their lives.

The characters who actually ran things in Las Vegas were very dangerous men. One leading figure was Marcello Caifano. A member of the Chicago Outfit under Sam Giancana, he had convictions for burglary, larceny, bank robbery, fraud and extortion. Giancana regularly rented him out for hits and he was the prime suspect in at least ten murders.

He had been arraigned for contempt of Congress in 1958 after citing his Fifth Amendment right 73 times before the McClellan Committee. Police investigations also connected him to the murder of the beautiful cocktail waitress Estelle Carey, girlfriend of Nick Circella, who had been jailed over an extortion ring in Hollywood.

When it was feared that Circella might talk, Carey was kidnapped, tied to a chair, tortured and then doused in gasoline and set on fire. After that, Circella's lips were sealed.

Later it was thought that Caifano had murdered corrupt cop turned gangster Richard Cain and oil tycoon Raymond J. Ryan. Caifano had been jailed for trying to extort $60,000 from Ryan, but after he was released Ryan was killed by a car bomb.

Eager to leave Chicago, Caifano gave his beautiful wife to Sam Giancana in exchange for being made 'Don' of Las Vegas. He then changed his name to John Marshall and moved to Nevada, where he is said to have planned the disappearance of Louis 'Russian Louie' Strauss, who was blackmailing former Dallas bootlegger and Las Vegas developer Benny Binion.

Caifano was eventually barred by the Nevada Gaming Control Board and he spent 20 years in jail for handling stolen securities. In 1971 he was replaced by Tony 'The Ant' Spilotro.

TONY 'THE ANT' SPILOTRO

An enforcer for the Chicago Outfit, Spilotro had learnt his trade from 'Mad' Sam DeStefano, an expert in torture and ice-pick slaying. Spilotro quickly gained notoriety when he crushed one of his victim's heads in a vice. After he was 'made' in 1963 he was assigned to run a bookmaking territory with his childhood friend Frank 'Lefty' Rosenthal. He then ran the Mob's betting operations in

Miami, following which he was sent to Las Vegas, where he brought in his own men and imposed a street tax on every bookmaker, loan shark, drug dealer and pimp in town. Bookmaker Jerry Dellman was one of the few who resisted him. He was shot dead in daylight and his body was left in the open garage area behind his house. It was a message that there was a real gangster in town.

After Spilotro took control, a series of murders took place. Victims were tortured and dumped out in the desert. He also extended the Mafia's tentacles into the sheriff's office, the courthouse and the telephone company, so he could have people's telephones tapped.

In 1973, Spilotro was indicted for murder alongside DeStefano, but he was acquitted after DeStefano was slain. DeStefano had acquired his 'Mad' Sam nickname because

Anthony Spilotro and his wife leave the federal building in Las Vegas after a mistrial was declared when he was up on racketeering charges

of his sometimes eccentric behaviour. In other trials he had done things like turning up in court wearing pyjamas or appearing in a wheelchair, feigning illness. And he can't have aided his defence, or that of his co-defendants, by shouting at the judge through a megaphone. Perhaps it was all an act, but it was enough to worry some of the Mob.

The following year he was indicted a second time, this time alongside reputed Mob boss Joseph Lombardo. Both men were acquitted when a key witness was murdered, but the Nevada Gaming Commission then barred Spilotro from entering its casinos. Undeterred, he diversified into burglary and protection. When he wasn't attending to business he hung out at a favourite bar, and he dined daily at the Food Factory, a hamburger joint owned by his brother John.

At one point, Spilotro was betting $30,000 a week at a bookmaker that was offering better odds than any other establishment in town. It was actually an IRS sting.

When the IRS agent running it had the nerve to ask Spilotro for collateral, Spilotro greeted him with a baseball bat. 'Do you know who I am?' he asked. 'I run this town.'

Spilotro's activities did not go unnoticed. He was put under surveillance 24 hours a day, using tails, telephone taps and hidden cameras and microphones. Even though he was indicted for murder, there was never enough evidence to convict though. The Mob was not amused, because it damaged the image of Las Vegas. Then some of the men Spilotro had brought to town turned informer, which led to the arrest and conviction of a number of leading mafiosi in Kansas City, Milwaukee and Chicago. The Outfit decided to have him killed.

They lured him back to Illinois where Spilotro and his brother Michael were beaten to death.

The FBI heard about this from the wife of one of the men who had dug their grave, but they did little to investigate and no one was ever arrested for the killings.

ATLANTIC CITY GETS DEALT IN

Despite the wholesale corruption that existed, the state of Nevada was making money out of Las Vegas, so other states wanted to join in. In 1976, the citizens of New Jersey voted to permit gambling in the rundown seaside resort of Atlantic City. When the Casino Act was signed into law in Atlantic City's convention hall two years later, Governor Brendan Byrne told organized crime to 'keep your filthy hands out of Atlantic City; keep the hell out of our state'. These were empty words. Mafiosi had been migrating across the Hudson from New York since the 1920s. There were seven families in the state and Atlantic City had been a Mob town since Nucky Johnson held the first conference of the national crime syndicate there in 1929.

In May 1978 Resorts International renovated a 1,000-room hotel on the Boardwalk and opened the first casino. A former incarnation of the company had been involved with casinos

Singer Steve Lawrence at Resorts International casino in Atlantic City

Even before the first casino in Atlantic City opened, Mafia boss of Philadelphia, Angelo Bruno, called a meeting. All leading members were ordered to put up $500,000, so the Mafia could monopolize all food, drink, linen and vending machines going into the hotels. Mafia contractors would build the casinos and the Mob would also control the unions. The man in charge, Nicodemus 'Little Nicky' Scarfo, had been sent to Atlantic City in 1964 because so many people in Philadelphia wanted to kill him. He took over Local 54 of the Hotel Employees and Restaurant Employees International Union, later telling a local plumber not to worry about trouble with his employees 'because we control the unions'.

Then looking out over the Boardwalk, Scarfo said: 'We'll own this city one day. That's what we're going to do.'

As in Las Vegas, money was laundered though the casinos and pay-offs were made by comping 'made' men. Soon New York's Five Families began to take an interest. But Atlantic City was traditionally the domain of the Philadelphia crime family. Angelo Bruno was not prepared to share it and Scarfo protected the family's territorial rights – and built a fearsome reputation – with a series of vicious murders.

In 1980, Bruno was gunned down by Alfred Salerno. The killing had been ordered by Bruno's *consigliere*, Antonio 'Tony Bananas' Caponigro, after Frank 'Funzi' Tieri, boss of the Gambino family, had assured him that the killing had the approval of the Commission.

in the Bahamas, where both Dino Cellini and Meyer Lansky had been involved, but this fact was ignored. Bally Manufacturing, by far the largest manufacturer of slot machines in the United States, was then granted a licence on condition that chairman and president William O'Donnell stepped down, due to his alleged criminal links. O'Donnell had taken over the company in 1963 with the help of Gerardo 'Jerry' Catena, underboss of the Genovese family. Another business associate was Dino Cellini.

Salerno and Caponigro were then summoned to New York. They expected to be told that they could take over the Philadelphia family – instead they were told that the Commission had not approved Bruno's removal. As with everyone that crossed the Commission, they were tortured and killed. Caponigro's body was punctured with 14 separate bullet and knife wounds and $20 bills were shoved into his orifices. It was the Mafia way of showing that he had been killed because he was too greedy. Salerno's body was found in the boot of a car, which was parked three miles (5 km) away.

Frank Tieri was awarded Caponigro's lucrative numbers operation in Newark, while Bruno's underboss, Phil 'Chicken Man' Testa, took over the Philadelphia family, with Scarfo as his *consigliere*. Scarfo was under indictment for murder at the time but he was surprisingly acquitted. Testa and Scarfo then began killing anyone they suspected might be disloyal.

Testa dug his own grave by trying to prevent the Five Families from moving into Atlantic City. He was killed by a nail bomb under his porch. Testa's underboss, Pete Casella, then told Scarfo that he was the new boss of the Philadelphia family, courtesy of 'Big Paul' Castellano, head of the Gambino family, and 'Fat Tony' Salerno. Scarfo had hopes in that direction himself, so he went to New York and told Castellano and Salerno that they could operate in Atlantic City if they made him boss instead. His ploy worked. Casella was then retired to Florida.

'LITTLE NICKY' SCARFO

Scarfo began his reign by imposing a 'street tax' on any criminals not working directly for the Mafia. Those who did not pay were killed. Family members who did not prove their loyalty to Scarfo also paid the price.

Seventy-year-old 'Harry the Hunchback' Riccobene soon fell foul of Scarfo. Riccobene ran a crew that was involved in gambling, vending machines, loan-sharking and drugs. For years, he had paid an annual tribute to Bruno and he was willing to continue the arrangement with Bruno's successors. But for Scarfo this was not good enough – he wanted paying weekly. Riccobene refused and a war broke out. The 70-year-old was shot five times while making a call from a phone booth to, it is said, his 23-year-old mistress. However, he survived, even managing to wrestle the gun from his assailant. Tit-for-tat shootings followed. These were seldom fatal, so Scarfo's faction became known in the press as the 'gang that could not shoot straight'. Nevertheless, the body count climbed. The list of corpses included Riccobene's half-brother and nephew. Finally, three of Riccobene's family were arrested and turned state's evidence. Harry was convicted of first-degree murder. In 2000 he died of natural causes in jail, after ceding his territory to Scarfo.

But Scarfo was riding for a fall. First of all he ordered his most competent hitman, Salvatore Testa, to be killed. Son of Phil 'Chicken Man' Testa, Salvatore had been a loyal henchman. He had run the family during

Atlantic City crime boss Nicodemo 'Little Nicky' Scarfo after being found not guilty of the execution-style slaying of cement contractor Vincent Falcone

Phil Leonetti, turned federal witness. In 1988, Scarfo and 16 others were convicted on murder and racketeering charges. He was sentenced to life imprisonment, which was reduced on appeal. If he makes it, he will be released in January 2033, when he will be 104 years old.

Scarfo continued to run the family through his cousin, Anthony 'Tony Buck' Piccolo. However, when he retired in 1991 at the age of 80, the Gambinos and the Genoveses installed Giovanni 'John the Dour Don' Stanfa as head of the Philadelphia family. The Second Philly War broke out in 1993 when the 'Young Turks' led by 'Skinny Joey' Merlino challenged the old-timers. In 1995, Stanfa was handed five life sentences and Merlino took over. He, in turn, went

the 'Riccobene War' when Scarfo was in jail on a firearms charge, he had taken a bullet in the line of duty and he had almost lost an arm to a shotgun blast. His reward was a bullet in the back of the head.

Young soldiers feared that they would be next in the line of fire so they began defecting to the FBI. Even Scarfo's favourite nephew and newly-appointed underboss,

down for 14 years in 2001 and was replaced by acting boss 'Uncle Joe' Ligambi. He has kept a much lower profile than the flamboyant Merlino and is said to have restored the sort of stability the Philadelphia family enjoyed under Angelo Bruno.

Merlino was released in March 2011 and is now said to live in Florida. He denies current involvement with the Mafia.

CARLO GAMBINO

Born in Palermo in 1902, Gambino stowed away on board the SS *Vincenzo Florida* at the age of 19. After working for a trucking company owned by his uncle in Brooklyn, he became a soldier for Joe Masseria. When Masseria was killed, he switched his allegiance to Salvatore Maranzano.

In the reorganization that followed the murder of Maranzano, Gambino and his brothers-in-law Paul and Peter Castellano became soldiers in the Mangano family. When Albert Anastasia took over, Gambino became his underboss. But it still wasn't enough – he wanted the top spot. The only way was to have Anastasia killed. He had a little help from Genovese, however, because it was said: 'Without Vito backing him, Carlo never would have went for it.'

Anastasia loyalist Aniello Dellacroce opposed Gambino's elevation, so Gambino simply eliminated Armand 'Tommy' Rava, another loyalist, and offered Dellacroce the position of underboss, which he wisely accepted. Together, they made the Gambinos America's most powerful crime family, though they would not handle drugs, believing they attracted unnecessary federal attention. The family motto became: 'Deal and die.'

In 1962, Carlo's eldest son Thomas Gambino married the daughter of Tommy Lucchese, so Lucchese cut Gambino in on the rackets at John F. Kennedy Airport. During the Banana War Gambino wanted Bonanno to be killed, but he was persuaded to let him retire instead.

Gambino was a fan and friend of Frank Sinatra. They were photographed sharing a drink with Luciano, Lansky and Anastasia at the Havana Conference in 1946. He also hung out with the Rat Pack (Sinatra, Dean Martin, Sammy Davis, Jnr., etc.) in Las Vegas in 1967.

After being named boss of bosses following the death of Luciano, Gambino is thought to have been responsible for many deaths, which brought him immense respect in the Cosa Nostra. This was a precious commodity. When Colombo soldier Carmine 'Mimi' Scialo drunkenly harassed him in a restaurant, Gambino did not respond. Not long afterwards, Scialo's body was found in the cement floor of Otto's Social Club in Brooklyn.

During his career in crime Gambino was arrested 16 times and convicted on 6 occasions, but he only went to jail once. He spent 22 months inside in 1937, after being convicted of tax evasion in connection with a million-gallon still in Philadelphia. In 1970 he was indicted for conspiring to hijack a vehicle that was transporting $3 million, but he was too ill to stand trial. Heart problems also prevented his deportation when it was established that he had entered the country illegally.

He denied being offered $1 million to assassinate Martin Luther King. No mobster would do such a thing, he declared.

Before he died of a heart attack in 1976, he went over the head of Dellacroce and named his brother-in-law Paul Castellano as his successor.

'Gambino was a fan and friend of Frank Sinatra. He also hung out with the Rat Pack'

Carlo Gambino

THE KENNEDYS VERSUS THE MOB

Democratic nominee Senator John Kennedy, with wife Jackie (to his right), addresses supporters in the run-up to the 1960 election

When John F. Kennedy ran against Richard Nixon in the 1960 presidential election he won by just 113,000 votes. A massive 68 million votes had been cast, so Kennedy had scraped home by a margin of less that two-tenths of a percentage point. Key to his victory was Cook County, formerly the playground of Al Capone. It delivered an overwhelming 450,000 votes to Kennedy, giving him 27 electoral votes from the State of Illinois and the presidency.

Kennedy's father Joe had been a bootlegger in the Prohibition era, so he had good connections with the Mafia. He used all his influence on behalf of his son. In particular he recruited Chicago's mayor, Richard Daley, the last of the big city bosses.

Mayor of Chicago Richard J. Daley with Lyndon B. Johnson

Daley was re-elected every four years from 1955 to 1975. John F. Kennedy would joke that on the eve of the election his father had asked him the exact number of votes he would need to win, because there was no way he was paying for a landslide.

John F. Kennedy had Mafia links of his own. In February 1960 he was at the Sands Hotel in Las Vegas when Frank Sinatra introduced him to a young woman named Judith Campbell. They became lovers. A week after their first assignation she met Sam Giancana, who was head of the Chicago Outfit from 1957 to 1966. Because of Giancana's 'shoot first, ask questions later' policy, there were 75 gangland murders in Chicago during his nine-year reign. He was also said to have several police chiefs on the payroll and he claimed to have Cook County 'locked up tight'.

One day, Kennedy told Campbell that he may need Giancana's help with his campaign. She acted as a liaison between the two men and a meeting was set up in a Miami Beach hotel that April. Kennedy was so pleased with the outcome that he promised to divorce his wife Jackie and marry Campbell if he failed to win the Democratic nomination. Later, Giancana promised to deliver the 'river wards' to Kennedy in the November election. According to Campbell, Giancana boasted that he had got her boyfriend elected – though Mayor Daley also claimed credit.

A few days after the failed Bay of Pigs invasion in April 1961, Campbell said that Kennedy called her and asked her to fly to Las Vegas. He needed her to pick up an envelope from Johnny Roselli, underboss in the Los Angeles Dragna crime family. The envelope was delivered to Giancana and another meeting between Kennedy and Giancana was set up at the Ambassador East Hotel in Chicago. After Fidel Castro had taken over in Cuba in 1959 he had closed down the Mafia's lucrative gambling operations there, so the Mob had every reason to throw their weight behind Operation Mongoose, a programme of assassination attempts on Castro.

Relations between John F. Kennedy,

Judith Campbell and Sam Giancana cooled after Kennedy's brother Robert F. Kennedy, the United States attorney general, began investigating the Mafia. The story of John F. Kennedy's Mafia connections died with his assassination in 1963, but they resurfaced in 1975. Just five days after Giancana had been gunned down in his home, Johnny Roselli was called in front of the Senate Intelligence Committee that was investigating the plot to kill Castro. Roselli revealed nothing to the committee but the Mob bosses considered him a security risk, so he was kidnapped, shot and strangled. After that, his legs were sawn off and his body was stuffed into a 55-gallon oil drum, which was weighted with chains and dumped in the sea off Florida. However, gases from his decomposing corpse caused the drum to float to the surface. His killers were never identified, though it is thought that Florida Mob boss Santo Trafficante, another of the Operation Mongoose conspirators, had ordered the hit. There were also rumours that Roselli had been involved in the assassination of John F. Kennedy, who had failed to honour promises made to the Mafia during his election.

Robert F. Kennedy was chief counsel to the Senate Labor Rackets Committee under John L. McClellan when he famously squared up to Jimmy Hoffa, president of the Teamsters union. Hoffa's predecessor, Dave Beck, cited the Fifth Amendment over a hundred times during his appearance before the McClellan committee in 1957 (the Fifth Amendment protects witnesses from being forced to incriminate themselves). Nevertheless, in 1959 he was prosecuted for embezzlement, labour racketeering and tax evasion and was jailed for three years. After Hoffa took over in 1957 the Teamsters were expelled from the AFL-CIO (American Federation of Labor and Congress of Industrial Organizations) whose leader, George Meany, said that he could only agree to the return of the Teamsters if Hoffa was dismissed as their president. Among other things, there were allegations that Hoffa had diverted $500,000 into Nixon's campaign fund.

In 1960, Robert Kennedy published *The Enemy Within*, an account of union malpractices. After running his brother's campaign, John made Robert attorney general. In that role, he began a successful campaign against organized crime – convictions rose 800 per cent during his term of office. He continued his pursuit of the Teamsters and confronted Hoffa again in televised hearings. Then in 1962 he tried to prosecute Hoffa for taking kick-backs from a trucking company, but the trial ended with a hung jury.

In 1964 one of Hoffa's union associates, Edward Partin, turned surprise federal witness and Hoffa was convicted of jury tampering. He was sentenced to eight years in jail. Later that year, he was also convicted of fraud in respect of the improper use of the Teamsters' pension fund and a further five

American union leader Jimmy Hoffa appearing before a senate committee, c.1960 – he was rumoured to have connections with organized crime. In 1975, he disappeared and his body was never found

meet in the parking lot of the Machus Red Fox Restaurant in Bloomfield Township, Oakland County, Michigan. Hoffa was never seen again. Giacalone and Provenzano denied meeting him, but few doubt that Hoffa's disappearance was the work of the Mafia.

According to former Teamster official Daniel Sullivan, Hoffa told him some time before that: 'Tony Pro threatened to pull my guts out or kidnap my grandchildren if I continued to attempt to return to the presidency of the Teamsters.'

Richard Kuklinski, a Polish hitman working for the Mafia, claims to have killed Hoffa. So does Donald 'Tony the Greek' Frankos, another freelance hitman for the Mafia. According to Frankos, he and some other Mafia killers picked Hoffa up at the Red Fox and took him to a house in Mount Clemens, Michigan.

'I pumped two slugs into Hoffa's forehead,' said Frankos.

Then they cut his body up with a chainsaw. The remains were bagged up to be disposed of in a Mob-run garbage disposal facility. However, the manager was worried about handling such a high profile case so the parts were left in the freezer until they were finally buried in the foundations of the Giants Stadium in Meadowlands, New Jersey. Hoffa's body was never found, so in accordance with the law he was declared legally dead seven years after his disappearance.

years was added to his sentence. However, he was released in December 1971 after serving less than five years of his 13-year prison term. President Nixon had commuted his sentence to time served. The Teamsters then gave him a $1.7-million lump sum pension, something they had never done before.

On 30 July 1975 Hoffa had an appointment with two Mafia leaders – Anthony 'Tony Jack' Giacalone from Detroit and Anthony 'Tony Pro' Provenzano, a *caporegime* for the Genovese crime family in New York. Provenzano was also Hoffa's former vice-president in the Teamsters. They were to

Chapter 11

THE PIZZA CONNECTION

When Luciano decided to go into business smuggling drugs into the United States, he had one major problem. While the Mafia and the Camorra were expert smugglers, there was a shortage of skilled chemists in Italy. So he turned to the Mafia's French counterpart, the *Unione Corse,* which operated largely out of Corsica and Marseilles.

During the Second World War, some members of the *Unione Corse* had been resistance fighters and others had been recruited as agents by the Allies, so it was only natural that the CIA should turn to gangster and former resistance leader Antoine Guérini at the end of hostilities. He was recruited to break the Communists' hold on the docks. He then became crime boss of Marseilles and with Luciano's help he went on to play a key role in the heroin trade. The morphine base would come in from Beirut, via Sicily, at around $1,000 a kilo and the refineries in Marseilles would then turn it into 90 per cent pure heroin, worth $7,000 a kilo.

By the time it arrived in the United States it would be worth $30,000 a kilo. On the streets, where it was cut with powdered milk, it would fetch $300,000 a kilo at 1950s prices.

Most of the heroin entered the United States via Montreal. Because the city was part of the French-speaking province of Quebec, it was easy for Corsican gangsters from Marseilles to work there. Montreal was also the Mafia capital of Canada. The city boss, Vincent 'Vic the Egg' Cotroni, was allied to the Bonanno family in New York. The link had been set up by the Corsican Antoine d'Agostino, a Luciano protégé, who supplied the Genovese family via what became known as 'Gino's Tours'. Italian holidaymakers would cross the Atlantic by liner to Montreal, bringing with them a car specially fitted out in Italy or France. From Canada they would then drive down to see the sights of New York, where the car would be stripped of the narcotics that had been stashed in its hidden compartments.

Agostino fled Canada after being arrested for possessing heroin and running a brothel. He settled in Mexico where he set up a new drug trafficking operation. The Canadian operation was taken over by Vic Cotroni's younger brother Giuseppe ('Pep') and Carmine Galante, until Galante was deported. By 1956, Cotroni and Salvatore Giglio, Galante's replacement, had teamed up with the Genovese family to control two-thirds of the heroin entering the United States, which had an estimated street value of over $50 million a month. However, the operation was exposed in 1961 and Galante and 'Pep' Cotroni were jailed.

The heroin route then adopted a southerly approach, courtesy of Meyer Lansky, who

> '*Montreal was the Mafia capital of Canada. City boss "Vic the Egg" Cotroni was allied to the Bonannos*'

Left: **Auguste Joseph Ricord flanked by federal agents**

was living in Miami, and Santo Trafficante, Jnr., the boss of Tampa. Santo Trafficante's father had long been an associate of Lansky and Luciano. He had taken over Florida's connections with Corsica and Marseilles following the murder of Florida crime boss Ignacio Antinori in 1940. Santo Trafficante, Jnr. managed the family's interests in Cuba for 13 years before he was arrested and expelled by Castro. After that he controlled an army of émigré Cuban hitmen and traffickers.

As the supply of morphine-base from the Middle East began to dry up, cheaper opium began to come out of Laos, courtesy of the CIA, who traded with the hill tribes as a bulwark against the Communists. Because Laos had formerly been part of French Indochina, the Corsicans and the Marseillaise already had contacts over there so in 1968 Trafficante visited Saigon, where he met up with some Corsican mobsters. Meanwhile Auguste Ricord, one of the founders of the 'French Connection', had set up bases in Argentina and Paraguay from where he ran the heroin over the Mexican border or flew it into Miami. He was formerly a member of the Carlingue (the French Gestapo under the Vichy regime). In the ten years up to his arrest in Asuncion in 1972, it is estimated that he moved five tonnes of heroin worth over $1 billion into the United States.

Italians who had emigrated to Buenos Aires or São Paulo in Brazil then took over, using what was left of Antoine d'Agostino's Corsican network in Mexico – which was then financed by wealthy businessman Jorge Asaf y Bala, who was known as 'the Al Capone of Mexico'. More heroin was being brought in through Montreal. This was also the route used by Carmine Galante when he imported illegal immigrants from Sicily. He needed them to staff the growing chains of Mafia-controlled pizzerias that were used as fronts for the drug-trafficking operations. The immigrants were known as 'Zips' because of their propensity for violence. Even Carlo Gambino, who was generally opposed to drugs, turned to the Zips when he needed reliable killers.

Venezuela was another haven for Mafia traffickers. It borders cocaine-rich Colombia and has a 1,750-mile coastline. The offshore islands of the Dutch Antilles – Aruba, Bonaire and Curaçao – have been the home of smuggling for centuries. According to the *Corriere della Sera*, Aruba was 'the first state to be bought by Mafia bosses'. Venezuelan citizenship could be obtained for as little as $500. The country had no exchange controls and it had no extradition treaty with any other nation.

Tuna fishermen from the Agrigento on the southern coast of Sicily then began to fish in the Caribbean. They bought up the tuna fisheries and canneries in Latin America. Soon heroin and cocaine was being smuggled into the United States in cans and frozen blocks of fish. The quantities involved were so great that the drugs became known as 'white tuna'.

By the late 1960s, the authorities began to

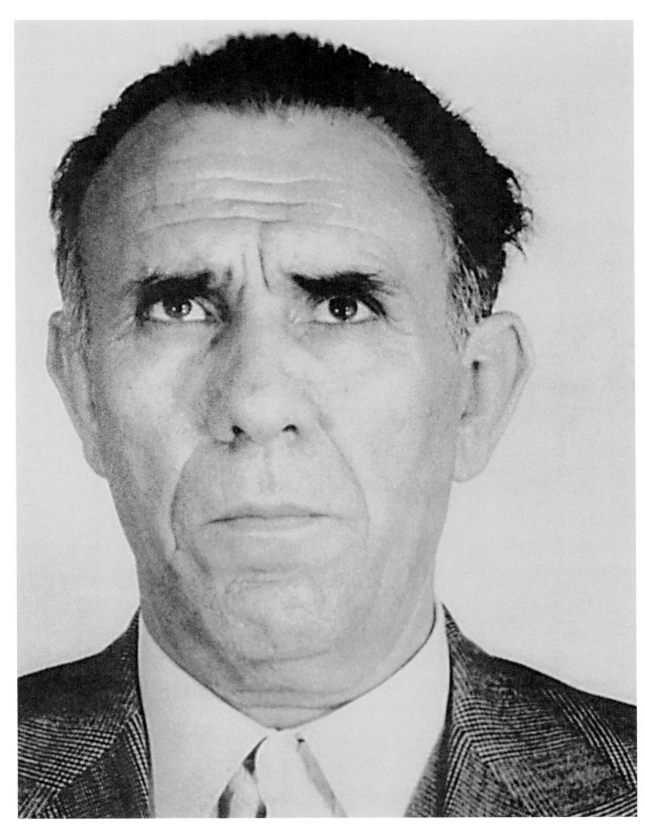

Gaetano
Badalamenti at the
age of 61

clean up Marseilles. Over 40 former French intelligence agents were arrested and eight drugs refineries were closed down. In 1967 Antoine Guérini was gunned down by two hired assassins outside a petrol station. The Corsican supplier Pascal Molinelli then tried to make a deal with the Camorra. This led to a short and bloody war with the Mafia, which left the Camorra as a junior partner.

THE PIZZA CONNECTION

With money flooding into Sicily from the Mafia's worldwide drugs operation, the Sicilians began building refineries of their own, staffed by unemployed chemists from Marseilles. From there the drugs were shipped directly to the States. In 1971, 82 kilos of 90 per cent pure heroin was found in a car that had been shipped to New York on an Italian cruise liner. The man who came to collect it was a member of the Gambino family who worked at Piancone's Pizza Palace, part of a chain owned by Michael Piancone. He was a business associate of Salvatore and Matteo Sollena, nephews of Sicilian crime boss Gaetano Badalamenti. The Sollenas also ran pizzerias and were suspected of involvement in the drugs trade.

In 1978 Salvatore Sollena's girlfriend was arrested in New Jersey. She was carrying counterfeit money and she also had in her possession over $50,000 in real money and $25,000 in cashier's cheques. An investigation revealed that the Sollena brothers had sent $330,000 worth of cashier's cheques to Palermo. They were drawn in amounts under $10,000, so they did not have to be reported. Over the following year $4 million was sent from New Jersey to Sicily, including $1 million from one small pizza chain in New York. Then nearly half-a-million dollars in banknotes was found in a suitcase in Palermo airport. The money was wrapped in a pizza apron that was traced back to one of the Sollenas' pizzerias in New Jersey. The brothers were later murdered.

From his prison cell, Carmine Galante had been planning to take control of the Bonanno family – and then the entire American Mafia. In 1974, he was released on parole after serving 12 years of his sentence. Forty-eight hours later, the tomb of Frank Costello was blown up. Then in 1978, Galante ordered eight of the top Genovese lieutenants to be gunned down. Others were told to fall in behind him or face the consequences. However, there was a secret meeting of the other Mafia bosses behind his back, who decided Galante had to go. The contract was given to Salvatore Catalano and his fellow Zips.

On 12 July 1979, Galante dropped in at Joe and Mary's Restaurant in the Bushwick section of Brooklyn. He had gone there to say goodbye to his cousin Giuseppe Turano, who was about to take a vacation back in Italy. With Galante was his bodyguard Leonardo 'Nina' Coppola and two younger soldiers, Baldassare Amato and Cesare Bonventre, both from Castellammare del Golfo. Galante had just finished his main course when three masked gunmen pushed through the restaurant and into the courtyard where they were eating. Galante was killed by a shotgun with his trademark cigar still in his month. Turano and Coppola also died. Although there were only three gunmen, ammunition from five guns was found. So it is thought that Amato and Bonventre joined in the slaughter.

In the autumn of 1980 the FBI, the DEA (Drug Enforcement Administration) and United States Customs were monitoring Salvatore Catalano and his partner Giuseppe Ganci, who were based at the Al Dente Pizzeria

'The other Mafia bosses decided Galante had to go. The contract was given to Salvatore Catalano and his fellow Zips...'

in Queens. Suddenly, the two men went off to a Mafia wedding in New York's Hotel Pierre. The leaders of many of the crime families in the United States, Canada and Sicily were there, so the authorities obtained a list of the telephone numbers that had been dialled from the hotel's payphones. This gave them the first clue that the Mafia was running a vast network of drug traffickers.

In 1983, undercover DEA agents in Philadelphia attempted to buy heroin from two suspected drug dealers, one of whom was the owner of a pizzeria which was again called the Al Dente. The surveillance of Ganci was stepped up.

By that time, the Mafia was having trouble with the amount of money it was making. It was estimated that between 1979 and 1984 pizzerias on the East Coast and in the Midwest were handling 330 lbs (150 kg) of heroin a year, with a street value of $1.65 billion. Under the old system, bagmen picked up the cash and then ran from bank to bank, changing it into small cashier's cheques, but this became impractical. Instead, private planes were hired to fly millions of dollars in cash to banks in Bermuda. The funds would then be forwarded to Switzerland. Later on, couriers flew in direct from Switzerland to pick up the money. Eventually, the Mafia had to co-opt major financial institutions. Tens of millions of dollars were deposited with Wall Street firms such as E.F. Hutton and Merrill Lynch. These large sums were then siphoned through a series of front companies until they reached some sort of Mafia-run operation in Sicily or a numbered bank account in Switzerland.

At that time the drugs were being provided by Gaetano Badalamenti, who was then living in Brazil, but by 1984 demand was outstripping supply. When an emergency meeting was called in Madrid on 8 April 1984 Badalamenti, his son Vito and his nephew Pietro Alfano were arrested. Then the police began raiding the pizzerias.

In New York, the 'Pizza Connection Trial' ran for 16 months. There were 22 defendants, all born in Sicily. Many could not speak English. Cesare Bonventre was indicted, along with pizzeria-owner Gaetano Mazzara,

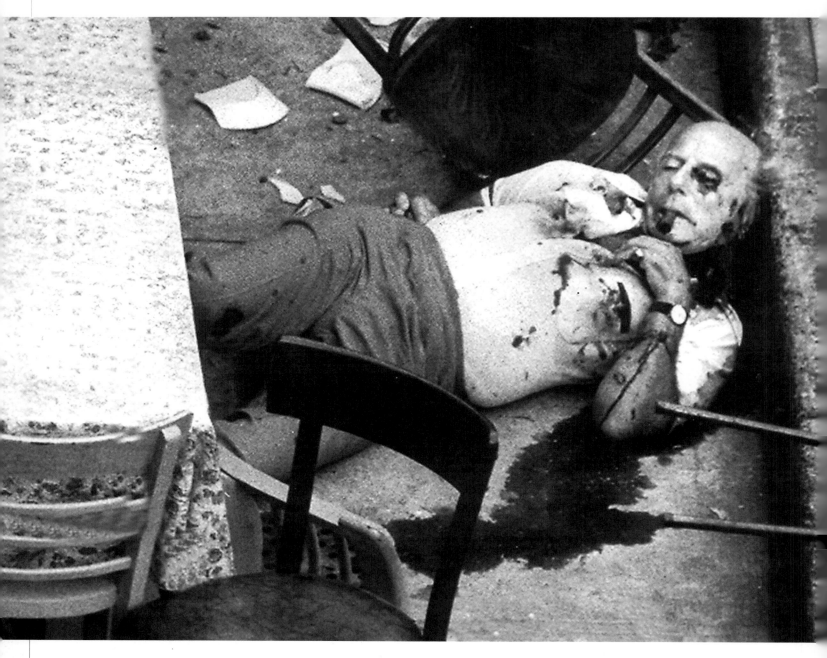

The body of Mob boss Carmine Galante, complete with trademark cigar

but he was murdered before he could stand trial. And Giuseppe Ganci died of cancer before proceedings started. The key witness was Tommaso Buscetta. Although he was not part of the pizza connection, he had set up some of the first pizzerias in America and had imported Zips to run them.

Gaetano Badalamenti was handed a 45-year sentence and died in jail; Salvatore Catalano was also jailed for 45 years after ordering the murder of his cousin and namesake Salvatore 'Saca' Catalano, when Saca became addicted to heroin; Pietro Alfano was shot and crippled while he was out on bail awaiting sentencing;

and Baldassare 'Baldo' Amato got away with a relatively light five-year prison term.

After he was released he was convicted of murder and sentenced to life. Giovanni Ligammari was sentenced to 15 years. He was released after eight years, but he and his son Pietro were then found hanged in their home in New Jersey. The verdict was double suicide. Others were also sentenced to long jail terms. Only Vito Badalamenti was acquitted. However, when he did not leave the country he was arrested by the immigration authorities. Later, in the mid-1980s Maxi Trial in Italy, he was sentenced to six years in jail. However, in

1995 he became a fugitive. He is thought to be hiding out in either Australia or Brazil.

THE MAFIA COMMISSION TRIAL

The 'Pizza Connection Trial' was not the only setback for the Mafia. In December 1984 the entire New York Commission was arrested: Phil 'Rusty' Rastelli of the Bonannos, Anthony 'Fat Tony' Salerno of the Genoveses, Paul 'Big Paulie' Castellano of the Gambino family, Tony 'Tony Ducks' Corallo of the Luccheses and Gennaro 'Gerry Lang' Langella, acting head of the Colombo family. Their average age was 70. Bail was set at over $2 million

Judge Giovanni Falcone, surrounded by armed bodyguards, arrives in Marseilles to meet his French counterparts fighting the Mafia

D.A. Rudolph
Giuliani

each, but it was raised in a matter of minutes.

Rastelli was granted a separate trial. After it was discovered that the Bonanno family had been infiltrated by FBI agent Joseph Pistone, under the alias 'Donnie Brasco', Rastelli was removed from the Commission. Convicted on extortion and labour racketeering charges with underboss Joey 'The Ear' Massino, he was sentenced to 12 years in jail, but he was released on humanitarian grounds in 1991. He died of liver cancer three days later. Massino was jailed for ten years after being acquitted of a triple murder. After he was released, he was known briefly as 'The Last Don', because the heads of the other Five Families were all in jail. However, in July 2005 he was convicted of extortion, arson, loan-sharking, money laundering, illegal gambling, conspiracy and seven murders. In order to escape the death penalty he turned state's evidence, the first of the official bosses to do so.

By the time the Mafia Commission Trial opened the defendants had been joined by Carmine 'Junior' Persico, the official boss of the Colombo family; Aniello 'The Lamb' Dellacroce, underboss of the Gambino family; Salvatore 'Tom Mix' Santoro, Lucchese family underboss; Christopher 'Christy Tick' Furnari, *consigliere* of the Luccheses; Ralph 'Ralphie' Scopo, a Colombo family soldier and president of the Cement and Concrete Workers District Council; and Anthony 'Bruno' Indelicato, the Bonanno family soldier who was thought to have been one of the hitmen who killed Carmine

Galante. They were charged with offences under the Racketeer Influenced and Corrupt Organizations Act (RICO), including labour racketeering, extortion and murder for hire. Prosecutor Rudolph Giuliani aimed to wipe out all Five Families.

The evidence against them had been collected by a series of bugs. One had been placed in the home of Paul Castellano. It revealed that the Mafia owned all of the companies that bid for construction contracts that involved cement or concrete and were worth over $2 million. Other bugs were in Anthony 'Tony Ducks' Corallo's car, a social club owned by the Genoveses and Ralph Scopo's union office. Even Jerry Langella's favourite table at a Brooklyn restaurant was bugged.

The accused were found guilty of all 151 counts of the indictment. They were each sentenced to 100 years in prison for belonging to 'an ongoing criminal enterprise', except for Indelicato who was jailed for 45 years for the murder of Galante. Released in 2000, he was returned to prison for parole violations.

Aniello Dellacroce died of cancer while he was out on bail on 2 December 1985. Two weeks later Paul Castellano, who was also on bail, was murdered. It was the work of an ambitious young *capo* named John Gotti. Having served time for hijacking, Gotti had returned to the Gambino family when Carlo Gambino's nephew was kidnapped. Part of the ransom was paid, but the boy was killed. The FBI arrested two suspects and Carlo Gambino put out a contract on the third. Gotti was one of a three-man death squad that killed the man in a Staten Island bar. After pleading guilty to attempted manslaughter, Gotti was jailed for four years.

THE TEFLON DON

Released after two years, Gotti became a 'made man' in the Gambino family. Promoted to *capo*, he became a close associate of Dellacroce, but Castellano feared him. Meanwhile, Gotti developed such a reputation for brutality that the police compared him to Albert Anastasia. He did not always get his own hands dirty, though.

In March 1980, Gotti's neighbour John Favara accidentally ran over and killed Gotti's 12-year-old son Frank. Favara was absolved of any blame for the accident, but he found the word 'murderer' spray-painted on his car. He was advised to move but he ignored the warnings. Four months after the accident some men bundled Favara into a car as he left work. He was never seen again. Gotti was away in Florida at the time.

Castellano discovered that Gotti was trafficking heroin, which was against the family rules, so he vetoed Gotti's plans to move into John F. Kennedy Airport, with its lucrative opportunities for labour racketeering and cargo theft. Instead, he tried to persuade Gotti to accept a contract to take out Roy DeMeo, an infamous killer who had murdered up to 200 people after first luring them to the Gemini Lounge in Brooklyn. Gotti politely declined,

which made him even more unpopular with Castellano. When Dellacroce died Gotti hoped to take his place as underboss, but Castellano picked his protégé Thomas Bilotti, leaving Gotti in the cold. Castellano's days

Paul Castellano lies dead on the pavement, not far from Thomas Bilotti

were numbered, however. At that time the 70-year-old Gambino family head was facing a long prison sentence and there was always the possibility that he might turn informer rather than spend his remaining years behind bars.

On 2 December 1985 Castellano had scheduled a meeting with Dellacroce's son Buddy, so a table was booked for 5.30 pm at Sparks Steak House on East 46th Street in Manhattan. The Gambino family boss was

Immaculately dressed, John Gotti arrives for the funeral of bodyguard Anthony J. 'Shorty' Mascuzzio who was killed in a West Side disco after pistol-whipping the owner. On the right is Salvatore 'Sammy the Bull' Gravano

going to offer his condolences and explain why he had not gone to the funeral. Castellano had just got out of his limousine when three men wearing trench coats and Russian fur caps rushed down the busy street. After pulling out handguns they shot Castellano and Bilotti repeatedly in the face, pausing only to deliver a final shot to the back of Castellano's head. Then they disappeared into the crowd. John Gotti watched everything from a parked car across the road.

Although it is against the rules of the Mafia to assassinate a boss without permission, no one was upset by Castellano's demise. He had been foolish enough to let the FBI bug his house and as a result the entire Commission had been arrested.

Transcripts of the tapes also showed that he blabbed about Mafia business to anyone who visited him, even if they did not belong to one of the crime families. He also discussed Commission business with his underboss. So there was no objection when Gotti took over the biggest Mafia family in the country, with Sammy 'The Bull' Gravano as his underboss.

Known for his handmade suits and his immaculate grooming, the newspapers soon dubbed Gotti the 'Dapper Don'. And a series of court cases kept him in the public eye. In September 1984 he assaulted refrigerator repairman Romual Piecyk, who had been in an altercation with Gambino family associate Frank Colletta. Piecyk reported the matter to the police and then identified Gotti and Colletta before a grand jury. However, when the case came to trial a year later, Piecyk said that he could not remember the two men who had assaulted him, prompting a famous headline in the *New York Daily News*: 'I FORGOTTI.'

A month later, Gotti was back in court on RICO (Racketeer Influenced and Corrupt Organizations Act) charges. The trial soon descended into chaos with a bomb scare, the car bombing of one of Gotti's co-defendants, Frank DeCicco, and allegations of the intimidation of witnesses. Consequently, the court case was suspended for four months and Gotti's bail was revoked.

The bomb under Frank DeCicco's car had been planted on the orders of Vincent 'The Chin' Gigante.

It had been intended to kill Gotti too. Castellano had been one of Gigante's closest friends, so he was looking to revenge his shooting. He also had another motive – with Gotti and DeCicco dead, Gigante figured that he could install his own man as head of the Gambinos. He also ordered the murder of Edward Lino, one of Castellano's killers, and 'Bobby' Boriello, a confidant of Gotti and his son, John Jnr.

Gotti was making moves of his own to control the Commission. He was backing Vittorio 'Little Vic' Orena as head of the

> *'Gotti was confident because he had bought one of the jurors for $60,000. After a trial that lasted seven months the jury, clearly intimidated, returned a not guilty verdict'*

Colombo family and he was lobbying for Joey 'The Ear' Massino, now head of the Bonanno family, to be returned to the Commission. Meanwhile, plans were still being made to get rid of Gotti. Louis Manna, a 59-year-old *capo* from New Jersey, and five Genovese soldiers had been heard discussing his assassination in a restaurant that was being bugged by the police. Gotti was informed and Manna and two others were later convicted.

During the trial, it became clear that several prosecution witnesses had been granted immunity and had even benefited financially from giving evidence. Gotti made scathing comments loud enough for the jury to hear and gave regular press briefings during recesses. He was confident that the jury would at least be hung, because he had bought one of the jurors for $60,000. After a trial that lasted for seven months, the jury withdrew for seven days. Clearly intimidated, they returned a not guilty verdict.

In January 1989, Gotti was arrested again, this time for an attack on John O'Connor, head of Local 608 of the United Brotherhood of Carpenters and Joiners. Philip Modica, a Gambino soldier, had paid O'Connor off with a $5,000 bribe so that he could use non-union labour to refurbish his restaurant in Battery

Park City but O'Connor had decided that it was not enough. He returned with some union thugs who did $30,000-worth of damage. Modica complained to Gotti who instructed Angelo Ruggiero to hire four gunmen from the Westies, a violent Irish street gang, to rough O'Connor up. O'Connor was shot four times in the legs, buttocks and hip. He survived, only to be arraigned for coercion and criminal damage.

When Gotti was arrested, he offered the police odds of three to one that he would be freed. After the arraignment, Gotti was given a standing ovation in the detention cell and when he was released on $10,000 bail he was met by a mob of journalists and cameramen.

By this time the FBI had installed bugs in Gotti's headquarters – the Ravenite Social Club on Mulberry Street in Little Italy, Manhattan and the Bergin Hunt and Fish Club in Ozone Park, Queens. Gotti's defence argued that tapes of his conversations could not be used because they were an invasion of privacy. However, when it was ruled that they could be used, Gotti's lawyers maintained that they revealed nothing more than their client carrying on normal conversations with his friends.

'You'll hear rough language,' said his

> *'When Gotti was arrested, he offered the police odds of three to one he'd be freed. He was given a standing ovation in the detention cell and upon his release he was met by a mob of journalists'*

defence counsel, 'and some threats that are meaningless.'

On the tapes, Gotti was heard to say: 'We're gonna bust him up.'

His defence team argued that he had actually said: 'We're gonna bust 'em up' – which could have an entirely innocent meaning. Besides, the tapes could have been tampered with.

The star witness was James McElroy. He had already been convicted for the attack on O'Connor, but he expected to benefit from the Witness Protection Program and have his sentence reduced. His evidence was shaky, however. Although he named Joseph Schlereth as the man who had actually fired the shots, in his own trial another gang member, Kevin Kelly, had been identified as the shooter.

O'Connor then took the stand – as a witness for the defence. He said there were internal conflicts in the union and he had many enemies. Later, 'Sammy the Bull' Gravano told author Peter Maas that O'Connor had been warned that it was not a good idea to testify against Gotti.

After three days' deliberation, the jury found Gotti not guilty. The Dapper Don had now become the 'Teflon Don' – nothing seemed to stick to him.

THE DOWNFALL OF JOHN GOTTI

On 11 December 1990, John Gotti was arrested again – this time by the FBI. He would be charged with the murders of Castellano and Bilotti. The key witness was Philip Leonetti, former underboss of the Philadelphia crime family, whose testimony had already ensured that Nicodemo 'Little Nicky' Scarfo would never walk free again. He claimed to have been at a meeting of Philadelphia crime bosses where Gotti had bragged about the Castellano hit.

The prosecutor then ordered Gotti's regular defence team to be banned from the trial on the grounds that they had been caught on tape and could be called as witnesses. Details of the FBI tapes then appeared in the press, including conversations between Gotti and his *consigliere* Frank LoCascio.

Their remarks about 'Sammy the Bull' Gravano would result in his turning against his boss. However, handbills depicting Gravano as a lying rat were found attached to chairs in the courtroom. A third witness for the prosecution was Peter Chiodo, a *capo* for the Genoveses, who admitted four murders. During the trial, his sister was shot and wounded after she dropped her children off to school. And there were at least two bomb threats against the courtroom.

The jury heard tapes which showed that Gotti had ordered the murders of Robert DiBernardo, Louis Milito and Louie DiBono – all Gambino family members suspected of double-crossing the family.

Two witnesses then swore that they had seen two associates of Gotti – Anthony Rampino and John Carneglia – outside Sparks Steak House on the afternoon of Castellano's assassination.

The prosecution also called an IRS investigator who testified that the expensively dressed Gotti had not filed a tax return for six years. A tax attorney called by the defence said that he had advised Gotti not to file a tax return while he was under indictment. Otherwise, all of Gotti's other defence witnesses were ruled ineligible. In all, three jurors were dismissed.

It took 13 hours for the remainder to find Gotti guilty on all counts.

He was sentenced to life

imprisonment without parole.

Frank LoCascio received the same sentence. When asked whether he had anything to say, he again denied all of the charges against him and then said: 'I am guilty though. I am guilty of being a good friend of John Gotti. And if there were more men like John Gotti on this earth, we would have a better country.'

Outside the courtroom up to a thousand people were involved in a demonstration.

They had been bussed in from Ozone Park and Howard Beach in Queens by Gotti's son, John Gotti, Jnr. He had already been made a *capo* by his father and he was named acting boss following his father's conviction.

After admitting to 19 murders Sammy Gravano was sentenced to just five years in jail, but because he had already been in jail for that length of time he walked free. He returned to court in 1997 to give evidence against Vincent Gigante. Gigante had feigned mental illness for years in an attempt to avoid prosecution, but it did not help him this time. He was sentenced to 12 years' imprisonment and he died in jail.

After successive appeals had failed there seemed no prospect that Gotti would ever be freed, so he was forced to relinquish his position as head of the Gambino family. Nicholas 'Little Nicky' Corozzo seemed set to take over, but he was soon embroiled in a series of racketeering charges.

In January 1998, John Gotti, Jnr. was indicted for extortion, loan-sharking and fraud. It is thought that his father gave him the nod to plead guilty in exchange for a shorter sentence. Four other Gotti family members went to jail. Shortly before John Gotti, Snr. died in jail in 2002, his elder brother, Peter Gotti, a retired sanitation worker, was indicted. Although he was the nominal head of the Gambino family, even the prosecutors claimed he was no more than a front. However, he had been caretaker at the Bergin Hunt and Fish Club and had relayed messages from the jailed John Gotti, Snr.

Although Peter protested that he had made no money from criminal activity he was convicted of extortion and money-laundering in 2003 and was sentenced to 20 years in jail.

In the following year, he was convicted on a second count of extortion and planning the murder of Sammy Gravano, which added another nine-and-a-half years to his sentence.

John Gotti, Jnr. also faced several more indictments, including one for attempting to kidnap the founder of the Guardian Angels, Curtis Sliwa. Gotti claimed that he had given up his life of crime after his conviction in 1999, for the sake of his children. After three mistrials, the federal prosecutors decided to drop the case. In August 2008, John Gotti, Jnr. was indicted on a list of RICO charges that included trafficking cocaine and the murder of three men. He was released after the jury failed to agree.

Handcuffed Joe
Colombo Sr. arrives
at Nassau District
Attorney William
Cahn's Mineola,
L.I., office after his
arrest

JOE COLOMBO

Born in Brooklyn in 1923, Colombo was still a teenager when his father was killed in a gangland war. After serving in the US Coast Guard during the Second World War, he worked as a strongman on the piers of New York and he also organized rigged dice games.

He then joined the Profaci family, becoming a 'made man' in the late 1950s.

After that he became a *capo* and an enforcer, one of a five-man hit team which was credited with at least 15 kills. When Profaci died, his brother-in-law Giuseppe Magliocco took over, but the man who pulled the strings was Joe Bonanno. When the word came from Bonanno that Lucchese, Gambino, Magaddino and DeSimone were to be taken out, Colombo went to Carlo Gambino and spilled the beans. Magliocco was then removed and Colombo took over what became the Colombo family. He was still only 40 years old.

When Colombo's son, Joe jnr., was arrested for melting down $500,000 worth of United States coins for their silver content, Colombo complained of police harassment. He then formed the Italian-American Anti-Defamation League, which later became the Italian-American Civil Rights League. After that he held a rally on 29 June – Italian Unity Day – in Columbus Circle, which attracted 50,000 people. His next move was to organize a benefit at Madison Square Garden. Headlined by Frank Sinatra, it raised $500,000. The idea was to persuade every Italian-American in New York to pay a $10 joining fee, which would raise $20 million. But most of the money that was raised found its way into Colombo's pocket. He forgot to share the money with the other families and some Mafia members did not appreciate all of the attention it was drawing to them. Worse, when the League's books were audited, it was bankrupt.

On 28 June 1971 Colombo held a second rally in Columbus Circle. By now the Mob wanted rid of Colombo, so they obtained press credentials for a young African-American named Jerome Johnson, which would enable him to get through the police cordon that surrounded the event. He was to be Colombo's assassin. Colombo's bodyguard was then instructed to make it easy for Johnson to get a clear shot at his boss. When Johnson got close he pulled the trigger, seriously wounding Colombo. While a cop wrestled Johnson to the ground, the bodyguard leapt from the platform and blew the assassin's brains out. The man behind the shooting was thought to have been Joey 'Crazy Joe' Gallo. The Gallos had been at war with Colombo for about a year and they had good contacts in Harlem.

Colombo was rushed to hospital with a bullet in his head. Although he survived, he suffered permanent brain damage. He died seven years later after lapsing into a coma.

'The Mob wanted rid of Colombo so Colombo's assassin pulled the trigger, seriously wounding Colombo. The bodyguard blew the assassin's brains out'

Chapter 12

THE ICE MAN

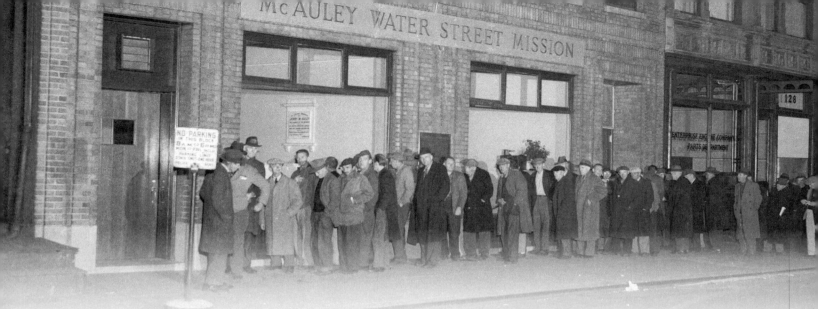

Left: **Ruchard Kuklinski, aka the 'Ice Man'**

Richard Kuklinski was a Mafia hit man who claimed to have killed over a hundred people. A professional assassin, he earned the soubriquet 'The Ice Man' because of his habit of refrigerating bodies to disguise the time of death.

Curiously for a Mafioso, he was not a Sicilian or an Italian. His father was Polish, his mother Irish and he was brought up in the projects of Jersey City. His father was an alcoholic who beat his children savagely for no reason. Richard's elder brother died as a result of these beatings. Kuklinski later regretted not killing his father. He actually went to a bar where his father hung out to put a bullet in his head, but he wasn't there.

Kuklinski tried to defend his mother from one of his father's beatings. This earned him a punch that put him out for half the night. But his mother beat him too, hitting him around the head with pots and pans, shoes, brushes and broom handles.

He was sent to a Catholic school where he was beaten by the priests and the nuns. Angry, he vented his rage on cats and dogs, torturing them and burning or beating them to death while enjoying their screams. Once he tied the tails of two cats together, hung them over a washing line and watched them tear each other to pieces.

TEENAGE KILLER

When his parents separated, Kuklinski supplemented the family's meagre diet by stealing. He also stole true crime magazines, which he studied obsessively. By the time he was 13, he had graduated to stealing cars. At 14, he committed his first murder.

Bullied by a gang headed by Charley Lane, Kuklinski beat Lane to death with a thick wooden pole. He put the body in the boot of a stolen car and dumped it in a river that ran through a vast, densely forested area known as Pine Barrens. First of all, though, he smashed the corpse's teeth and cut off its fingertips to prevent identification. Back in the Jersey City projects, Kuklinski tracked down the rest of Charley Lane's gang one by one and beat them up viciously.

After quitting school, he hung out in pool halls where he learned that you could win any fight if you struck first with full force, usually wielding a pool cue. Anyone who got the better of him was later knifed.

He formed a gang whose members were tattooed with the words 'Coming Up Roses' on their left hands – the idea being that anyone who crossed them would end up as plant food. They planned robberies and stick-ups and Kuklinski armed himself with a .38 revolver with a six-inch barrel. When his father visited to administer another beating to his mother, he put the gun to his head and pulled back the hammer. His father did not bother the family again.

Then an Irish policeman named Doyle called Kuklinski a 'dumb Polack' in a bar. When Doyle went out to his car, Kuklinski poured petrol over it and struck a match.

The Gambino family chart reveals the hierarchical structure of the Mafia. It was shown at a Senate crime inquiry in October 1963.

PRACTISING HIS ART

The Coming Up Roses gang quickly came to the attention of the DeCavalcante New Jersey crime family and Carmine Genovese invited them to his house. Over spaghetti and meatballs he hired them for a hit. They immediately drove out to the mark's home. When another gang member funked it, Kuklinski walked up coolly to the target as he sat in his car and blew his brains out. The gang members got $500 each.

Genovese then employed them as hijackers, but when two of his gang held up a card game run by a made man in the DeCavalcante family, Kuklinski quickly dealt with the situation. He

shot them in the head before they knew what was happening.

Now a lone wolf, he practised his art as an executioner by taking the ferry over to Manhattan and murdering down-and-outs and homosexuals on the run-down lower West Side. He killed with a knife, a gun, a rope and an ice-pick, figuring out the most efficient way of inducing death. He reckoned that he had killed more than fifty men there over the years.

SETTLING PERSONAL SCORES

In February 1956 he was playing pool in a bar in Hoboken when a truck driver called him a

Polack. Kuklinski smashed a pool cue round his head and KOed another man with an eight ball. When he left, three men went after him. The truck driver attacked him with a length of pipe but Kuklinski shot him in the head and then killed the other two. He dumped their bodies down a sinkhole in Bucks County, Pennsylvania, and pushed their car into the Hudson.

Kuklinski beat Linda, the woman he was living with, even when she was pregnant. But he never laid a finger on their children. Anyone who did was given a severe beating. Later Kuklinski killed a friend of his when he asked him to kill his wife and child, explaining: 'I don't kill women and I don't kill children. And anyone who does doesn't deserve to live.'

When Kuklinski discovered that Linda was having an affair, he broke down the door of the guilty couple's hotel bedroom, broke every bone in the man's body and then cut Linda's nipples off.

KILLER ON A SHORT FUSE

Carmine Genovese then commissioned Kuklinski for another hit. This time the mark was to suffer. Kuklinski tied the man to a tree and cut his fingers off one by one, then took a hatchet to his feet and legs. Finally he cut his head off to take back to Genovese, to show him he had done the job.

His reputation was soon so formidable that other Mafiosi steered clear of him. He always carried a knife and two guns, favouring a .38 Derringer. It was easy to conceal and lethal

at close range – and Kuklinski liked to do his killing up close. He often used two different guns so that the police would think there was more than one gunman.

Genovese sent Kuklinski to Chicago to pick up some money. The mark kept telling Kuklinski that the money was coming. When he did eventually hand it over, Kuklinski killed him anyway for wasting his time.

A crooked police officer paid him to collect a suitcase from Los Angeles. Later he discovered that it contained a kilo of heroin and he had risked a long prison term. He killed the cop and buried him out in the middle of nowhere.

On another occasion, a man who aimed to welch on a $5,000 gambling debt had his brains splattered over the side of his car with a tyre lever. Another target was having sex with his girlfriend on board a boat. Not wanting to hurt the girl, Kuklinski waited half the night, then went and killed the mark, forgoing any torture as he was feeling in a good mood.

By the age of 24, Kuklinski was drinking heavily and getting into bar fights. When someone asked him to settle a difference outside, Kuklinski stabbed his opponent under the chin so hard that the blade penetrated his brain. Then a bouncer who kicked him out for being loud had his head beaten in with a hammer the next day.

BRIEF HIJACKING CAREER

Kuklinski briefly went straight and married Barbara Pedrici. To keep her in style he turned back to crime, stealing a truckload of jeans direct from a depot. While on his way to the buyer, he inadvertently cut up two guys in a red Chevrolet. After an altercation they came at him with a baseball bat. He shot them both in the head.

After Kuklinski had stolen a truck full of Casio watches, the buyer tried to renegotiate the price. He shot him in the head, along with the three men unloading the truck.

Another hijacked truck disappeared from a farm where he had left it. With a flare, he burned the farmer's foot off, then his testicles, until he finally admitted that a friend had taken it. He shot both of them in the head.

BOOTLEGGING PORN

Kuklinski then went to work at a film laboratory, where he also developed hardcore porn which he began to bootleg to the Gambino family. When a union official at the laboratory berated Kuklinski for hogging all the overtime, Kuklinski punched him. He went down hitting his head and another body disappeared into the Hudson.

Kuklinski was only arrested after he intervened when his brother Joe was being held hostage over a gambling debt. Loading his Derringers with dumdum bullets, Kuklinski fired them into the car driven by the men who were holding him, but had got rid of the guns by the time the police arrived. The men spent the night in the cells but were freed in the morning, after Kuklinski had arranged to get $3,000 to the judge.

The film laboratory where Kuklinski worked was just a block away from the famous Peppermint Lounge. One evening Kuklinski had trouble with a bouncer there. Three days later he arrived with a .22 revolver in a lunch sack, pulled out the gun, shot the bouncer in the head and walked away.

FULL-TIME CONTRACT KILLER

Now in the porn industry, Kuklinski ran across Roy DeMeo, who put the squeeze on him. Ambushed by DeMeo's crew of seasoned killers, Kuklinski could do nothing while DeMeo savagely pistol-whipped him. Later they agreed to go into the contract-killing business together. But first Kuklinski was put to the test. DeMeo gave him a .38 revolver and pointed out a man walking his dog. Kuklinski shot him in the back of the head.

For his first assignment, Kuklinski was given an address in Queens, a photograph of the mark and $20,000. He followed the mark, parked next to him and punctured his front tyre. When the man returned, Kuklinski offered to lend a hand, then pulled a gun and forced the man into the boot of his Cadillac. He drove him out to Pennsylvania, shot him in the head and dropped him down a sinkhole.

As he was not a made man, Kuklinski did not hang out with other mobsters and after a hit he went home to his family. They moved into a middle-class neighbourhood in Dumont, New Jersey, where Kuklinski was known as a good neighbour who gave extravagant poolside barbecues. Indoors, he still had bouts of uncontrollable rage and warned his children

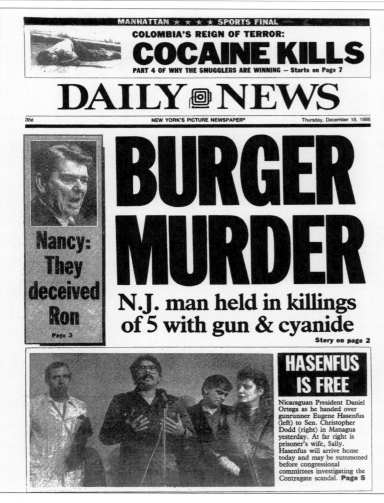

The New York *Daily News* front page dated 18 December 1986 with the story of a Kuklinski murder where the perpetrator used his preferred method – cyanide

that if he killed their mother he would have to kill them too.

The next on the list was Paul Rothenberg, the lynch-pin of the porn business. Kuklinski shot him down in a busy street while DeMeo looked on. While making his getaway, a man in a red Mustang cut him up so he shot him dead at the next stop sign.

TORTURE WAS A GAME

DeMeo then sent Kuklinski after a man in Florida who had raped a fellow Mafioso's daughter. 'Make him suffer,' he said.

Kuklinski abducted the man, tore his testicles off with his bare hands, removed his penis, stripped him, carved away his flesh, poured salt in the wounds, disembowelled him and then put him in a life jacket and floated him out to sea for the sharks to finish off.

On the way home through South Carolina, he was taunted by three rednecks. When they went for him with a club, he shot all three of them dead and drove off.

Back in Brooklyn, he handed DeMeo the victim's severed penis in a ziplock sandwich bag he had taken for the purpose. While the two men shared a plate of antipasto, DeMeo enjoyed Kuklinski's description of how the mark had met his end. By then Kuklinski had begun collecting torture ideas from movies and *Road Runner* cartoons, detailing them in a notebook. When a man in Los Angeles owed him $10,000, he went to his shop, handed him the pin from a grenade and dropped the grenade behind the counter. The blast threw people out of windows eight stories up.

A Sicilian Mafia boss did not like the man his daughter was seeing, so Kuklinski took the boyfriend out to the caves in Bucks County, wrapped in wet rawhide, with one strip around his testicles. He photographed his agony as the rawhide dried, then left him to be eaten – alive – by rats. Later he filmed these torture sessions and would watch them at night when everyone else had gone to bed. Even DeMeo could not bear to see them.

When a mark in LA proved elusive, Kuklinski rang his front doorbell, waited until he put his

Merrick and Barbara Kuklinski, daughter and wife of the Ice Man

eye to the spyhole and then pulled the trigger. Contracted to kill a lieutenant in the Bonanno family, Kuklinski approached him in a disco with a syringe of cyanide. Everyone thought he had suffered a heart attack.

FAVOURED KILLING METHOD

Cyanide then became his favourite method of murder. He slipped it in drinks or sprinkled it on pizza or on a line of cocaine. He always used just enough to kill, but not enough to be detected. Ex-Special Forces man Robert Pronge taught Kuklinski how to use cyanide. After his arrest he said his favourite way of using cyanide was to spray cyanide solution into the victim's face using a nasal-spray bottle. Pronge also taught him to keep the corpse in a freezer for a couple of months before dumping it, confusing the police about when the victim had died.

HIGH-PROFILE COMMISSIONS

On the spur of the moment, Kuklinski shot a friend named George Malliband five times, then dumped the body in a back alley. It was known that Malliband had gone to meet Kuklinski that day.

After a meeting with John Gotti, 'Sammy the Bull' Gravano asked Kuklinski to kill a man named Paul Calabro, who cautiously took the back roads to his home in New Jersey. Kuklinski parked his van so Calabro would slow down and then shot him with both barrels of a shotgun. It was only the next day that Kuklinski learned that his victim was a decorated NYPD detective.

According to Kuklinski, John Gotti also had a special job for him. He went with John's brother, Gene Gotti, to abduct John Favara. Kuklinski said that he burnt Favara's genitals off with a flare and then stuffed them up his rectum, before Gotti cut him up.

Kuklinski then killed small-time crook Louis Masgay for one of his few friends, a fence named Phil Solimene who ran 'the store' in Paterson, New Jersey.

POLICE HAD HIM TAPED

Things began to unravel when a small-time burglar named Percy House told the police that he had been part of a burglary gang run by 'Big Rich'. The gang had dispersed after Kuklinski had poisoned a member named Gary Smith. Then when Kuklinski killed another gang member named Danny Deppner, Percy House began to talk.

Checking out Kuklinski, the New Jersey police found he had a reputation for punching a hole in the windshield of the car of any driver that offended him. Meanwhile, he killed Paul Hoffman, the chemist who supplied him with cyanide. Then he claimed to have killed DeMeo, pistol-whipping his corpse in revenge.

As more bodies that had connections with Kuklinski were found, Pat Kane, a single-minded New Jersey detective, contacted the NYPD's organized crime unit, and discovered that Kuklinski was linked to DeMeo, who was now dead.

Although the police were on to him, the killings continued. He murdered a hitchhiker who gave him the finger and he killed a man in a secluded street just to try out a new mini-crossbow he had bought.

Solimene then came to the attention of the law and Kane persuaded him to let an undercover police officer named Dominick Polifrone, aka Provanzano, hang around 'the store'. But Kuklinski was on money-laundering business in Zurich, where he killed rivals with a cyanide spray and a knife. Back in New Jersey he killed the members of a ring of child abusers.

In 1985, Gotti and Gravano were planning to eliminate Paul Castellano. Kuklinski was called in to kill his bodyguard and driver Tommy Bilotti. When Castellano's car pulled up outside Sparks Steak House, two men approached wearing trench coats and Russian fur caps. Job done, Kuklinski and the other assassin then disappeared into the crowd.

With Kane on his trail, Kuklinski decided that the only way he could get rid of the nosy cop was with a cyanide spray and he asked Solimene if Provanzano could get him some of the poison. Polifrone telephoned Kuklinski and trapped him into admitting using cyanide in a spray, while the call was taped. They met at a service station where Kuklinski sold Polifrone a .22 revolver with a silencer. Polifrone then got Kuklinski to agree to a hit. He also talked of the murders of Smith, Deppner and Masgay. Everything was taped.

When Polifrone delivered the cyanide, Kuklinski spotted that it was not the real thing and took off. The police then stopped him driving away from his home. He did not pull the .25 automatic from under the seat of his car for fear that Barbara, who was in the car with him, might get hit. It took four men to wrestle him to the ground and handcuff him.

Kuklinski was formally charged with the murders of Deppner, Malliband, Masgay and Smith. When he discovered that Polifrone had been a plant, he knew he was sunk and mounted no defence. He was found guilty on all counts, but was spared the death sentence because there had been no eyewitnesses to his horrific crimes.

Already serving five life sentences, he pleaded guilty to the murder of Peter Calabro, earning himself another 30 years. Kuklinski was scheduled to testify against Gravano in the case when he died on 5 March 2006, aged 70.

Chapter 13

THE SNAKE

American mobster Carmine Persico, age 17, after being arrested on charges of fatally beating another youth in Brooklyn, New York, 1951

Carmine Persico is the last of the old-time New York Mafia bosses. He rose through the ranks from street thug to the head of the Colombo family, a position he held for forty years, though for much of that time he has been behind bars.

During the Depression, the Italian and Irish denizens of the Carroll Gardens and Red Hook neighbourhoods of Brooklyn, where Persico was brought up, scraped a living by working on the nearby waterfront or in factories. The Persico family was well off. His father was a stenographer for a prestigious Manhattan law firm and brought home a weekly pay packet even in the hardest of times.

The area was run by the Profaci crime family. The big bankrolls of the wiseguys drinking coffee and playing cards outside the local

Left: Carmine Persico, aka 'The Snake'

social or athletic clubs impressed the Persico brothers – Alphonse, Carmine and Theodore. At 16, Carmine dropped out of school and joined a street gang called the South Brooklyn Boys.

JOINING THE WISEGUYS

At 17, he was arrested for the fatal beating of another boy during a brawl in Prospect Park, his first felony. The charges were dropped, but they brought him to the attention of Profaci *capo* 'Frankie Shots' Abbatemarco, who employed the skinny, 5-foot-8-inch teenager as an enforcer. Persico then worked his way up through bookmaking and loan-sharking rings to burglaries and hijacking. By his mid-twenties, he was a made man.

During the 1950s, Persico stacked up over

a dozen arrests. His rap sheet ran the whole gamut of mob activity – running numbers, dice games, assault, harassing a police officer, burglary, loan-sharking, hijacking and possessing an unregistered firearm. But he never spent more than two weeks in jail. Profaci lawyers got felony charges reduced to misdemeanours, while plaintiffs and witnesses changed their minds or were out of town at the time of the trial. Fines were considered a business overhead.

LEAD-UP TO THE GALLO WAR

Persico was tight with the Gallo brothers – Larry, Albert and 'Crazy Joe'. When Albert Anastasia, the head of Murder, Inc., was gunned down while having a shave in the barber's shop of the Park Sheraton Hotel, Joey Gallo claimed it was the work of his 'barbershop quintet'. One of them was thought to be Carmine Persico.

When Frankie Shots was murdered, Persico and the Gallo brothers expected to inherit a large part of his Brooklyn rackets as a reward for icing Anastasia. Instead, Profaci's cronies were rewarded. The Gallo faction responded by kidnapping Profaci's brother-in-law and underboss Joe Magliocco, along with Joe Colombo and four other *capos*. The hostages were released after Profaci lifted the higher tribute payments he demanded from the Gallos. But Profaci quickly reneged on the deal and war broke out.

Recently retired mob boss Frank Costello convinced Persico that his loyalties lay with

Joseph Profaci, founder of the Colombo crime family, controlled prostitution, loan-sharking and narcotics trafficking in Brooklyn

Profaci. On 20 August 1961, a police sergeant on a routine inspection of the Sahara Lounge, a bar in South Brooklyn, found Persico strangling Larry Gallo with a rope. Persico fled and Gallo refused to press charges. This perfidy earned Persico the soubriquet 'the Snake'.

The Gallos struck back, peppering Persico's car with bullets. He was hit in the hand and arm, but he too obeyed the rule of *omertà*. While his supporters said that he had been hit in the face and had spat out the bullets, Persico himself referred to his wounds as paper cuts. In fact, he never regained the full use of his left hand.

In the 'Gallo War' that ensued, nine combatants were killed and three more disappeared, presumed dead.

A RISING STAR

When Profaci died of cancer in 1962, Magliocco took over, but the other dons intervened, forcing out Magliocco and installing Colombo as boss of the Profaci crime family. Persico was promoted to *capo*. A rising star, he now wore well-tailored suits and his crew became one of the most profitable in the newly renamed Colombo family.

But a federal indictment for a 1959 hijacking was still hanging over him. A battery of expensive lawyers dragged the case out for 12 years. After five separate trials, he was convicted, thanks to the testimony of Mafia 'rat' Joe Valachi, and sentenced to 14 years. However, he was cleared of running a multimillion-dollar loan-sharking business when a key witness vanished before the trial started and another 12 failed to identify him in court.

In 1971, Joe Colombo was shot and paralyzed at an Italian-American civil rights rally. Although he was in prison, Persico took over the family with Tommy DiBella as acting boss.

Paroled in 1979, Persico was charged with attempting to bribe an agent of the IRS. Federal marshals looking for his brother Alphonse 'Allie Boy', then a fugitive, crashed a meeting Persico was holding in Brooklyn. He was immediately charged with violating his parole by associating with other known criminals.

In a plea bargain, he went away for another five years.

SURROUNDED BY THE FBI

Released after just three years, he got wind that a RICO indictment was being prepared, alleging that he was the head of the Colombo family. He went into hiding in the house of Fred DeChristopher, whose wife Katherine was the sister of Andy 'Fat Man' Russo, Persico's cousin and a capo in the Colombo family. Terrified of Russo – who once, at dinner, held a fork to a man's eye and said 'Next time you f*** up, I'll push this fork right into your f*****g eye' – DeChristopher confessed all to the police. One morning soon after, DeChristopher's phone rang. A voice said: 'Can I speak to Mr Persico?' DeChristopher handed over the phone.

Persico said: 'Who is this?'

The voice on the phone said: 'This is the FBI. We have the house surrounded. Come out with your hands up.'

Persico did.

At the ensuing 'Colombo trial', DeChristopher testified that, while preparing pasta with garlic and olive oil, his uninvited guest had boasted that he had run the Colombo family from jail and had stashed away enough money from his crimes to 'last ten lifetimes'. He also said 'I killed Anastasia' and bragged that he was one of Joey Gallo's 'barbershop quintet'. Persico went down for 39 years. His son Alphonse, 'Little Allie Boy', was sentenced to 12 years for being one of his father's lieutenants. In a separate trial, Persico was convicted of being a member of the Mafia Commission and was sentenced to another hundred years.

THIRD COLOMBO WAR

From jail Persico put out contracts on US Attorney Rudolph Giuliani, later mayor of New York, and other federal prosecutors. He also bribed prison guards for favours and arranged to have sex with a female attorney who visited him.

Running the family business from behind bars, Persico installed Victor 'Little Vic' Orena as acting boss until Little Allie Boy got out of jail. But Little Vic had ambitions of his own. After two years, he asked his *consigliere* Carmine Sessa to poll the *capos* to see who favoured him taking over permanently. Instead, Sessa informed Persico. On the evening of 20 June 1991, Orena returned to his home in Cedarhurst, Long Island, to find a five-man hit squad waiting outside. He sped away.

For three months, Orena's and Persico's factions negotiated. Then bullets began to fly, in the third Colombo war. Orena was backed by Joe Profaci's son, Salvatore – aka 'Sally Pro' or 'Jersey Sal', as he ran the family's interests in New Jersey. He said that the Snake had gone crazy.

Persico's faction was led by Gregory 'the Grim Reaper' Scarpa, who was also an FBI informant. In 1964, when three civil rights workers disappeared in Mississippi, the Bureau employed Scarpa to find out what had happened to them. Scarpa kidnapped a Ku Klux Klan member, beat him up, shoved a gun barrel down his throat, and said: 'I'm going to blow your head off.' Realizing that Scarpa was serious, the klansman revealed that the bodies had been buried under an earth dam.

That December five Colombo mobsters were gunned down – one while hanging a Christmas wreath on his front door. Eighteen-

Gregory Scarpa before the Senate Investigations Subcommittee; he took the Fifth Amendment 60 times, refusing even to say where he was born. He was subpoenaed after two convicted men named him as a principal 'mob-fence'

year-old Matteo Speranza was murdered in the bagel shop where he worked by an Orena gunman who mistakenly thought he was a Persico supporter. Innocent civilians also died in the gunfire.

In an attempt to halt the war, Brooklyn District Attorney Charles J. Hymes subpoenaed 41 suspected Colombo family members before a grand jury. Only 28 showed up and none of them would talk.

As the body count climbed, Scarpa contracted AIDS through a blood transfusion and lost an eye in an unrelated dispute over narcotics. The Persico faction then had to apologize to the Genovese family for accidentally killing 78-year-old Gaetano 'Tommy Scars' Amato, a retired soldier who had mistakenly been at an Orena social club when Persico gunmen paid a visit.

The FBI then subpoenaed Kenneth Geller,

an accountant who worked for the Colombos. He had borrowed $1 million from their loan-sharking operation for a business deal that went sour and sought to escape his debt via the Federal Witness Protection Program. Geller delivered Orena, who was arrested at his mistress's home where agents found four loaded shotguns, two assault rifles and six handguns.

Orena was handed life imprisonment without the possibility of parole on the RICO charges of murder, conspiracy to murder and heavyweight loan-sharking. Sixty-eight *capos*, soldiers and Colombo associates also went down, including Orena's two sons.

Andy Russo, Persico's younger brother Theodore and enforcer Hugh McIntosh were also sentenced to long prison terms. Persico's elder brother Alphonse, 'Little Allie', who was already serving 25 years for extortion, died in jail. Finally Gregory Scarpa was arrested. His work for the FBI did not save him from a ten-year sentence for three murders and conspiracy to murder. He, too, died in jail. Nevertheless, the arrests ended the war and left Persico in charge.

In 2001, Little Allie Boy Persico went down for 13 years for loan-sharking. A life sentence for murder followed in 2007. Even so, Carmine Persico continued to run the Colombo family from the Federal Correctional Complex in Butner, North Carolina. The war he waged to maintain control cost 12 lives and led to some 70 wiseguys and their associates landing in jail.

Chapter 14

BABY SHACKS

During his six decades as a career criminal, Luigi Manocchio worked his way up to being head of La Cosa Nostra in New England. Then, in the FBI's biggest ever one-day raid on organized crime, his empire came tumbling down.

Manocchio was first arrested in the 1940s, before he enlisted in the US Army in 1946. Being a soldier clearly did not suit him as he was discharged after just 14 months. Nevertheless, he still takes advantage of medical care at the VA Medical Center in Providence and he receives a military pension of $985 a month.

In 1948, he was arrested for robbery and was given a five-year suspended sentence. Four years later he was charged with two counts of assault and robbery, illegal possession of a firearm and driving a stolen car. His charge sheet already listed two of his nicknames – 'Baby Shanks' and 'Baby Face'. Everything but the weapons charge was dropped and he received another five-year suspended sentence. However, in 1955 he went to jail – for just 11 days.

In April 1968, bookmaker Rudolph 'Rudy' Marfeo was gunned down with his bodyguard Anthony Melei in Pannone's Market in Providence's Silver Lake district. Marfeo was found holding a .38 revolver, but he had been unable to loose off a single round. The hit had been on the orders of the gang boss at that time, Raymond L.S. Patriarca, who had told Marfeo to close down his rogue gambling operation.

Left: **Luigi Manocchio, aka 'Baby Shacks', 'Baby Shanks' 'Baby Face'**

ON THE RUN

The gunman, John 'Red' Kelley, joined the Federal Witness Protection Program, while Patriarca and several of his men were given ten-year sentences for conspiracy to murder. Manocchio was also arrested as an accessory, but was let out on bail. He then disappeared, spending ten years on the run in Europe, largely in France and Italy. It is thought that he returned to the United States several times, using a fake passport and wearing a disguise. It is said that on one occasion he dressed as a woman to escape arrest.

In July 1979, Manocchio returned to Rhode Island and gave himself up. He was convicted of being an accessory to murder and conspiracy, and was given two life sentences plus ten years. However, a key witness suffered from Alzheimer's disease and was found to have lied in a related case. Manocchio was released on bail. The ensuing court battle went all the way to the Supreme Court. Manocchio then cut a deal. He pleaded no contest to conspiracy and was sentenced to the two-and-a-half years he had already served.

Manocchio had earned himself something of a reputation among the Patriarca family, who referred to him simply as 'that guy'. While the headquarters of the New England family had moved to Boston when Francis 'Cadillac Frank' Salemme became boss, Manocchio remained in Providence as *capo* of a crew of thieves, loan-sharks and bookmakers.

In January 1995, a major push against organized crime nailed Salemme, Stephen 'the Rifleman' Flemmi and the Irish-American hoodlum James 'Whitey' Bulger. The power then shifted back to Rhode Island and Manocchio became boss.

THE SIMPLE LIFE

Manocchio is the very antithesis of the ham-fisted, cigar-chomping godfather. A small man, he is said to be a health nut. Rising early, he would jog around Providence golf course, stopping at a tree to do a series of pull-ups. He was also an accomplished skier.

'People watch mob movies and see these guys smoking cigars and living the good life. Louie Manocchio stayed in tremendous shape,' said Rhode Island State Police Colonel Brendan Doherty. 'He watched what he ate and would even recommend to his other mob associates they go on a diet.'

He did not dress flashily and maintained a low profile, like old-style Sicilian Mafia bosses. Until his arrest in 2011, he lived in a small apartment above a café in the Federal Hill section of central Providence and ran his crime family's operations from a Laundromat on nearby Altwells Avenue. He remained unmarried, but is thought to have three adult children.

He was also thought to have had a financial interest in several restaurants, though his name did not appear on any official document. But he had been seen chatting to customers – in Italian to those who understood it – and recommending wines.

After his plea bargain in 1988, he tried to

Raymond L.S. Patriarca's crime family controlled racketeering operations in New England for more than three decades

steer clear of the law. But the police would keep tabs on him and make random visits to the Laundromat.

'He was always a gentleman to me and to law enforcement,' said Doherty. 'But he made his point known that we were on the other side of the fence, and "catch me if you can".'

However, in 1996 Manocchio was arrested at his elderly mother's home in Mount Pleasant, where he was installing appliances stolen from a store in Connecticut. He entered a no contest plea and was given three years' probation.

This was frustrating for Doherty as the police and the FBI knew Manocchio was a crime boss. He took care to avoid being seen around other gangsters, but in 2006 was photographed having dinner with underboss Carmen 'the Big Cheese' DiNunzio, who later got six years for bribery.

EXTORTION WITHOUT THREATS

Manocchio eventually stepped down as boss of the Patriarca family, and the power shifted back to Boston under Peter 'Chief Crazy Horse' Limone. This may have been because he was over 80, or because federal investigators were getting too close for comfort.

In 2008, two FBI agents approached him in a restaurant on Federal Hill after he had been handed an envelope by an employee of a local strip club. It was found to contain cash, protection money from the strip club's boss. Manocchio was with Thomas Iafrate, who worked as a bookkeeper at the Cadillac Lounge strip club. Iafrate was arrested along with Manocchio during the 2011 round-up that took 127 Mafia suspects into custody.

Manocchio pleaded guilty to extorting between $800,000 and $1.5 million in protection money from strip clubs including the Satin Doll and the Cadillac Lounge, but maintained he did not threaten anyone.

'By virtue of my position, I inherited the deeds of my associates,' said Manocchio. 'I don't want my family or any of my friends to believe I personally threatened anyone.'

'The envelope contained cash, protection money from the strip club's boss'

However, Assistant US Attorney William J. Ferland said that after a strip club owner reduced his payment to the mob, Manocchio visited him and informed the owner he needed to pay $4,000 a month.

'It's his personal appearance. It is who he is and what he represents that constitutes a threat,' Ferland said. 'He fails to recognize that because of his position, these businesses were willing to pay. They weren't making charitable donations to La Cosa Nostra.'

He was sentenced to five-and-a-half years. The judge recommended that the 85-year-old serve his sentence in North Carolina or Florida, where the climate would be better for his health.

'I think you are going to make it through this prison sentence and come out on the other end,' the judge said.

There are conflicting stories about how Manocchio got his nicknames. One story told that he was called 'Baby Shanks' because he liked slim young women; another said the moniker referred to his short legs.

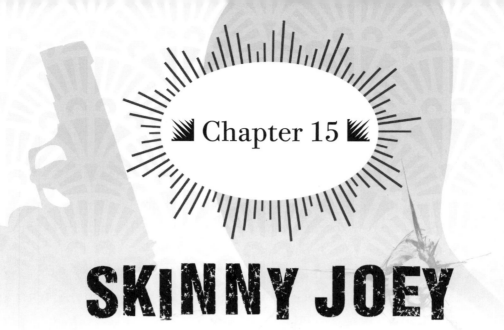

Chapter 15

SKINNY JOEY

Nicky Scarfo, Jr., son of crime chief Nicodemo Scarfo, survived an assassination attempt in Luigi's, a Philadelphia restaurant, in 1989. Scarfo was shot by a lone assailant armed with an automatic pistol as he was eating dinner with two friends

Left: **Joseph Merlino, aka 'Skinny Joey'**

Joseph 'Skinny Joey' Merlino was born to the mob. His father Salvatore 'Chucky' Merlino rose to be underboss to Nicodemo 'Little Nicky' Scarfo, boss of the Philly mob after the death of Angelo Bruno (see page 223). Scarfo used Merlino Sr.'s bar to plan his takeover. Skinny Joey was also the nephew of Lawrence 'Yogi' Merlino, a Scarfo capo jailed for racketeering and murder. His sister was engaged to Scarfo hitman Salvatore 'Salvie' Testa. And he was at school with Michael 'Mikey Chang' and Joseph 'Joey Chang' Ciancaglini, who both became made men under Scarfo.

Joey Merlino used to hang out on the streets with Mikey Ciancaglini, Georgie Borgesi and Gaetano 'Tommy Horsehead' Scafidi, who was younger. 'They used to beat up girls, they used to rob people,' said Horsehead. 'They used to go into clubs and start fights.'

In August 1982, Joey Merlino and Horsehead's older brother Salvatore 'Tori' Scafidi stabbed two men at the Lido Restaurant in Atlantic City. Merlino was convicted of two counts of aggravated assault and one count of possessing a weapon for an unlawful purpose.

According to another friend: 'Joey Merlino was mob royalty and no way he wasn't going into the life . . . Joey was born to follow in his father's footsteps. How could he not? He was the son of an underboss. People on the street respected and feared him. Girls went crazy over him. There was always plenty of money and the best tables in expensive restaurants and no waiting on line at the nightclubs. Big time sports celebrities and movie stars wanted to hang with him.'

FEUD WITH THE SCARFOS

In 1984, Joey and his father were barred from New Jersey casinos, and when Salvatore Merlino was stopped for drink-driving he attempted to bribe the police officer who pulled him over. Scarfo decided that the family did not need this heat and demoted Merlino Sr. for his drinking. This started a feud and Joey broke off his friendship with Nicky Jr., Scarfo's son. Scarfo Sr. was then convicted of conspiracy to commit extortion in 1987. RICO convictions the following year put him away for 45 years.

On Halloween night in 1989, Nicky Scarfo Jr. was shot and wounded eight times by a masked gunman inside a South Philadelphia restaurant. For years, police sources claimed that Joey Merlino was the masked gunman, but Merlino and his attorneys have always denied his involvement and no one has ever been charged with the attempted hit. Scarfo Jr. went to live in North Jersey and law enforcement sources claimed his father arranged for the Lucchese crime family to

'Big time sports celebrities and movie stars wanted to hang out with him'

safeguard the younger Scarfo from further attempts on his life.

Convicted of robbing an armoured car in 1989, Merlino spent his time in jail plotting with Ralph Natale, a former friend of Angelo Bruno, to take over the Philadelphia crime family – then headed by John Stanfa in Scarfo Sr.'s absence. According to Natale, Merlino admitted in prison that he had been the shooter in the 1989 Halloween night attempt on Nicky Jr.'s life.

Natale said he authorized and helped Merlino plan the gangland murders of Louis 'Louie Irish' DeLuca in 1990 and Felix Bocchino and James 'Jimmy Brooms' DiAddorio in 1992. He also said that other members of Merlino's organization, including defendants Steven Mazzone, George Borgesi and Martin Angelina, visited him at different times in prison to discuss those plans.

TAKING OVER THE FAMILY

At the time, neither Natale nor Merlino had been formally initiated into the mob, so they decided to initiate themselves.

'We'll make ourselves,' Merlino said. 'What's the difference if we have the button or not? We'll take over Philadelphia and kill John Stanfa.'

Merlino was formally initiated into the mob by Stanfa in 1992, while Natale was formally initiated by Merlino after he had been

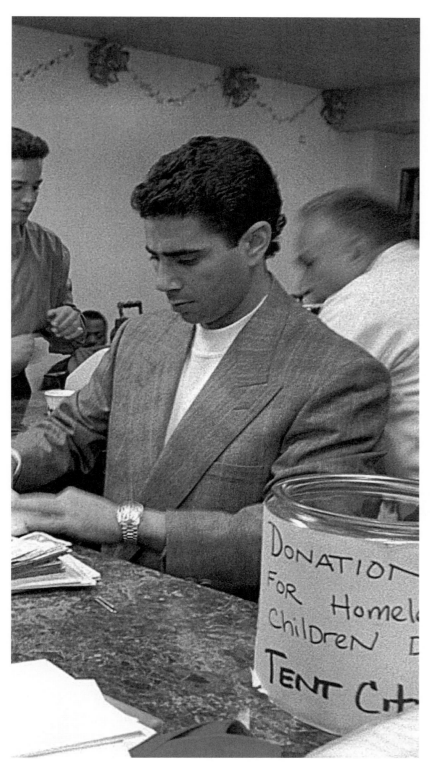

In November 1995, Joey Merlino busies himself with charity work. Earlier that day, Merlino's rival, John Stanfa, had been convicted of murder, extortion, kidnapping and racketeering charges

released from prison in 1994.

In 1993, war broke out between Stanfa and the Merlino faction. Merlino was injured in a drive-by shooting with a bullet in the buttocks, while Mikey Chang, who was with him, was killed. Stanfa's son Joseph was shot in the face in another drive-by shooting, this time in the rush hour on the Schuylkill Expressway.

Merlino went back to jail briefly for parole violation. Then Stanfa was convicted of labour racketeering, extortion, loan-sharking, murder and conspiracy to commit murder and was sentenced to five consecutive life sentences. When Merlino got out of jail he took over the Philadelphia family, with Natale as titular boss because he had connections with the Genovese family in New York. But when Natale went back to jail for parole violation in 1998, Merlino took his place.

'LIKEABLE GUY' EVERYONE WANTS TO KILL

Merlino's men gave drug dealer Louis Turra a severe beating when he refused to pay the mob's 'street tax'. Louis was then found dead in a prison cell, having apparently hanged himself. In retaliation for the beating, his father Anthony Turra suggested throwing grenades into Merlino's house to kill him and his 'scumbag' girlfriend. But Turra then went on trial for racketeering and drugs offences. At 61, he was confined to a wheelchair. On the way to the court, he was shot dead outside his home by a gunman wearing a black ski mask.

Merlino himself survived at least ten

assassination attempts – two of which were thwarted by the FBI – and there was a $500,000 contract out on him.

'I honestly don't know why so many people are seeking his demise,' said his lawyer, Joseph C. Santaguida of Philadelphia. 'He's really a likeable guy.'

CHARITY WORK

Despite his violent reputation, Merlino was also known for his charitable work.

'I thought he was a gentleman, always been a gentleman with me, and I understand he's done a lot of nice things for underprivileged children and, for that, I commend him,' said South Philadelphia resident Pat Bombito.

In 1999, Natale was facing fresh drugs charges that would have put him away for life, so he decided to turn state's evidence. He admitted ordering three killings in a gang war for control of the Philly LCN's multimillion-dollar gambling and loan-sharking empire, a business enterprise that stretched from Philadelphia to Atlantic City.

Two years later, Merlino faced Natale in court while standing trial on 36 counts of racketeering, including murder, attempted murder, extortion, illegal gambling and trafficking in stolen property. Merlino also faced a drug-trafficking charge. He was acquitted of three counts of murder, two counts of attempted murder and the drug-dealing charges. Nevertheless he was still sentenced to 14 years for racketeering. 'Ain't bad,' he said. 'Better than the death penalty.'

NEIGHBOUR FROM HELL

After 12 years in jail, Merlino was released. He was no longer skinny, having spent much of his prison time in the gym bulking up. Although he went to live in a cul-de-sac in an upper-class area of Boca Raton, Florida, he showed little intention of settling down.

'We've had the police come several times,' said one neighbour. 'It's been very stressful living near them. There is always screaming and fighting.'

The neighbours said that what they found most disturbing were the banging noises in the middle of the night, as if furniture or equipment was being moved about.

'I'm not easily frightened,' another neighbour said, when told a convicted mobster lived a few doors away. 'I don't know who he is, but he does have a lot of visitors.'

Merlino appeared to work out of his home and named his wi-fi connection 'Pine Barrens'. This is a reference to the heavily forested area near Atlantic City, where Richard Kuklinski often disposed of bodies. It was the scene of one of the most famous episodes of *The Sopranos*.

'I can tell you that I would not want to live next door to Joey Merlino,' said Stephen LaPenta, a retired Philadelphia police lieutenant who had worked undercover as a mob informant, and had infiltrated Merlino's inner circle. LaPenta, who was spending his retirement in Florida, still kept tabs on the flamboyant mobster.

'The Joey I know was a hard-drinking,

womanizing, gambling drug user who would strangle you,' he said. 'If Joey sneezed, 20 people would hand him a handkerchief.'

EARLY RETIREMENT

Merlino was no stranger to Florida, having spent time there when working for Nicky Scarfo, who had a house in Fort Lauderdale. There was speculation that Merlino was still living 'the life'. While he was prohibited from associating with known felons, communication was easy enough in the digital age. He had been replaced as head of the Philly mob by Joseph 'Uncle Joe' Ligambi, though the law enforcement authorities speculated he was just a front for Merlino.

But Merlino insisted he is happy in Florida.

'It's beautiful down here,' he said. 'Great weather. No stress. People come here, they live to be a hundred.'

And he said he had no intention of returning to a life of crime.

'Too many rats,' he said. 'I want no part of that.'

In July 1999, Joey Merlino's mother and wife leave court in Philadelphia after an appeal by Merlino's lawyers asking for his release from prison pending his trial on drugs charges.

Chapter 16

THE GENTLE DON

Angelo Annaloro, the Gentle Don, was born in Villalba, Sicily, and went as an infant to the United States in 1911. His father, Michele, ran a grocery store in south Philadelphia. Young Angelo first came to the attention of the police when he turned in an extortionist who had tried to extract protection money from his father.

When he turned to crime, he changed his name, taking the maiden name of his paternal grandmother. Police records from the 1930s reveal that he gave his name as Angelo Bruno when he was arrested on illegal gambling and bootlegging charges. He was introduced to Philadelphia Mafia boss Salvatore Sabella by Michael Maggio, owner of the cheese factory in which he worked. In his thirties, Bruno became a made man.

FORCED RETIREMENT

When Sabella stepped down at the end of the Castellammarese War, Joseph 'Bruno' Dovi pushed aside John Avena to take over the family. He was succeeded by Joseph Ida. Under his regime, Bruno graduated from small-time bookmaker and gambler to major numbers writer and loan-shark, and was made *capo*. With underboss Marco Reginelli and *capo* Peter Casella, he ran the Greaser Gang whose bookmaking, gambling and loan-sharking operations turned over $50 million a year.

In 1953, a police raid uncovered 17,000 numbers slips in Bruno's headquarters. Convicted, he was fined and given two years'

Left: **Angelo Annaloro, aka Angelo Bruno, 'the Gentle Don'**

Annaloro maintained a successful gambling operation at the Plaza Hotel in Havana, Cuba

probation. But that did not stop him gambling and loan-sharking and he managed to escape several other prosecutions.

When Ida was deported to Italy, he had to choose between Bruno and Antonio 'Mr Miggs' Pollina as his successor. He chose Pollina. By then Bruno had his own loyal following, so Pollina sought to eliminate his rival. He gave the contract to underboss Ignazio 'Natz' Denaro. But Denaro told Bruno, who appealed to the Mafia Commission in New York. It was a dangerous move. If the Commission had found against him, he would have written his own death warrant. However, by asking for the Commission's arbitration, he had shown them respect.

Pollina had not asked permission to whack Bruno, who had already forged an alliance with Carlo Gambino. The Commission found in Bruno's favour, naming him the new boss of the Philadelphia mob and giving him permission to whack Pollina. Instead, Bruno forced him into retirement. This was typical of 'the Gentle Don', who sought to resolve disputes by diplomacy rather than murder.

By the mid-1960s, the Commission was headed by Carlo Gambino, who gave Bruno a seat. Bruno's alliance with Gambino enhanced his status and for two decades he maintained a 'Pax Mafia' in Philadelphia. As the Gentle Don kept violence to a minimum, this was largely tolerated by the authorities. Neil Welch, who later became Special Agent in charge of the FBI's Philadelphia office, said that for years the Bureau did not pursue Bruno with great vigour.

HITTING THE JACKPOT

Bruno maintained a front as a legitimate businessman, running the Atlas Extermination Company in Trenton, New Jersey and the Aluminum Products Sales Corporation in Hialeah, Florida, as well as retaining an interest in a casino at the Plaza Hotel in Havana, Cuba. Nevertheless, he chalked up further arrests for interstate tax conspiracy and filing false income tax returns.

When family member Nicky Scarfo stabbed a longshoreman over a seat in a restaurant, Bruno banished him to Atlantic City, then a depressed area. But in 1976 laws were passed to allow gambling there, in an attempt to revive the city. The rush was on to build casinos. Bruno had contacts in several steel companies in Pittsburgh and the Philly mob took a major hand in the construction work. They then moved in on all aspects of the gambling industry. Suddenly Scarfo was cock of the walk.

By then Bruno's hold on the family was weakening. He spent two years in jail for refusing to testify before a grand jury during an investigation into corruption in Atlantic City, involving a number of high-ranking officials. Instead of maintaining his monopoly, he allowed New York and New Jersey families to move in on the casinos in New Jersey. He also refused to become involved with the lucrative drugs trade. This caused resentment among the younger soldiers and *capos*.

TIME TO GO

The 69-year-old Bruno was not in the best of health and faced indictments for racketeering. His *consigliere*, Anthony 'Tony Bananas' Caponigro, conspired with New York and New Jersey crime families to have Bruno wasted. He consulted Frank 'Funzi' Tieri, the acting boss of the Genovese family. Tieri gave his word that he would support Caponigro in front of the Commission.

On the evening of 21 March 1980, Bruno's driver, John Stanfa, took his boss home. As Stanfa pulled up outside Bruno's house at 934 Snyder Avenue, a man was waiting in the shadows. Stanfa pushed the button, lowering the passenger window next to Bruno. The man in the shadows moved swiftly towards it. He pulled a 12-bore shotgun from under his coat, put it to the back of Bruno's head and pulled the trigger. As Bruno slumped lifelessly, the gunman ran to a waiting car and sped off.

Stanfa was wounded when some pellets hit him in the arm. He was later charged with perjury relating to the testimony he had given in front of the grand jury investigating Bruno's shooting.

At Bruno's funeral, the cortege consisted of 17 limousines and 35 other cars. More than a thousand people filled the pavements outside the church.

Caponigro was summoned before the Commission, who said they had not given permission for the hit, nor had they even considered it. He turned to Tieri who, he said, had sanctioned the killing. Tieri denied it. As Caponigro had killed a Commission member without the Commission's consent, he was sentenced to death. On 18 April 1980, his body was found in the boot of a car in the South Bronx. He had suffered 14 bullet and knife wounds. His executioner was Joe 'Mad Dog' Sullivan, a Bronx enforcer.

POWER STRUGGLES

Over the next five years, 28 members or associates of the 60-strong Philadelphia family would die. After Caponigro's death, Bruno's underboss Philip 'Chicken Man' Testa took over the family with Scarfo as his *consigliere*. A year later, Testa was returning home when a remote-controlled bomb blew up his house. Testa's underboss Pete Casella claimed that he had been made boss at a meeting with Paul Castellano and Fat Tony Salerno. Scarfo discovered that he was lying. In exchange for allowing the Gambinos and the Genovese to operate in Atlantic City, Scarfo obtained their backing to become boss of the Philly mob and Casella went into retirement in Florida.

Then war broke out with Harry 'the Hunchback' Riccobene. War continued on and off for the next 20 years until the family was stabilized under Joseph 'Uncle Joe' Ligambi in 2001 – a far cry from the 20 years of profitable peace Angelo Bruno had given them.

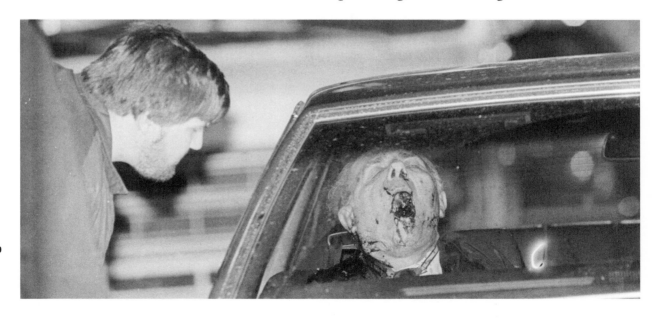

A Philadelphia policeman checks the body of Angelo Bruno, who lies shot to death in his car.

Chapter 17

THE LAST DON

046944 07:59 0 1:09:03 5.10

Below left: **Joseph Charles Massino, aka 'The Ear', 'Big Joey'**

Born to Italian-American parents, Joey Massino was brought up in Maspeth, a working-class area of Queens, New York. He dropped out of high school before graduating and went instead into the lunch-wagon business, selling snacks and soft drinks at factories and construction sites. But his trucks were a cover for illegal gambling, loan-sharking and selling stolen goods. He soon became known to the police as a rookie wiseguy.

A burly 5 feet 9 inches, he ate too many of his own sandwiches and doughnuts. His weight ballooned to 250 pounds and he became known as 'Big Joey'. In 1960, he married Josephine Vitale and his brother-in-law Salvatore 'Good Looking Sal' Vitale became his right-hand man.

The Manhattan skyline from Queens: Joe Massino, John Gotti and Charlie Carneglia all operated out of this borough

A teenage friend was the nephew of Philip 'Rusty' Rastelli, a *capo* in the Bonanno family who was based in Maspeth. Rastelli was the kingpin of a hijacking operation that pulled off five or six road robberies every week in the New York area. Maintaining his thriving 'roach coach' business, Massino and his team successfully branched out into hijacking. As a protégé of Rastelli, Massino was 'made' in the Bonanno crime family.

SUPPLY AND DEMAND

Most heists took place with the gang blocking the truck and a team member jumping on to the running board and sticking a gun in the driver's face. Massino used a different method. Thanks to his loan-sharking business, he could organize 'give ups', when

Joseph Massino appeared as a defendant in the Rastelli-Bonanno family trial, September 1986

a teamster, or truck driver, could not afford to pay. That is, the truck driver handed over the goods without fuss. Using this method, he is thought to have got away with $100,000 worth of coffee, $500,000 worth of clothing on its way to Saks Fifth Avenue and $2 million worth of Kodak film.

The key to his success was organizing 'drops' – empty warehouses or lots where the contraband could quickly be off-loaded on to smaller trucks for delivery to fences or pre-arranged clients. Massino's contacts were so good that he organized drops and fences for other hijackers. Soon he was running an underground clearing house for stolen goods – everything from lobsters to air-conditioners. This brought him into contact with another hijacker, John Gotti. They became neighbours when Massino moved his family out to Howard Beach.

However, the FBI were on his trail. On one occasion, they thought they had him cornered in a warehouse full of stolen goods. But as they rushed in at the front door, Massino vanished out the back, down a pre-planned escape route. Another time it was discovered that he was off-loading expensive suits via a rope line from the warehouse to a clothes shop, when a customer dropped in for a cut-price purchase.

'He was smart and feared and nobody would give him up,' said one agent.

FBI agent Patrick F. Colgan spotted a hijacked truck outside a diner in Maspeth one night. He tried to follow it, only to be blocked by a car that then sped off. When the car caught up with the truck, Massino jumped out of it and then climbed up on to the truck's running board. He had a word with the truck driver, then leapt back into the car and took off.

Colgan assumed that Massino had told the driver to dump the rig and then try to escape. He managed to catch up with the truck before that happened and was holding the driver, Ray Wean, at gunpoint when Massino turned up and asked what was going on. Colgan told Massino that he was under arrest, but Massino said that he needed to relieve himself first. He then drove off. Two days later, Massino gave himself up. He stood trial on his first felony charge for theft from an interstate shipment. While Wean was convicted and spent a year in prison, Massino's attorney argued that his client had innocently stopped to find out if Wean, a casual acquaintance, was having trouble. He was acquitted.

FAILED TAKEOVER BID

While Carmine Galante was in jail in the 1970s, Rastelli took over as boss of the Bonanno family. But when Galante was paroled, Rastelli was in jail, and he took over again. Nevertheless, Massino remained loyal to Rastelli and visited him in prison. This enraged Galante and Massino feared that Galante might whack him. But before this could happen the Commission gave Rastelli permission to take out Galante. Massino was outside the restaurant as back-up when the hit was made.

Massino had previous experience of murder. He and John Gotti had killed and dismembered Paul Castellano's daughter's boyfriend, Vito Borelli, after he said that Castellano looked like Frank Perdue, the well-known purveyor of poultry. Joseph 'Do Do' Pastore, a cigarette smuggler and loan-shark, was also whacked by Massino, just because Massino owed him $9,000.

With Galante dead, Rastelli became boss of the Bonanno family again. But he was in jail, so he made the *capo* Salvatore 'Sally Fruits' Ferrugia acting boss. Massino was also promoted to *capo*, but the Bonanno soldiers knew that Massino had the direct line to Rastelli.

In May 1981, Massino heard from a Colombo soldier that three Bonanno *capos* – Philip 'Phil Lucky' Giaccone, Alphonse 'Sonny Red' Indelicato and Dominick 'Big Trin' Trinchera – aimed to take over. Massino consulted Paul Castellano and Carmine Persico, who told him to 'do what you have to do'.

The three renegade *capos* were invited to an 'administration meeting' in a Brooklyn social club run by the Gambinos. Weapons were traditionally not carried at these events, so it was all the more of a surprise to them when they were gunned down by masked men.

LEND ME YOUR EARS

At the time, undercover FBI agent Joseph Pistone had penetrated the Bonanno family under the alias Donnie Brasco. By then he had collected enough evidence to put the key players away for a long time. When Massino discovered this, he ordered a hit on Dominick 'Sonny Black' Napolitano, who had nominated Pistone.

When the first wave of indictments was handed down in the wake of the Donnie Brasco investigation, Massino's name was not on the list. He had been wary of Pistone from the beginning and had always been cautious about government surveillance. He would not even let people refer to him by name. Instead, when they spoke about him they were to tug their ears – hence his nickname.

Nevertheless, he figured that it would only be a matter of time before he was arrested, so he went into hiding. He still managed to run the family during this period – first from the Hamptons, then from the Pocono Mountains in Pennsylvania.

DODGING THE MURDER RAPS

In July 1982, Massino was indicted for conspiracy to murder the three *capos*. Two years later, in 1984, Rastelli was released from prison. He and Massino then arranged the murder of Cesare Bonventre, a Bonanno soldier. Their complaint was that he had not helped Massino while he was on the run. By this time, most members of the Bonanno family considered Massino the boss, though Rastelli remained titular head.

After consulting a lawyer, Massino handed himself in on 7 July 1984, confident that he could beat the rap. He was released on $350,000 bail. But more indictments followed.

He was charged with conspiracy to murder Do Do Pastore and labour racketeering. He and Rastelli had controlled Teamsters Local 814, where they ran a scam in moving and storage. Found guilty, he was sentenced to ten years.

Although Wean and Pistone testified against him, Massino was cleared of the murder charges. He was found guilty of a 1975 hijacking, but it fell outside the RICO act's five-year statute of limitations, so he was cleared of that as well.

LIFE FOR 'THE LAST DON'

When Rastelli died in 1991, Massino became boss of the Bonanno family. He was released the following year, at a time when other crime bosses such as John Gotti, head of the Gambino family, were going to jail. So the newspapers started calling him 'the Last Don'. In proper godfather style, he held court in the CasaBlanca restaurant in Maspeth. But then, to save himself, his underboss Salvatore Vitale agreed to testify against him. Others followed.

On 9 January 2003, the FBI picked up Massino at his home in Howard Beach, Brooklyn, to face 19 federal charges. More charges soon followed. FBI assistant director Pasquale J. D'Amuro said: 'Massino is the most powerful mobster in the country.'

He went on trial the following year, facing charges related to seven murders, loan-sharking, arson, gambling, money laundering and extortion. The trial lasted for nine weeks and featured more than 70 witnesses,

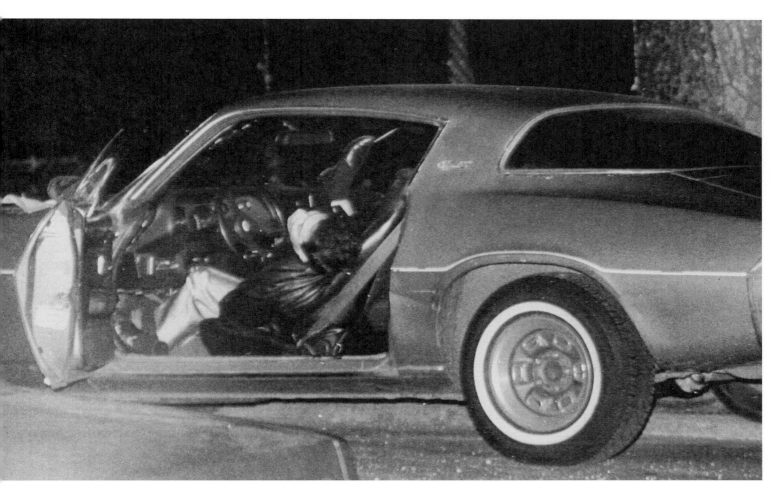

Mobster Louis Tuzzio lies slumped in the driver's seat of his Chevrolet Camaro with a bullet in the back of the head. He was murdered by the Bonanno family on 3 January 1990

including Massino's brother-in-law and six other members of the Bonanno family. He was convicted on 11 counts, including the murders of the three *capos* and Dominick Napolitano.

The FBI was not finished with him yet. Massino was to be tried for the 1999 murder of a Bonanno assassin named Gerlando 'George from Canada' Sciascia, who had been in on the murder of the three *capos*. This time the US Attorney General John Ashcroft sought the death penalty.

When the authorities also made it clear that they planned to strip him of all his assets, leaving his family homeless and penniless,

Massino reconsidered his position and began to co-operate, giving evidence against Vincent 'Vinny Gorgeous' Basciano, who had become acting head of the Bonanno family.

In 2005, Massino pleaded guilty to the murder of Sciascia and received a life sentence on top of the life sentence he had received for his previous convictions. However, his forfeiture was lowered from $10 million to $9 million.

Basciano was also sentenced to life imprisonment and other top players ended up in jail. The Bonanno family never recovered from the investigative work of Donnie Brasco.

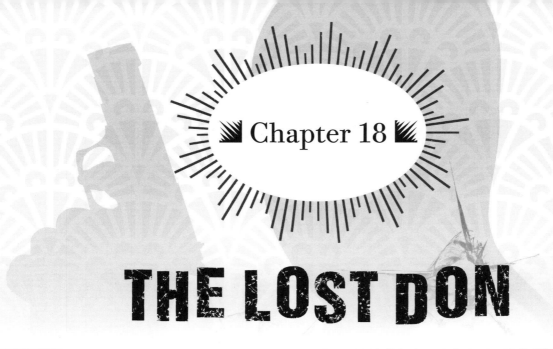

Chapter 18

THE LOST DON

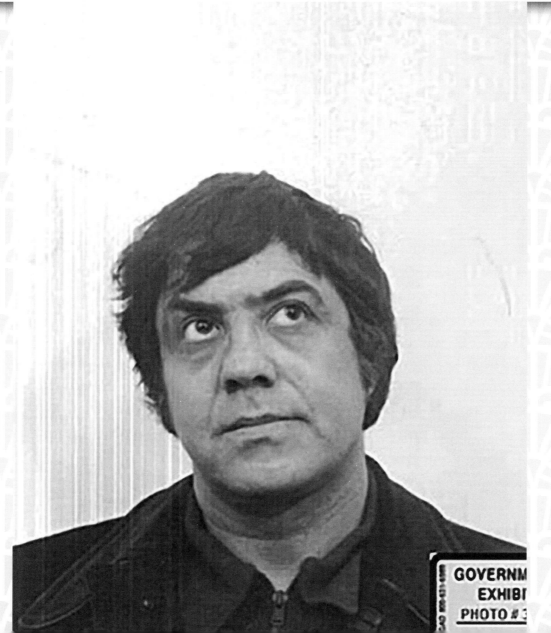

GOVERNM
EXHIBI
PHOTO # 3

In October 1957, members of the Teamsters labour union (with a jackass mascot) root for the election of Jimmy Hoffa, an activist with mob connections. By the 1950s, organized criminals had infiltrated the Teamsters and corruption had become endemic

Left: **Joseph Lombardo (born Giuseppe Lombardi), aka 'The Clown', 'Pagliacci'**

Born to Italian immigrants, Lombardi dropped out of school. He committed his first theft at 18 so that his mother could get an operation. Known for his humour – earning him the nickname 'the Clown' or 'Pagliacci' – he changed the last letter of his name to an 'o' when he joined the Outfit. On the streets he was known as 'Lumpy', because he was so good at giving people lumps on their heads.

Lombardo made his way up the crime ladder as a jewel thief, a juice loan collector and a hitman. Quickly rising to become *capo* of the Grand Avenue crew on Chicago's North Side, he had 30 soldiers under him and ran the same streets in the Grand-Ogden area as Tony 'the Ant' Spilotro and Tony Accardo's Circus Café Gang.

YOUNG ENTREPRENEUR

At the age of 25, Lombardo owned a construction company. Over the years, he also owned a trucking company, was said to be a worker for a hot-dog stand manufacturer, and had hidden holdings in restaurants and real estate. Meanwhile he was racking up arrests for burglary and loitering, though in each case he avoided conviction.

In 1963, his name was linked with John 'No Nose' DiFronzo, later boss of the Chicago

Outfit, in a West Side loan-sharking ring. Lombardo and five others were accused of abducting a factory worker who owed $2,000, tying him to a beam in a basement and beating him unconscious. In court the man could not identify his assailants and Lombardo walked free – his 11th acquittal following 11 arrests.

Lombardo's activities included loan-sharking, illegal gambling and selling pornography. He even ran a ring dealing in stolen furs that operated at four Midwestern airports, including O'Hare. His men wore overalls so that they looked like airport workers.

Identified as a rising star, Lombardo was one of a thousand guests invited to a party honouring West Side overlord Fiore 'Fifi' Buccieri at the Edgewater Beach Hotel. This was 'the largest assemblage of mobsters ever staged in Chicago', the police said. They were entertained by crooner Vic Damone and a 20-piece band.

While the Chicago mob moved into Las Vegas, Lombardo stayed at home in the Windy City making so much money that he was a regular reader of the *Wall Street Journal*. He oversaw Tony Spilotro and Frank 'Lefty' Rosenthal in Las Vegas and liaised with Allen Dorfman, whose father had introduced Jimmy Hoffa to the mob. Dorfman ran the Teamsters' pension fund, which was used to buy new casinos.

DIPPING INTO THE PENSION FUND

Meanwhile Lombardo was keeping his hand in as a hitman. In 1973, two men carrying shotguns walked into Rose's Sandwich Shop on Grand Avenue, lined the customers up against the wall and picked out disgraced police officer Richard Cain. He was Sam

In 2013, a detective gathers up crime scene tape during the search in a field near Detroit for the remains of former Teamsters union president Jimmy Hoffa, who went missing in 1975. The police were acting on a tip from Tony Zerilli, a former mobster

Giancana's bag man and did other work for the mob, while acting as an informant for the FBI. The gunmen put their shotguns under Cain's chin and blew his head off. One of the trigger men was said to be Lombardo.

In 1974, Lombardo, Spilotro and Dorfman were charged with defrauding the Teamsters' pension fund of $1.4 million. The money was being siphoned through the American Pail Company, a front organization run, some say unwittingly, by 29-year-old Daniel Seifert. Tony Accardo, who was then running the Chicago Outfit, told Lombardo to take Seifert out. He was shot dead by four masked gunmen in front of his wife and child. Again Lombardo was said to be one of the trigger men. Without Seifert, the fraud case fell apart and the defendants were acquitted.

According to FBI informants, Lombardo had authorized the killing of Indiana oilman Ray Ryan, a millionaire, when he stopped paying off one of Lombardo's associates. Another informant asked Lombardo's permission to whack a man who had damaged his disco in Schiller Park.

'Break the guy's arms, legs and head instead,' Lombardo replied. 'But if the problem occurs again, do whatever you have to do.'

SHARING A JOKE

Lombardo and James 'Legs' D'Antonio were sitting in a car when the police went to raid an illegal gambling den. They sped off. Officers pursued them. After a six-minute high-speed chase, they stopped the car and tried to walk innocently away, while Lombardo threw some notebooks over a fence. The police arrested the two men and recovered the notebooks. They contained the licence plate numbers of the cars that were chasing them and a number of off-colour jokes. Lombardo was, after all, 'The Clown'.

Six thousand dollars was found in his pocket; another $6,000 in his shoes. In court, explaining their frantic flight, Lombardo said: 'I had $12,000 on me. Those guys might have been robbers or killers.' He was found guilty of resisting arrest.

CASH FOR FAVOURS

The FBI put a phone tap on all the lines from Dorfman's office, seeking to prove the Outfit's ownership of several casinos in Las Vegas. Instead they listened in on a bribery scheme. The Teamsters would sell a plot next to the Las Vegas Hilton, to US Senator Howard Cannon of Nevada, at a knock-down price. In return, he would kill a bill deregulating the trucking business.

Lombardo, Dorfman, Teamsters' president Roy Williams and others were indicted. As the trial progressed, jurors were approached by menacing strangers. Nevertheless, they found the defendants guilty of 11 counts of bribery, fraud and conspiracy. While out on bail awaiting sentence, Dorfman was killed by

> *'Break the guy's arms, legs and head . . . do whatever you have to do'*

a shotgun blast. Apparently the mob thought he was too soft to serve time and might inform on them.

Lombardo told the judge: 'I never ordered a killing. I never OK'ed a killing. I never killed a man in my life. I never ordered or OK'ed any bombing or arson in my life.'

The judge praised his eloquence and sentenced him to 15 years. From behind bars, Lombardo continued to protest his innocence.

'I have no faith in the system,' he said.

Soon after, Lombardo was convicted of skimming almost $2 million from Las Vegas casinos and was sentenced to another 16 years, running concurrently. Tony Spilotro was also facing trial. He and his brother Michael were found in a shallow grave in Indiana. The man who was supposed to have disposed of the bodies, John Fecarotta, was then killed for his incompetence.

ADVERTISING HIS INNOCENCE

Lombardo was paroled in 1992, only to make his most public joke yet. He put a small ad in a number of Chicago papers that said: 'I never took a secret oath with guns and daggers, pricked my finger, drew blood or burned paper to join a criminal organization. If anyone hears my name used in connection with any criminal activity please notify the FBI, local police and my parole officer, Ron Kumke.'

Nevertheless, back in the old neighbourhood, Lombardo still played the big-time mob boss. His pal Chris 'the Nose' Spina lost his job as a foreman at the First Ward sanitation yard in 1993, when the city alleged he was spending his time chauffeuring Lombardo around town while he was clocked in at work. In 1997, a Cook County judge reinstated Spina – with back pay.

'He's seen as a spy of the Clown,' the *Chicago Tribune* reported.

After several years, DNA evidence tied the death of Big John Fecarotta to mob enforcer Nick Calabrese, who was already serving time in Michigan. Confronted with this, Calabrese flipped and told the FBI the inner workings of the Outfit. He gave details on 18 gruesome gangland murders and the FBI started Operation Family Secrets.

THE MISSING CLOWN

In 2003, the FBI approached Lombardo in the masonry shop where he worked and took a saliva swab and a hair sample. They were hoping to match the DNA to a strand of hair found in a ski mask left in the getaway car used in the Seifert murder. Agents also warned Lombardo that his life was in danger.

Lombardo was indicted for his role in at least one murder, as well as for illegal gambling and loan-sharking. But before the arrest warrant was issued, he disappeared. While 14 other defendants appeared in court, everyone wondered where the 'Lost Don' was.

The *Chicago Tribune* put a picture of a cigar-chomping man on the front page of their Metro section under the headline: 'Have you seen this "Clown"?' Only it wasn't Lombardo, just someone who looked like him.

Lombardo, Frank Calabrese Sr. and James Marcello in court in 2007, facing charges stemming from Operation Family Secrets

happened to be Tony Spilotro's brother, Patrick.

Lombardo pleaded not guilty. In court it was revealed that he was suffering from atherosclerosis, but had not seen a doctor.

'I was unavailable,' he explained.

Unusually, Lombardo took the stand in his own defence, claiming that he was in a police station reporting the loss of his wallet at the time of Seifert's slaying. But employees of an electronics store identified Lombardo as the man who had bought a police scanner used during the murder, and Lombardo's fingerprint was found on the title application of the car used.

The Clown himself then began to write to the judge, claiming he was innocent and spelling out terms for his surrender. He signed himself: 'Joe Lombardo, A Innocent Man.' In the letter, he made it clear that he was not going to flip. This was a message to the mobsters who might be on his tail.

JOKE OVER

A $20,000 reward was put on Lombardo's head and after nine months he was captured following a visit to his dentist – who just

He was found guilty of murder, racketeering, extortion and loan-sharking. At his sentencing, he complained: 'I was not given a fair trial and now I suppose the court is going to sentence me to life in prison for something I did not do. I did not kill Daniel Seifert and also I did not have anything to do with it.'

He was right. He did get life. It was 33 years to the day since Daniel Seifert had been killed. His son Joseph was in the courtroom. It was his turn to laugh.

Chapter 19

THE SIXTH FAMILY

Vincenzo 'the Egg' Cotroni was 14 years old when his family emigrated from Calabria to Montreal. They lived in a shabby apartment at Saint-Timothée in Ontario. Cotroni did not attend school in Canada. Instead, he worked as an assistant to his father, a carpenter, then became a professional wrestler under the name Vic Vincent.

With his brothers Francesco – 'Frank' – and Giuseppe – 'Peppe' or 'Pep' – he became a petty criminal. By the time he was 20 he had built up a long rap sheet that included minor crimes such as theft, possessing counterfeit money, the illegal sale of alcohol, and assault and battery. He was also charged with the rape of Maria Bresciano, but she dropped the charge and became his wife. They had a daughter and stayed together until Maria's death, though Cotroni also had a son with his French-Canadian mistress, a teacher.

DRUGS ON THE MARKET

The three brothers moved into bootlegging, prostitution, gambling and drugs. By 1945, they had become powerful enough to use extortion to buy votes and intimidate officials at polling stations during elections. This brought them to the attention of Joseph 'Joe Bananas' Bonanno, who had taken over the Maranzano family in 1931 and made it the Bonanno family. He sent his underboss Carmine Galante to Montreal, which was to become the hub of the Bonanno family's narcotics importing business.

Left: **Vincenzo Cortoni, aka 'The Egg'**

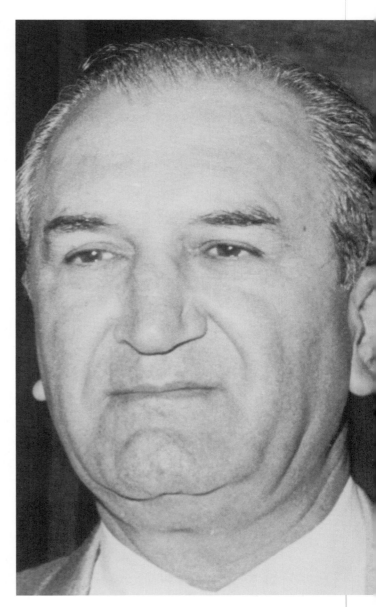

'Joe Bananas' Bonanno at a federal court hearing in June 1966, two years after his disappearance in 1964. FBI recordings captured angry Bonanno soldiers saying, 'That son-of-a-bitch took off and left us here alone'

Galante soon found there were restaurants and nightclubs that had not been shaken down thoroughly enough and pimps, prostitutes, madams, back-alley abortionists, illegal gambling houses and after-hours lounges who were paying a mere pittance. So he imposed a 'street tax' on them. Cotroni and Galante grew close and Vic became godfather to one of Galante's children.

The drugs operation ran smoothly. Later a government witness, a little-known criminal named Edward Smith, described meetings with Galante and Vic, Pep and Frank Cotroni. In a Montreal apartment, Galante would open a suitcase on the coffee table. Smith's partner would count the bags of white powder inside and Smith would take the suitcase to Frank's Bar & Grill in Brooklyn, where the contents would be cut and distributed.

In 1956, the Canadian authorities began to crack down on American gangsters in their midst and Galante became a target because of his strong-arm tactics. Notorious for his cruelty, Galante would smash beer glasses on the floor in a restaurant he owned and make a busboy dance barefoot on the shards. Galante was deported to the United States. His associate Salvatore 'Little Sal' Giglio, who set up the drugs pipeline between Marseilles and Montreal, was caught with 240 Cuban cigars and 800 American cigarettes he had failed to declare and similarly ousted.

THE GOOD LIFE

The Bonannos' Montreal interests were left in the hands of Vic Cotroni and the Sicilian Luigi 'Louie' Greco. According to Joe's son, Salvatore 'Bill' Bonanno: 'Cotroni was the head honcho. He was captain of the crew. Louie was his right-hand man. We had to have a couple of sit-downs to straighten that out,

In this FBI surveillance photo taken in September 1977, Bonanno soldier Anthony Mirra speaks to another family member

but we got it down. They trusted and listened to my dad . . . Louie was big enough to respect that. Louie knew it was best for everyone . . . If any of Louie's guys made trouble, Louie knew he had New York to answer to.'

In 1959, Pep Cotroni pleaded guilty to drug trafficking and was jailed for ten years. Galante was also arrested. The trial was repeatedly delayed; one postponement occurred when one of the defendants absconded the day before the trial was scheduled.

Cotroni could neither read nor write, but in the 1960s he owned a limousine, along with a duplex in Rosemont and a house outside the city in Lavaltrie. This had marble floors, six bathrooms, a huge conference room, a walk-in refrigerator, crystal chandeliers and a cinema. He was also a pillar of the community, making large donations to Montreal churches and various charities.

INFLUENCING THE JURY

After six months of what an appeal court judge would later call 'every conceivable type of obstruction and interruption', Galante's trial was halted on the eve of the summations to the jury. The foreman of the jury had broken his back. He seemed to have fallen down the stairs of an abandoned building in the middle of the night.

A retrial in 1962 began with one of the defendants, Salvatore Panico, shouting abuse before the jury had even been selected. Panico would later clamber into the jury area to rough up the front row while screaming abuse at them and the judge. Then Anthony Mirra, another Bonanno soldier – later whacked for introducing 'Donnie Brasco' Pistone to the family – picked up the witness chair and flung it at the prosecutor. This did not help their case and Galante was sentenced to 20 years. There weren't any witnesses, so the judge couldn't prove anything. The most he could do at that stage was sentence Galante to 20 days in jail for contempt of court.

KEEPING A LOW PROFILE

By now Cotroni was keeping a low profile and when *Maclean's* magazine referred to him as the godfather of Montreal, he sued for $1.25 million. However, the judge ruled that Cotroni's name was 'tainted' and awarded him $2 for the English-language edition of *Maclean's* and $1 for the French-language edition.

In the 1970s, Cotroni turned over the day-to-day running of the family to the hot-headed Paolo Violi, another immigrant from Calabria. In 1955 Violi had pumped four bullets into fellow immigrant Natale Brigante in a car-park row about a woman in their home country. Brigante died, but not before he had stabbed Violi under the heart. Violi showed the stab wound in court, claiming he had acted in self-defence. The manslaughter charge against him was then dropped.

In the early 1960s, Violi hooked up with Vic's younger brother, Frank 'Le Gros' Cotroni. He ran an extortion racket in the Italian community of St Leonard and then went into counterfeiting and bootlegging. In 1965, he married the daughter of Giacomo Luppino, a member of the 'Ndrangheta from Calabria who had become boss of Hamilton, Ontario. Vic Cotroni and Ontario mobsters Paul Volpe and Johnny 'Pops' Papalia were godfathers to their children. When an underworld figure was forced to give testimony before a government commission about Violi's standing, he said: 'My Lord, his name, it's like a god . . . everyone is afraid of him. Violi, he's not one man – he's a thousand men.'

Vic Cotroni (centre, white shirt) with his brother Frank (on the right) and Paolo Violi (left) in an Acapulco nightclub in 1970

SHARED TELEPHONE LINE

In 1973, war erupted between the Cotronis and the French-Canadian Dubois gang. On a wiretap, Violi was heard saying they should go into the Dubois' club, 'clients or no clients, line everybody up against the wall and rat-a-tat-tat'. Cotroni had a cooler head and persuaded him to make peace.

The following year, Cotroni was called before the Quebec Police Commission's inquiry into organized crime and was sentenced to a year in prison for giving testimony that was 'deliberately incomprehensible, rambling, vague, and nebulous'. His lawyers won a reversal, but not before he had spent several months in jail.

Cotroni and Violi were then caught on a further wiretap. They were threatening Papalia, who had used their names in a $300,000 extortion plot without notifying them or cutting them in. They demanded $150,000, but Papalia insisted that he had only netted $40,000. Cotroni was then heard to say: 'Let's hope so because, eh, we'll kill you.'

The three men were sentenced to six years, but Cotroni and Violi had their convictions quashed on appeal.

After Luigi Greco was burnt to death in an accidental fire at his pizzeria, the Sicilian faction of the family under Nicolo Rizzuto made a bid for power. On 14 February 1976, Violi's *consigliere* Pietro Sciara was gunned down leaving a cinema with his wife. They had just seen *The Godfather*.

The following year, Violi's brother Francesco was on the telephone when he received a shotgun blast to the face. Then he was finished off with a couple of bullets from a handgun.

LAST CADILLAC RIDE

Violi was in jail for contempt of court at the time, for refusing to testify to the Police Commission. When he got out, Nick Rizzuto sought sanctuary in Venezuela. But on 22 January 1978, Violi was playing cards in a bar when two masked men walked in. One put a 12-bore shotgun to the back of his head and

The family of reputed Mafia member Joe Di Maulo release doves following his funeral in Montreal on 14 November 2012. Di Maulo was shot in his driveway. He had been very close to Frank Cotroni

pulled the trigger.

At Violi's funeral, 31 black Cadillacs carried tributes from mobsters in North America and Italy. Three Sicilians were jailed for the slaying.

For weeks afterwards, Cotroni stayed inside his fortress in Lavaltrie while Rizzuto took over the family. It seems Cotroni had at least approved the hit on Violi.

Vincenzo Cotroni died of cancer in 1984. There were only 23 cars carrying floral tributes at his funeral. However, 17 brass bands turned out to mark the passing of Montreal's legendary 'man of respect'. By then, Galante was dead and the Bonanno family was in decline, their links with the Cotronis severed. The Montreal mob was gearing up to become North America's 'sixth family'.

Chapter 20

THE CHARNEL HOUSE

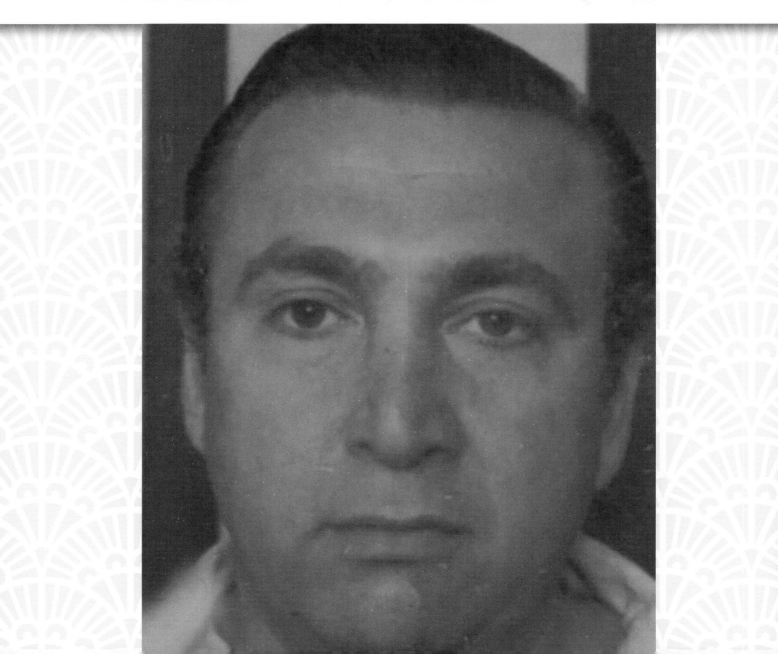

A made man in the Gambino family, Roy DeMeo was one of the most feared hitmen in the mob. He killed over a hundred men and disposed of their bodies with assembly-line efficiency.

THE GEMINI METHOD

Victims would be lured to a charnel house called the Gemini Lounge in Brooklyn, where DeMeo and his gang of assassins hung out. Entering through a side door, they would be taken to an apartment at the back of the building. As soon as a victim walked in, he would be shot in the head using a gun with a silencer. A towel would quickly be wrapped around his head to catch the blood and someone would stab him in the heart to stop it pumping.

The body would then be dragged into the bathroom, put in the shower and drained of blood. Then the corpse would be laid out on a pool liner in the living room where DeMeo, who had been an apprentice butcher in his youth, had shown the crew how to take bodies apart bit by bit. The smaller the bits the better, because it hindered identification – the head would even be consigned to a rubbish compactor. The body parts would then be dumped at the huge Fountain Avenue landfill in Brooklyn, where it was unlikely that any trace of them would ever be discovered.

DeMeo enjoyed the business of dismembering his victims. Some, though, had to be left intact – as proof of death, for instance. All knew that an invitation to the Gemini Lounge was likely to be a death warrant.

ASSEMBLING THE TEAM

After dropping out of school at 17, DeMeo involved himself in legitimate businesses while making the bulk of his money from loan-sharking, which he had learned from the sons of local Mafia boss Joe Profaci. DeMeo had no qualms about using violence on those who did not pay up on time. Gambino associate Anthony 'Nino' Gaggi got to hear about him and invited him to his home. DeMeo knew of the Gambinos through family associations with the Lucchese and set his heart on becoming a member.

Under Gaggi, DeMeo set up his own crew with his cousin Joseph 'Dracula' Guglielmo, marijuana dealer Harvey 'Chris' Rosenberg, Anthony Senter, Freddy DiNome, 'Dirty' Henry Borelli and Joey and Patrick Testa. They loan-sharked, sold stolen cars and laundered drugs money through the Boro of Brooklyn Credit Union, after DeMeo had talked his way on to the board. Gaggi and DeMeo also muscled their way into the X-rated movie business.

BUTCHERED IN THE MEAT DEPARTMENT

When Andrei Katz, a body shop owner involved in a stolen car ring, testified to a grand jury, DeMeo decided that he had to go. The crew abducted him. Taking him to the meat department of a supermarket in Queens, they stabbed him in the heart, dismembered

Left: **Roy Albert DeMeo, aka 'The Rooster**

him, and dumped the remains beneath some rotting vegetables in a rubbish bin. But the body parts were discovered by a homeless man searching for food.

Borelli and Joey Testa were arrested and tried, but acquitted. These were the early days, before the 'Gemini method' had been perfected. From then on, the crew decided to be more careful.

When their X-rated movie business was raided, Gaggi and DeMeo feared that one of their partners, Paul Rothenberg, might turn informer. DeMeo invited Rothenberg out to dinner and then shot him in the head in an alleyway.

When Carlo Gambino died and Paul Castellano took over, DeMeo expected promotion, particularly as Gaggi was close to Castellano.

Gaggi put in a good word for DeMeo, but Castellano did not trust him and refused to make him a made man. However, when DeMeo arranged a lucrative alliance with the Westies, an Irish-American gang from Hell's Kitchen, Castellano finally gave in and gave DeMeo his 'button'.

DeMeo continued dealing in drugs, despite the Gambino family's rule against it, but by then he had become too useful as a hitman. He even used murder to discipline his own crew. Danny Grillo, a gambler who was heavily in debt to DeMeo, was disposed of in the Gemini Lounge.

'DeMeo invited Rothenberg out to dinner and then shot him in the head in an alleyway'

STUDENT MAKES ERROR

Next to go was Chris Rosenberg, one of DeMeo's oldest associates. Introducing himself as Chris DeMeo, he had set up a cocaine deal in Florida. When a four-man team – including the girlfriend of the Cuban supplier known only as 'El Negro' – arrived in New York to deliver the drugs, Rosenberg had them shot and dismembered. But El Negro and his Cuban gang were well connected. They threatened a war with the Gambinos unless Rosenberg was very publicly killed.

DeMeo was reluctant to whack an old pal and procrastinated, but when the Cubans appeared in town he became paranoid. When an 18-year-old student named Dominick A. Ragucci, who was selling vacuum cleaners door-to-door to pay for his education, turned up outside his house, DeMeo took him for a Cuban hitman. He and Guglielmo came out wielding guns. Seeing them, Ragucci slammed his car into gear and sped away. The two gunmen jumped into DeMeo's Cadillac and chased after him, firing as they went.

At an intersection, Ragucci crashed into another car. Despite two flat tyres, Ragucci made it another 500 feet before his disabled vehicle shuddered to a halt. DeMeo then jumped from his Cadillac and emptied his pistol into the unfortunate teenager.

Gaggi then insisted that DeMeo kill Rosenberg before some other innocent civilian got hurt. So DeMeo shot Rosenberg in the head in the Gemini Lounge. But Rosenberg did not die immediately. As he rose to one knee, Sender finished him off with four more shots. To make sure the murder made the newspapers – so that El Negro would see it – the body was dumped in a car near the Gateway National Recreation Area and riddled with bullets, old style, with a Thompson sub-machine gun.

FAKE CHARITY AND THE FIRST LADY

But there was friction in the family, in the form of James Eppolito and his son James Eppolito Jr., two made men in the Gambino family. Eppolito Sr. told Paul Castellano that Gaggi and DeMeo were selling drugs.

But Jimmy Jr. was out of favour with Castellano after he had appeared on *60 Minutes* with the First Lady, Rosalynn Carter, at a dinner for his crooked children's charity. If this was exposed, Castellano feared that President Jimmy Carter might react by sending a large contingent of FBI agents to New York to smash the Gambinos, so he gave Gaggi and DeMeo permission to whack the Eppolitos.

They were duly invited to the Gemini Lounge for a sit-down. Gaggi, DeMeo and Brooklyn wiseguy Peter 'Petey 17' Piacenti went to collect them. On the way, Jimmy Sr. wanted to stop so he could relieve himself. As he got out of the car on the service road of the Belt Parkway, Gaggi and DeMeo opened fire, killing both Eppolitos and putting a bullet through the windshield.

A witness alerted an off-duty police officer. As DeMeo made off, the officer approached Gaggi and Piacenti. Gaggi opened fire – and missed. The cop fired back, hitting Gaggi in the neck and Piacenti in the leg. They were arrested, but DeMeo had made his escape from the scene and was not implicated.

HITTING THE HIT MAN

Nevertheless, he was experiencing difficulties from another direction. He had expanded his auto-theft operation and was shipping stolen cars to Kuwait and Puerto Rico. However, his partner in the operation, Vito Arena, had been picked up and had agreed to turn state's evidence.

This meant that DeMeo would have to appear before a grand jury. Castellano, who had never trusted DeMeo because of his thirst for murder, put out a hit on him. The problem was that DeMeo had such a fearsome reputation that even John Gotti turned down the contract.

Richard Kuklinski claims to have killed DeMeo. Other sources say that Gaggi put seven bullets in DeMeo's head in the Gemini Lounge. His body was dumped in the boot of his Cadillac and a chandelier he was taking to be repaired was placed on top of it. The car was then abandoned outside the Varnas Boat Club in Sheepshead Bay. A week later it was towed away by the police, who noticed dark stains on the seats. When they got it to the police garage they opened the boot and found the body.

Carlo Gambino's coffin is carried from Our Lady of Grace Roman Catholic church in Brooklyn on 18 October 1976. About 150 relatives and close friends, including top Mafia lieutenants, attended the funeral Mass for Gambino, 74, who died of a heart ailment at his home in Massapequa, New York

Chapter 21

CASINO

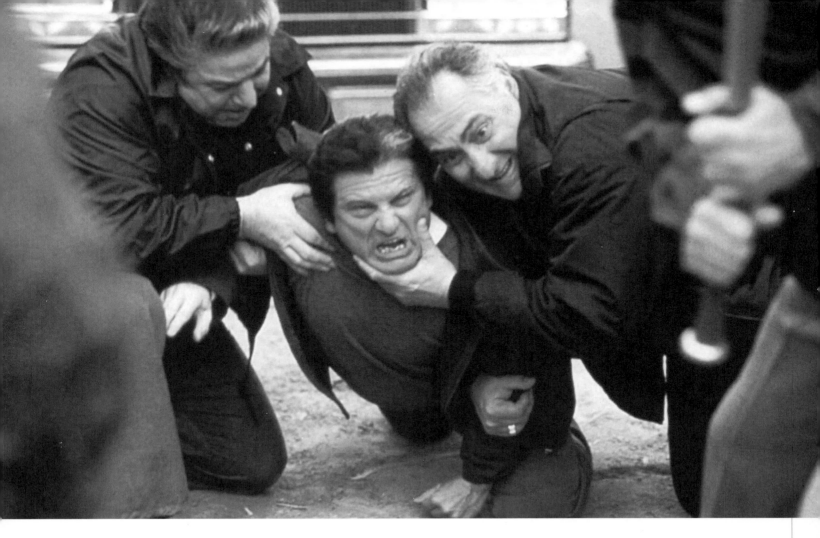

After emigrating to Chicago from Puglia, Italy, in 1914, Anthony 'the Ant' Spilotro's parents ran Patsy's restaurant in Chicago, where such well known criminals as Frank Nitti, Paul 'the Waiter' Ricca and Sam Giancana regularly dined. Patsy's car park was often used for mob meetings.

Spilotro dropped out during his second year in high school and made money shoplifting and purse-snatching. Then he teamed up with childhood friend Frank Cullotta. They would rob Jewish kids and ride around together in stolen cars.

'Tony was the toughest kid I knew,' said Cullotta. 'He was so tough that his brother Victor used to offer guys $5 to see if they could beat him up. Usually, Victor got a taker and the guy would try to kick Tony's ass, but if it looked like Tony was gonna lose, we'd all jump on the kid and break his head.'

In a fight with some black boys, Spilotro pulled out a knife and stabbed one of them, but the victim did not press charges.

At the age of 17, Spilotro was fined $10 for stealing a shirt. He was arrested another 12 times for petty crimes before the age of 22.

When Cullotta and some other youths shot three men in a tavern, Spilotro helped them get rid of the guns.

He then roped them into a scheme whereby they waited outside banks and robbed anyone carrying a large amount of cash.

By the age of 18, they were making $25,000 a month each. But when Cullotta bought a new Cadillac, Spilotro told him to get rid of it. He had already made contact with the Chicago Outfit, who wanted them to continue driving around in inconspicuous Fords and Chevrolets.

ONE OF HIS EYES POPPED OUT

Spilotro hung out with Vinnie 'the Saint' Inserro, who introduced him to Jimmy 'the Turk' Torello, Charles 'Chuckie' Nicoletti, 'Milwaukee Phil' Alderisio, Joey 'the Clown' Lombardo and Joseph 'Joey Doves' Aiuppa, who would go on to become head of the Outfit – a job Spilotro had coveted from an early age.

On one occasion, two hold-up men named Bill McCarthy and Jimmy Miraglia had an argument with Philly and Ronnie Scalvo. The Scalvos were then found dead, along with a woman, but no one had given permission for the hit, so retribution was ordered.

Spilotro, Nicoletti and Alderisio abducted McCarthy. They took him to a workshop to torture him but he would not talk, even when they stabbed an ice-pick through his testicles. So Spilotro put McCarthy's head in a vice and tightened it until one of his eyes popped out. He then put lighter fuel on McCarthy's face and set fire to it.

Unimpressed, Nicoletti ate pasta throughout.

Before he died, McCarthy gave up Miraglia's name. Eleven days later, the bodies of Miraglia and McCarthy were found in the boot of Miraglia's car.

THE BOOKMAKING YEARS

After these murders, Spilotro hooked up with Outfit enforcer 'Mad' Sam DeStefano, collecting debts for him. As part of Milwaukee Phil's crew, he began shaking down bookies. Then he became a bail bondsman, bailing out soldiers for Lombardo, Alderisio and Torello.

By 1963, Spilotro was a made man in the Chicago Outfit, controlling the bookmaking in the northwest side of Chicago. He quickly attracted the attention of law enforcement officers and the media, who called him 'the Ant' because he was just 5 feet 2 inches tall.

The following year Spilotro was sent to Miami to work with childhood friend Frank 'Lefty' Rosenthal, a mob-backed bookmaker, handicapper and match-fixer. In 1961, Rosenthal had appeared before the McClellan committee on Gambling and Organized Crime, where he took the Fifth Amendment 37 times – refusing even to say whether he was left-handed (the origin of his nickname).

JEWELLERY STORE HQ

In 1971, Spilotro was sent to run the Outfit's interests in Las Vegas. Again he worked with Rosenthal, who was in charge of the skim. His job was to siphon off as much cash as possible before it was recorded as revenue.

Working out of a jewellery store called The Gold Rush with his brother Michael, Spilotro imposed a street tax on all criminal activities,

Frank 'Lefty' Rosenthal adjusts his tie while refusing to answer questions before the Senate Rackets Subcommittee. Rosenthal was brought before the committee for bribery and match-fixing in 1961

enforcing this with five murders where the victims were brutally tortured before they were killed. But even before Spilotro arrived in Las Vegas the FBI in Chicago had alerted the bureau there that he was on his way. He was only in town two weeks before they had a wiretap on him. The local police picked him up every three or four months 'on general principle'. It was a hassle, but Spilotro enjoyed the publicity.

REMOVING THE EVIDENCE

In September 1972, Spilotro had to go back to Chicago to face trial alongside 'Mad' Sam DeStefano and his brother, Mario, for the 1963 murder of real estate agent Leo Foreman. One of the killers, Charles 'Chuckie' Crimaldi, had turned state's evidence. Spilotro was also worried about fellow defendant Sam DeStefano who, it was said, had cancer and was afraid of dying in jail.

Spilotro and Mario DeStefano went to visit Sam on the pretext that they had discovered where Crimaldi was being held by the authorities. They told Sam they had bribed the guards to turn their backs while they whacked him. DeStefano was gloating about exacting his revenge on Crimaldi when his brother, Mario, stepped aside. Spilotro was standing behind him with a double-barrelled shotgun. One blast took off Mad Sam's arm. The second hit him square in the chest, killing him instantly. Thanks to an alibi provided by his sister-in-law, Spilotro was acquitted in the Leo Foreman case and returned to Las Vegas.

Then Spilotro was indicted alongside Lombardo for defrauding the Teamsters' pension fund. This was solved by the murder of the only witness, 29-year-old Daniel Seifert. Both men were acquitted.

HOLE IN THE WALL GANG

Although Spilotro's job in Las Vegas was to keep an eye on Rosenthal and other Outfit interests, he began running a team of burglars known as the 'Hole in the Wall Gang', because they often gained entry by making a hole in a wall or roof.

Meanwhile, West Coast Mafia turncoat Aladena 'Jimmy the Weasel' Fratianno testified against him and the Nevada Gaming Commission blacklisted Spilotro. He was barred from being physically present in any Nevada casino. As a result, he expanded the Hole in the Wall Gang's activities to

'They were beaten with baseball bats and buried alive'

encompass the entire tri-state area.

But the gang's burglar alarm specialist Sal Romano was picked up on another charge. He flipped, and the crew were arrested on their next outing. Hearing that there was a contract out on him, Cullotta also turned state's evidence, but his testimony was not enough to convict Spilotro on conspiracy charges.

FATAL AFFAIR

Nevertheless, the bosses of the Chicago Outfit were not pleased with Spilotro. As well as operating without their authority, he was gaining a dangerously high profile. Then came news that Spilotro was having an affair with Rosenthal's wife. Mafia bosses don't approve of such things. Rosenthal was then car-bombed. Although it was thought that Milwaukee boss Frank Balistrieri – aka the 'Mad Bomber' – was responsible, Spilotro was also a suspect. FBI wiretap evidence in which Spilotro mentioned Joseph 'Mr Clean' Ferriola, then running the Chicago Outfit, had also been heard in court.

Spilotro was about to face trial for skimming profits at the Stardust casino and violating the civil rights of a government witness he was thought to have murdered – not to mention a retrial of the Hole in the Wall case. At the same time, Spilotro's brother, Michael, faced extortion charges in Chicago. On 14 June 1986, the two men were summoned to a meeting where they believed Michael was

The first Mafia-financed casino of Las Vegas – the Flamingo – opened on 26 December 1946. By the 1950s, the mob's skim at the Stardust was $7 million a year

going to be a made man. Instead they were beaten with baseball bats and buried alive in a cornfield in Enos, Indiana, some 60 miles southeast of Chicago.

Their remains were unearthed by a farmer. The grave was just four miles from a hunting lodge owned by Mafia boss Joe Aiuppa,

who was in prison at the time on charges of skimming profits from Las Vegas casinos.

Nicholas Pileggi's 1995 book, *Casino*, describes the Las Vegas careers of Spilotro and Rosenthal and was used as the basis for a movie of the same name directed by Martin Scorsese.

Chapter 22

GASPIPE

Left: **Anthony Casso, aka 'Gaspipe'**

Anthony 'Gaspipe' Casso is the highest-ranking member of the American Mafia to turn state's evidence. Once the head of the Lucchese family, he says that La Cosa Nostra is 'not an honored society of men anymore, it is a society of self-servicing scumbags that would give up their mother to turn a buck.' But still he hates himself for betraying it.

GROWING UP WITH THE MOB

Casso's grandparents were from Naples and his father was connected. Thanks to his childhood friend Salvatore 'Sally' Callinbrano – later Anthony's godfather and a *capo* in the Genovese family – the family did not go hungry during the Depression. Callinbrano

New York City longshoremen prepare to strike in December 1962. Up until the 1990s, International Longshoremen's Association Local 1814 was a bastion of Mafia power on the Brooklyn waterfront

made sure that Michael Casso had regular work as a longshoreman in the Brooklyn docks and access to the pilfering that went on. A tough guy, Casso Sr. always carried an eight-inch length of lead gas pipe that he used as a weapon. As a result, he was give the nickname 'Gaspipe', which his son inherited.

One of the younger Casso's earliest memories was visiting Callinbrano's club on Flatbush Avenue with his father, where everyone treated the well-dressed *capo* with respect. With the death of Albert Anastasia in 1957, Casso Sr. took over the International Longshoremen's Association Local 1814. When Anthony graduated from the Francis Xavier Catholic Elementary School, Callinbrano gave him a $50 bill. Later he gave

him a gold, diamond and sapphire pinkie ring – clearly an essential piece of jewellery for a made man.

On Sundays in summer, the family would go for picnics to Allendale Lake in New Jersey with the families of Joe Profaci, Vito Genovese and Albert Anastasia. There would be target practice with .22 rifles. Casso liked firearms and was a good shot.

In south Brooklyn, Casso was surrounded by the Mafia ethos. Disputes would be settled with the gun or the ice-pick and dead bodies turned up regularly, dumped in Flatbush or in the bays and estuaries around the coast.

In 1954, Casso saw the murder of Joe Monosco on 4th Avenue, followed by Donald Marino's murder on the corner of 5th Avenue and Sackett Street. The next year he witnessed the murder of Frank 'Shoes' De Marco in Costello's Bar. Murder was a way of life in Brooklyn.

BUYING SILENCE

Casso's father took him hunting at the farm of Mafioso Charlie LaRocca in upstate New York. The slaughter of wild animals, Casso later saw, was part of his training for organized crime. He joined a gang named the South Brooklyn Boys and became a notorious street fighter. As a result of one of these fights, Casso was arrested for the first time.

When Casso dropped out of school, Callinbrano supplied him with a forged birth certificate so that he could join the longshoremen's union; he also found him a

Vincent Gigante

$250-a-week 'no-show job' on the docks.

Through Callinbrano, Casso met Lucchese *capo* 'Christie Tick' Furnari and Paul Castellano, who got him another, more lucrative 'no-show job'. He also collected bookmaking money and loan-sharking receipts, sometimes heavy-handedly.

In 1961, Casso saw a junkie hassling a girl.

He intervened and an argument ensued. Casso pulled out a .32 pistol and shot the man in broad daylight. The incident was witnessed by the uncle of Carmine and Allie Persico, Ralph Salerno. While Casso hid out in New Jersey, his father tried to pay off the police, but did not have the $50,000 they demanded. Vincent 'the Chin' Gigante, then a *capo* in the Genovese crime family, offered to pay, but Casso did not want to join the Genovese. Meanwhile, the junkie, who had been badly wounded, was looking for Casso, saying he would kill him. Casso returned to Brooklyn to confront him. But the junkie was also connected. His uncle was a *capo* in the Genovese family and wanted no trouble. Money changed hands. Casso was arrested, but the victim did not identify him and he was acquitted.

COPS ON THE PAYROLL

Casso then went into the hijacking business, arranging for drivers to give up their loads for $10,000, rather than at gunpoint. He also bribed guards so that he could steal from the piers. Soon he was so busy he brought others – including Frankie DeCicco – into the operation.

Casso married and moved into a garden apartment in Bensonhurst and bought his parents a retirement home in the Catskills. By this point he was robbing banks by tunnelling into basement vaults. He carried out a hit for Lucchese made man Christopher Furnari in front of other made men. Then he and DeCicco gunned down a man in the street who had robbed them. Gradually, he built his own crew.

With Vic Amuso, he began importing marijuana from South America. He was soon a wealthy man. But in 1972, on the word of an informant, Casso was arrested. Through Greg Scarpa, he found out who the informant was and bought him off. This made him realize he needed information from the other side. He managed to put two crooked police officers, Louis Eppolito and Stephen Caracappa, on the payroll, along with others including an FBI agent.

SETTLING SCORES

In 1974, after a long hiatus, the Gambino family books were open again. But Casso became a made man in the Lucchese family instead, and was a member of Vincent 'Vinnie Beans' Foceri's *borgata* (branch of the family), which had its headquarters on 116th Street in Manhattan and 14th Avenue in Brooklyn.

Selling marijuana and cocaine, Casso dealt with Roy DeMeo and Sammy 'the Bull' Gravano. He also took on private work. When the daughter of a friend was raped, he waited until the rapist was out on bail, abducted him, mutilated his genitals, then killed him. And when his wife's 16-year-old nephew was killed by a member of the Colombo family, Casso demanded, and succeeded in getting, his killer's death.

When Furnari became *consigliere* of the Lucchese family, he wanted Casso to become a *capo* and take over his crew. But Casso preferred to be the one soldier a *consigliere* was allowed and recommended *Amuso* for the post of *capo*. Casso was running a lucrative bootleg gasoline scam with Ukrainian mob boss Marat Balagula in Brighton Beach. When the Russian gangster Vladimir Reznikov tried to muscle in, Casso set him up to be hit by DeMeo's crew.

'After that, Marat didn't have any problems with other Russians,' said Casso.

When Castellano decided that DeMeo had to go, John Gotti and Frankie DeCicco gave the contract to Casso. He, in turn, approached the Testa brothers and Anthony Senter, who did the job.

CHILLY HIDING PLACE

The so-called Commission Case followed in 1985, when 11 top Mafiosi, including the heads of the five families, went on trial for racketeering. John Gotti decided that it was time to make his move by hitting Castellano and becoming boss. Casso was against the coup and tried to talk DeCicco out of it, but Gotti had promised to make him underboss.

For killing their boss without permission, Gotti and DeCicco were sentenced to death by the Commission. Casso and Amuso were given the contract and they were told to use a bomb. They learned that Gotti and DeCicco were going to visit a social club in Bensonhurst. When DeCicco's car arrived, Herbie 'Blue Eyes' Pate slipped a bag containing C-4 plastic explosive under it. It was detonated by remote control. DeCicco was killed instantly. Another

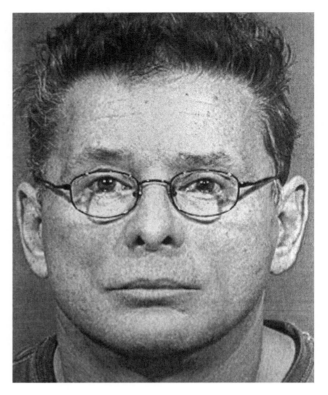

Salvatore Gravano, alias Sammy 'the Bull'

man with him was badly injured, but Gotti had cancelled at the last moment. They did not get a second chance because Gotti courted publicity and was almost always surrounded by the press. Meanwhile Gotti gave a contract on Casso to a hit team led by James Hydell. Gaspipe was shot at outside the Golden Ox restaurant and sought refuge – from the assassins and the police – in the restaurant's freezer. Hydell paid with his life.

RUNNING THE FAMILY ON THE RUN

The boss of the Lucchese family Tony 'Ducks' Corallo realized that the Commission Case was going to put the leadership of the family away for the rest of their lives. Because Casso was the family's biggest money-maker, Corallo suggested that he should be the new boss. But Casso refused and the leadership passed to Amuso, with Casso as *consigliere* and, later, underboss.

The Mafia had moved in on a $150 million deal from the New York Housing Authority to install replacement windows. In the resulting

'DeCicco was killed instantly . . . another man with him was badly injured'

racketeering investigation, Amuso and Casso were indicted. Tipped off by a mole in the FBI, they went on the run, leaving 'Little Al' D'Arco as acting boss.

Even though he was a fugitive, Casso still ordered hits. When 'Fat Pete' Chiodo decided to plead guilty, Casso and Amuso were in danger of being implicated. The two men ordered D'Arco to kill Chiodo. When he failed, Amuso ordered, for the first time in Mafia history, a hit on D'Arco's wife, but she and her children were taken into the

An FBI surveillance photo of Casso (right) with Amuso

Witness Protection Program.

Amuso was captured in a shopping mall in Scranton, Pennsylvania. This left Casso in charge of the Lucchese family. D'Arco realized that he was in danger now and turned himself in to the FBI. Casso continued to run the Lucchese family from the back of a van, but made the mistake of buying new mobile phones that were just being introduced. He was arrested in the shower in his girlfriend's home in Mount Olive, New Jersey.

An attempt to bribe his way out of jail was foiled at the last moment. Casso also planned an ambush on the van that brought him back from court, as well as a hit on the judge.

When these ploys failed, he offered to turn state's evidence and pleaded guilty to 72 counts of racketeering, including 15 murders – though it was thought he was responsible for at least 44.

He was sent to a special prison unit for co-operating witnesses, but he would not behave. He got into fights with other prisoners and bribed the guards for favours. The prosecutors decided that he was too unreliable to take the stand against Vincent 'the Chin' Gigante and relied instead on the testimony of D'Arco and Gravano. Casso then wrote a letter claiming they were lying. Clearly, he was not a co-operative witness and he was dropped from the programme. Returned to a regular prison, he was kept in solitary confinement for his own protection. Having broken the terms of his plea bargain, he was sentenced to 13 terms of life imprisonment, plus 455 years.

Chapter 23

DIABOLIK

Trapani on the west coast of Sicily – Diabolik's birthplace

Left: Matteo Messina, aka 'Diobolik'

Matteo Messina Denaro is a new type of Mafia don, not least because he has slipped the old Mafia's moral straitjacket and has emerged as a ladies' man – in defiance of the old Sicilian proverb that giving orders is better than sex.

LEGEND IN HIS OWN TIME

Some Mafiosi worship Messina Denaro as a saint. Others see him as James Bond – he is said to have an Alfa Romeo 164 armed with machine guns that can be activated at the push of a button. He boasts that he has filled a cemetery all by himself. It is said he is the guardian of Totò Riina's treasure which includes not only a fabulous collection of jewellery, but also the Mafia archive. This is purportedly held in a secret vault under a jeweller's shop in Castelvetrano, which can only be entered using an elevator built into the strongroom. However, his police files give his profession as 'farmer'.

His father, Francesco Messina Denaro, aka Don Ciccio, was a member of the Cupola, or Mafia Commission, and an ally of the Corleone faction led by Totò Riina and Bernardo Provenzano. He and his two sons, Matteo and Salvatore, were on the payroll of one of the richest families in Trapani. Among its number is Senator Antonio D'Ali, who claimed he had no idea that the Messina Denaros were involved in the Mafia. Francesco and Matteo were employed as estate managers – a traditional job for Mafiosi – while Salvatore was a clerk in the senator's family bank.

Matteo's brother-in-law, Giuseppe Guttadauro, was also a Mafia boss, even though he practised as a doctor. He received patients in his surgery each evening between 5 and 7 pm, after it had been open to the *picciotti* who had been collecting protection money.

MYOPIC KILLER

Taught to shoot at 14, Matteo killed for the first time at 18. His father found him a job as an armed guard to the D'Ali family. During the Mafia wars, he worked for Totò Riina. When Riina ordered the execution of Vincenzo Milazzo, Denaro killed him and strangled his pregnant girlfriend for good measure.

He served as Riina's chief intelligence officer and spied on anti-Mafia judge Giovanni Falcone and former justice minister Claudio Martelli, while both were living in Rome in the early 1990s. He also plotted the attack on the TV host Maurizio Costanzo.

In 1993, on Riina's orders, Denaro carried out car bomb attacks on the Uffizi Gallery in Florence and the Basilica of St John Lateran in Rome, which killed ten people and injured 93 others. Law enforcement officials also hold Denaro directly responsible for the murder of another six people, though he claimed to have killed more than 50.

After the bombing campaign, he went underground, using the pseudonym 'Alessio'

in his clandestine correspondence with Bernardo Provenzano. It is thought that he attended a clinic in Barcelona, Spain, to treat his myopia.

However, while being on the list of the world's ten most wanted fugitives, he remained curiously well known. Addicted to video games, he rejoices in the soubriquet of 'Diabolik', after an Italian comic strip character.

THE PLAYBOY DON

According to the press, Messina Denaro is a notorious womanizer who revels in the high life, with an extensive collection of Porsches, designer watches and sharp suits. A detective at Trapani police headquarters said: 'Messina Denaro is generous, he's an effortless conversationalist and he can judge the *perlage* of a fine champagne.'

He can afford to. He is worth an estimated $3.7 billion.

Time magazine called him the 'playboy don'.

Giacomo Di Girolamo, author of *The Invisible*, a book on the mobster, says: 'Denaro is a modern Mafia boss, the opposite of the traditional image of *The Godfather*. He has numerous lovers and a child out of wedlock. He knows which businesses to get involved in – and this is primarily drugs.'

His daughter lives with her grandmother in Castelvetrano, along with her mother – who dare not look another man in the eye because she needs to preserve the reputation of her

In 1993, Denaro carried out a car-bomb attack on the Uffizi Gallery in Florence

errant lover and her own life.

In 2001 the Italian news magazine *L'Espresso* put him on their cover with the caption: 'He is the new boss of the Mafia.' The magazine also reported that Denaro had killed a Sicilian hotel owner who had accused him of bedding young girls.

GREEN ENERGY CHAMPION

But it was only with the arrest of Provenzano in 2006 that Denaro became 'don of dons'. He did so only then as the result of a vicious Mafia war. According to Di Girolamo: 'Denaro is without doubt a very powerful and ruthless man who will stop at nothing to ensure he has utmost control of his territory.'

The FBI say Denaro is the Mafia's principal connection with the South American drug cartels and masterminds the importation of heroin and cocaine into Europe. As well as loan-sharking and extortion, Denaro has moved the Mafia into a new area of moneymaking – renewable energy.

Land is bought at a fraction of its true value and sold at a huge profit to developers who want to build solar and wind farms. Then the European Union hands out millions of euros for their construction. Investments are used to launder Mafia money.

The scale of the operation was revealed when police seized assets worth $1.8 billion from Sicilian businessman Vito Nicastri, who is nicknamed the 'God of the Wind' and is said to be a frontman for Denaro. They included more than 40 companies, nearly 100 properties, seven sports cars and luxury yachts. It was said to be the 'biggest ever seizure of assets linked to Denaro'.

Sicily is dotted with these giant windmills and solar panels, but they have never been connected to the grid. All are sitting there, laundering mob money.

All the police have to go on are snapshots of Denaro taken 20 years ago. In a bid to track him down they have used a special computer programme to age his image, but they admit that this may be of very little use as he is believed to have undergone extensive plastic surgery.

FOLK HERO

The other strategy open to them is to strip him of his assets. Building firms, cement companies, houses and shops worth around £455 million have been confiscated, along with supermarkets, which are one of the Mafia's main outlets for money laundering. But the forced closure of many branches has angered locals, who see Denaro as their benefactor. He provides job for them in the supermarkets and distribution centres that the Mafia have built for money laundering.

'The problem is many people in Sicily feel they have been abandoned by the Italian state,' said Di Girolamo, 'and see Denaro as a heavenly provider. He has given them jobs and money where the state has given them nothing so that's why many are attracted to the Mafia.'

Denaro's name has also been linked to a money-laundering account in the Vatican bank. In all, the state has seized $3.8 billion from him since 2009.

Di Girolamo is convinced Denaro has politicians and police officers on his payroll. He says: 'How else do you explain the fact that Denaro has been on the run for almost 20 years? He has a network of allies and is always on the move – I doubt he is abroad. If he left his home territory then it would be a sign of weakness and he could lose his grip. I am certain that senior figures within Italian politics and the police are doing their utmost to keep him in hiding.'

Denaro was in the news again in May 2013, when a trial opened in Palermo. It involved senior politicians, who were accused of entering into secret talks with the Cosa Nostra during Denaro's bombing campaign in the 1990s.

The elusive Denaro remains a folk hero. People reminisce about giving him a lift or having smoked with him and he is said to have the same appeal as the charismatic Mexican revolutionary Emiliano Zapata. One local mobster, caught on a wiretap planning to abandon his wife and daughter to join his idol on the run, said: 'Better one day as a lion than a hundred as a sheep.'

A composite 'age progression' identikit image of Denaro, who has been on the run since 1993

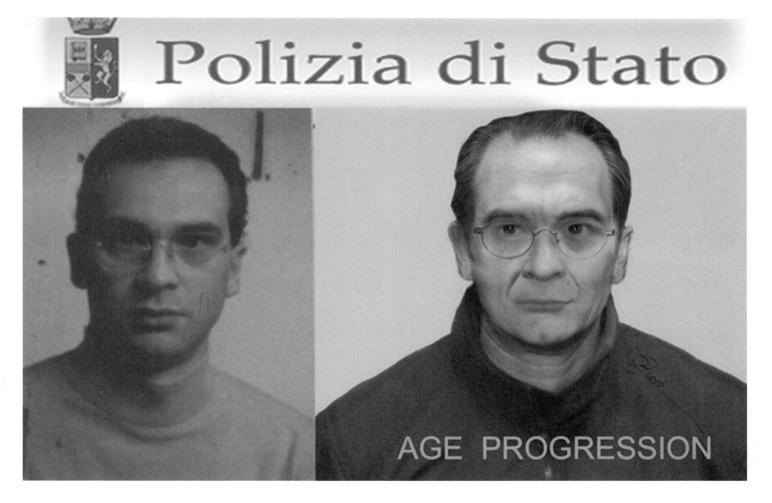

Polizia di Stato

AGE PROGRESSION

Chapter 24

THE PENTITI

On 30 April 1982 Pio La Torre, the head of the Italian Communist Party in Sicily, was gunned down in Palermo. His death was hardly surprising, because he was hugely unpopular with the Mafia. In 1962 he became a member of the first Antimafia Commission and in 1972 he was elected to the Italian chamber of deputies, where he attempted to pass a bill that outlawed members of the Mafia.

As a result of La Torre's murder, Christian Democrat Prime Minister Giulio Andreotti appointed General Carlo Alberto Dalla Chiesa prefect for Palermo. The general was the man credited with the destruction of the Red Brigades. Dalla Chiesa soon realized that he

Right: **General Carlo Alberto Dalla Chiesa who was murdered in a drive-by shooting**

Left: **Catholic penitents**

had been handed a poisoned chalice, because the Christian Democrats were in league with the Mafia. On 3 September 1982, Chiesa and his young wife were killed in a drive-by shooting. The murder weapon was the same AK-47 that had been used to kill Stefano Bontade and Salvatore Inzerillo. It was Pino Greco's weapon of choice. That day, La Torre's anti-Mafia law was finally passed.

Chiesa's death had come at the end of a series of murders, in which all of the victims had been law officers. Boris Giuliano, the police chief who had discovered the heroin connection between Sicily and America, had been shot four times in the back while enjoying his morning cappuccino on 21 July 1979. That autumn, Judge Cesare Terranova, who had been in charge of the Bari trial, was sent to Palermo. He was shot dead after just two days. In the following May, Emanuele Basile, a captain in the *carabinieri*, was also gunned down. He had issued 55 drugs-related arrest warrants to members of the Bontade and Inzerillo families.

The anti-Mafia law gave two investigating magistrates cause for optimism. Giovanni Falcone and Paolo Borsellino had both been born in Palermo and they had both worked in the Mafia strongholds of Monreale, Agrigento and Trapani before being transferred back to their home town. Once there, Falcone took up a position in the bankruptcy section, where he became an expert in forensic accounting.

When Tommaso Buscetta and Salvatore Contorno began to talk, the deputy chief

Anti-Mafia
judges Giovanni
Falcone and Paolo
Borsellino

of the investigative squad, Antonio 'Ninni' Cassarà, drew up the 'Michele Greco+161' report. It recommended arresting Michele Greco and 161 others who were involved in heroin trafficking, including the Salvo cousins. Falcone was then moved into the investigative office, where he started looking into the affairs of Rosario Spatola, who was a cousin of Salvatore Inzerillo and John Gambino. He was able to prove that the Spatola Construction Company was a front for drug smuggling. After analysing five years of bank records by hand, he managed to jail the rest of the Spatola family, obtaining 74 convictions in all. His cases depended only

on financial records, so no witnesses could be intimidated, and he only prosecuted cases that could be heard before a tribunal of three judges, so no jurors could be bought.

Borsellino concentrated on prosecuting the killers of Captain Basile, but the judge declared a mistrial, allowing the suspects back on to the street. Borsellino's boss, Rocco Chinnici, was so concerned for his subordinate's safety that he removed him from the Mafia investigation. But it was Chinnici himself who was killed, along with his two bodyguards and the concierge of his block, when Pino Greco organized a car bomb attack. His replacement, Antonino Caponnetto, let

Falcone and Borsellino work together and share information with other investigating magistrates. And when Bettino Craxi became prime minister in 1984 his new minister of justice allowed them to buy computers so they could deal with the huge amounts of financial data that flooded in.

MAFIA MAXI TRIAL

The information that had been supplied by Buscetta and Contorno enabled 474 defendants to face justice in the so-called Maxi Trial of the mid-1980s. A special courtroom bunker the size of a small sports stadium was built near Ucciardone prison in Palermo. The reinforced concrete near-fortress was then surrounded by barbed wire and guarded by 3,000 troops, plus a tank. Thirty cages, each big enough to house 20 defendants, were set into the inner walls of the building while a dozen tables had been provided for the lawyers and witnesses. Overlooking the entire spectacle was a public gallery, where 1,000 spectators could sit behind bullet-proof glass and view the proceedings.

As well as Buscetta and Contorno, there were over a thousand witnesses. The trial went on for 22 months, during which time 344 of the defendants were found guilty and sentenced to a total of 2,665 years in jail, not

The 474 people accused of Mafia activity are locked in steel cages in a specially built courthouse in Palermo, 1986

counting the 19 life sentences that had been handed down to the most important bosses in Sicily. They included Michele 'The Pope' Greco and – *in absentia* – Totò Riina and Bernardo Provenzano. Life sentences were also handed down to several of the 'Room of Death' killers (see page 196): Vincenzo 'The Tempest' Sinagra and his brother Antonio, and Salvatore Rotolo. Sinagra's cousin, also named Vincenzo Sinagra, supplied much of the evidence in that part of the trial.

His reward was a relatively light 21-year prison sentence.

Others were dealt with by 'Mafia justice'. Mario Prestifilippo, who was still at large during the trial, was gunned down in the street before the verdicts were returned. Antonio Ciulla was acquitted despite five *pentiti* testifying that he ran a heroin ring in northern Italy, but his delight was short-lived. Intending to celebrate, he stopped to buy champagne and pastries when he left Ucciardone prison, but he was shot and killed before he reached home. At least eighteen of those who had been acquitted were later murdered.

Some defendants had already been jailed for other offences, so the court's verdict counted for little. Luciano Leggio was acquitted of running the Corleonesi family from behind bars and ordering the murder of Judge Terranova, but he would not be leaving his prison cell. And Giuseppe Calò would continue to serve two life sentences, even though he had been cleared of killing Roberto Calvi.

However, many of those convicted did not stay behind bars. Corrupt politician Salvo Lima handed the hearing of appeals to Corrado Carnevale, who became known as *l'ammazzasentenze* or 'The Sentence Killer' after quashing over 400 sentences. He was suspended from office after the Andreotti trial and was sentenced to six years' imprisonment for conspiring with the Mafia, but his conviction was overturned on appeal and he returned to work as a judge.

By 1989 only 60 of those convicted in the Maxi Trial were still in prison and even they

Judge Giovanni Falcone, his wife Francesca and three bodyguards died on the motorway near Palermo after a roadside bomb exploded as they were passing, 23 May 1992

Pietro Aglieri, thought to be the mastermind behind the assassination of Italian anti-Mafia judge Paolo Borsellino

were given an easy time. However, when Caponnetto stood down, Falcone did not take over his position. Instead he moved to the ministry of justice in Rome, where he drafted legislation that would enable the establishment of a nationwide anti-Mafia organization.

Nevertheless, the 'Palermo spring' seemed to be over. This fact was brought home when a small businessman named Libero Grassi gave a television interview in which he denounced Mafia racketeering and publicly refused to pay protection money.

Soon afterwards he was shot down outside his house and no one, except his immediate family, dared turn up to his funeral. However, the outcry prevented Andreotti from releasing any more of the mafiosi who had been convicted at the first Maxi Trial.

In the summer of 1991 the Court of Cassation was to consider appeals according to what was known as the 'Buscetta theorem' – that those sitting on the Commission had approved, and were therefore culpable of, any murders that took place during that period. After pressure had been applied by parliament, the ministry of justice and the judiciary, Carnevale was prevented from becoming president of the court. Another judge sat in his place and the sentences were upheld.

Totò Riina, who had hoped to get his own life sentence overturned, was keen to take his revenge. First of all Salvatore Lima, the Mafia's man in Rome, was gunned down and then it was Giovanni Falcone's turn. On 23 May 1992 Falcone and his wife were paying a

The distorted wreckage of the car in which anti-Mafia judge Paolo Borsellino died when a remote-controlled bomb exploded in Palermo, July 1992, a few weeks after the death of his ally Falcone

visit to their holiday home in Palermo. They travelled in secret on a government plane and were met at the airport by a police escort, but as the convoy headed down the autostrada towards Capaci a bomb in a culvert under the motorway exploded. It was powerful enough to kill the policemen in the first car and Falcone and his wife in the following vehicle. The bomb was detonated by Pietro Aglieri and Giovanni Brusca – who was then given the

name '*lo scannacristiani*' ('the man who kills Christians').

There were cheers among the inmates of Ucciardone prison and someone phoned the Palermo newspaper *Giornale di Sicilia* to say that the bombing was a 'wedding present for Nino Madonia' – the eldest son of the Madonia family, who had been married in the chapel at Ucciardone earlier that day.

For the public though, it was a killing too

many. As pictures of the bomb site made the front pages of newspapers around the world, the Italian parliament called for a day of mourning and the current session was suspended until after the funeral. Forty thousand people turned out in Palermo for the service; a general strike was called, closing all stores and businesses; people hung sheets out of their windows bearing anti-Mafia slogans; and the politicians who turned up were berated as 'murderers' and 'accomplices'.

Borsellino was moved to Marsala, but even there he was approached by more *pentiti*. Then on 19 July 1992, less than two months after the death of Falcone, he met his end at the hands of the Mafia. It was known that he was going to visit his mother in Palermo on that day, so a car bomb was placed outside her home. When it exploded, Borsellino and his six bodyguards were killed. But even that did not stop more *pentiti* coming forward.

Seven thousand troops had to be sent to Sicily to keep order. In the following January the *carabinieri* arrested Totò Riina as he was being driven through Palermo, where he had been living for 23 years as a fugitive. There are two conflicting versions of his capture. The first revolves around Baldassare Di Maggio, who was acting head of the San Giuseppe Jato *cosca* while Giovanni Brusca and his father Bernardo were in jail. When Giovanni was released, Di Maggio feared that he was going to be eliminated, even though he had committed numerous murders for Riina. Riina tried to reassure him that he was not going to be thrown away like 'a used orange', but Di Maggio knew that Riina was at his most dangerous when he was being charming – so he fled. He was picked up on minor charges in the northern Italian city of Novara. Convinced that Riina was going to kill him, he turned *pentito*. The alternative version is that Riina was shopped by Bernardo Provenzano, so that he could seize compromising material held in Riina's apartment.

Riina had already been given two life sentences when he was tried and convicted of ordering many murders, including those of Falcone and Borsellino, along with Provenzano. In 1998 he picked up another life sentence for the murder of Salvo Lima.

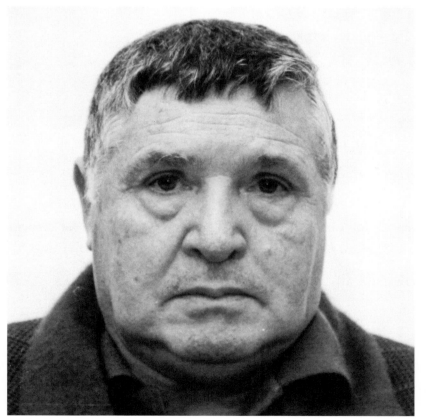

Mafia boss Totò Riina

THE PHANTOM DON

Riina's arrest meant that Bernardo Provenzano was now Sicily's boss of bosses. Luciano Leggio had once said of him: 'He shoots like a god, shame he has the brains of a chicken.' But Leggio had been in jail for over 30 years before Provenzano was arrested. Once known at 'The Tractor' for his ruthless killing, Provenzano later became known among the Corleonesi as 'The Accountant', for the bureaucratic way in which he ran his criminal empire.

During the Corleonesi war Provenzano was indicted for the murder of one of Navarra's men, so in 1963 he went on the run. That way he would escape arrest and also dodge the inevitable vendetta. With Leggio in jail, Provenzano became Riina's second in command. While continuing to build a considerable reputation as a gunman, Provenzano dealt efficiently with money brought in by heroin trafficking and other criminal enterprises. He also took over the Palermo suburb of Bagheria – where the 'Room of Death' was situated – as his personal fiefdom. The fugitive lived with his wife and two sons in a luxurious hideaway in the park of the 18th-century Villa Valguarnera, surrounded by associates who had also built houses there. Riina and the Grecos lived not far away. In order to avoid capture, Provenzano would go to meetings in an ambulance.

'As Provenzano grew older, he became more religious. Giving his consent to a murder, he might say, "Let the will of God be done"'

After Riina's arrest in 1993 it was clear that he would never again be a free man, so Provenzano succeeded him. By then he had been in hiding so long that the other mafiosi could not be sure that he was still alive, especially when his wife and children came out of hiding. His sons were never involved with the Cosa Nostra – he was most insistent on that score. Provenzano then put an end to the speculation by the simple device of writing to the prosecutor in Palermo, a move that generated massive publicity. But not everyone was convinced. Mafiosi members who had not yet seen Provenzano began to call him 'The Phantom'.

Provenzano was not without his rivals. The first of them was Riina's brother-in-law, Leoluca Bagarella, who was probably responsible for over 300 murders. Buscetta said he had 'mental problems'. He had killed Buscetta's nephew because he was related to a *pentito*. It is also said that he hanged his wife because her brother, Giuseppe Marchese, became an informer. With Riina dead, he tried to take over a section of the Corleonesi. However, in 1995 he was arrested and sentenced to life imprisonment on several counts of murder.

The second was Giovanni Brusca. Provenzano dealt with him by killing or co-opting his allies. Then in 1996 Brusca was also arrested. He had already been sentenced *in*

Italian police officers conceal their identities as they parade long-term fugitive Bernardo Provenzano

absentia to life imprisonment for the murders of Falcone and Borsellino. While he was in court, he admitted to planting the bomb under the motorway to Capaci and detonating it by remote control. He also admitted many other murders, including that of Giuseppe Di Matteo, the 11-year-old son of a rival, after holding him prisoner in a bunker for two years. The body was then dissolved in acid. Brusca was never granted the full status of a *pentito*. However, after eight years in jail it was reported that he was allowed out for one week every 45 days, so that he could see his wife and child.

As boss of bosses, Provenzano had learned the lesson of Riina's full-out assault on the state.

Under Provenzano, the Mafia would keep a low profile, avoid attacks on high-profile targets and try to resolve territorial disputes through negotiation.

The *Pax Mafiosa* was so complete that it was rumoured that 'Uncle Bernie' had done a deal with the authorities, trading peace in exchange for his liberty. His whereabouts were known to a small number of trusted associates. He never used the telephone for fear that it might be tapped and he communicated through small notes called *pizzini*, which were folded into half-inch squares, sealed with Sellotape and delivered by hand. He even contacted his family in this fashion. As he grew older, he became more religious and his notes often contained pious language, even when they referred to violence. Giving his consent to a murder, for instance, he might simply say, 'Let the will of God be done'. There was even a theory that he used biblical quotes as a code. And according to the Cosa Nostra's first female supergrass, Giuseppa Vitale, he sometimes appeared dressed as a bishop.

The latest known photograph of Provenzano dated from 1959, which meant he could travel relatively unhindered. He even made two trips to a clinic in the south of France, using forged documents, where he was treated for a prostate tumour. But the authorities were closing in. At dawn on 25 January 2005, doors were kicked down all over Palermo in an operation involving over 1,000 police officers

and *carabinieri*. It was the culmination of an investigation that lasted three years. Forty-six people who were thought to have helped the fugitive Mafia boss were arrested. The idea was to cut Provenzano off from his support. Only one close associate, Stefano Lo Verno, was left at large. The police reasoned that someone would have to deliver food to Provenzano, so they followed Lo Verno closely. But they gave up when he made no attempt to contact his boss after a couple of days. Lo Verno was then arrested, followed by another 84 suspects in March.

Some of the jailed mafiosi had more to fear than the investigators. Provenzano's closest aide, Francesco 'Ciccio' Pastoia, was horrified to learn that his house had been

The farmhouse where Sicilian Mafia chief Bernardo Provenzano was arrested

bugged when he had boasted about double-crossing Provenzano. Fearing what the Mafia might do to his family, he hanged himself with a bedsheet. Later his grave was desecrated and his remains were set on fire.

One informer led the authorities to a copy of Provenzano's forged ID. It had an up-to-date picture on it, which was then shown on *Chi l'ha visto?* ('Who has seen it?'), Italy's equivalent of *Crimewatch* or *America's Most Wanted.* When this avenue led nowhere, the authorities set up a new task force that was dedicated to the capture of Provenzano. With no fresh leads, all they could do was keep Provenzano's wife and sons under constant surveillance. But Provenzano had returned to Corleone. He trusted the shepherds who respected the old way of life and he lived in a cottage supplied by Giovanni Marino, a farmer without Mafia ties who just made ricotta.

With Provenzano out of the way, a power vacuum developed. Salvatore Lo Piccolo, the boss of Palermo – who had himself been in hiding for 20 years – began to court the survivors of the Inzerillo clan, who had fled Sicily during the 1980s. But the *capo* Antonio 'Nino' Rotolo, an ally of Riina's, feared their return. He had been sentenced to life but had been diagnosed with a heart condition, so he was allowed to serve his sentence under house arrest. However, the supposedly ailing *capo* was seen jumping over a garden fence to hold meetings in a builder's hut that his associates had 'swept' with anti-bugging devices. But the

Salvatore Lo Piccolo is escorted away by Italian police after his arrest in Palermo, 5 November 2007

surveillance crew had merely taken the simple precaution of turning their bugs off during the sweep. When they turned them back on again they heard Rotolo reading out Provenzano's small notes, or *pizzini*. Rotolo wanted to kill Lo Piccolo and his son Sandro, but Provenzano wanted to keep the peace. Later on, a conversation between Provenzano's two brothers was bugged. It revealed that he was living in Corleone.

It was all but impossible to mount a surveillance operation in the small country town. Any stranger would be noticed. However, investigators managed to install a miniature camera in a street light opposite the house where Provenzano's wife lived. They noticed a bag of washing being delivered and collected. After it left the house, the bag was passed from hand to hand, making it almost impossible to follow. But after months of observation, one of the mafiosi carrying the washing stopped to buy some ricotta from Giovanni Marino, whose house was then put under surveillance.

It was noticed that each morning at seven o'clock Marino opened the door to the little cottage in his yard, but no one emerged. Then one day, they glimpsed an arm passing something out.

On 11 April 2006, the authorities swooped. Inside was Provenzano, who put up no resistance. He congratulated his captors and asked them if he had been betrayed by informers. The police assured him that he hadn't. They noticed that his clothes were packed and that he slept in a sleeping bag, fully clothed and ready for flight. His meagre accommodation was decorated with religious pictures. On a small table lay his Bible, which he had annotated over the years. Beside it were a Brother typewriter and paper and Sellotape for his *pizzini*, along with incontinence pads for his prostate problem.

No trial was necessary because Provenzano had already been sentenced to life imprisonment *in absentia* many times over.

REPENTANCE

Few of the *pentiti* showed real repentance. However, Nino Gioè, who was with Giovanni Brusca when he killed Giovanni Falcone, showed a genuine change of heart in prison. This might have been because some of his conversations had been bugged by the police, so he had inadvertently broken the *omertà*. Whatever the reason, he stopped shaving and cleaning his clothes and those around him feared he was about to break. On 23 July 1993 he hanged himself in his cell. In his suicide note, he wrote:

'This evening I will find the peace and serenity that I lost some seventeen years ago [when he was 'made']. When I lost them, I became a monster. I was a monster until I took pen in hand to write these lines... Before I go, I ask for forgiveness from my mother and from God, because their love has no limits. The whole of the rest of the world will never be able to forgive me.'

March against the Mafia, Milan, 20 March 2010: this protest is held every year in memory of victims of the Mafia

ADDIOPIZZO

The basis of Mafia power has always been the *pizzo*, the small 'tax' extorted from every business so that the mafiosi could wet their beaks. When five graduates wanted to open a bar in Palermo in the summer of 2004 the Mafia came calling as usual, but this time the would-be bar owners refused to pay up. In fact they fought back by plastering the city with stickers that said: *'Un intero popolo che paga il pizzo è un popolo senza dignità'* – 'A whole people who pays the pizzo is a people without dignity.'

When this seemed to strike a chord with the populace, they set up the Committee *Addiopizzo* – which means 'goodbye pizzo'.

They organized demonstrations and printed *Addiopizzo* T-shirts on which the slogan *'consumo critico'* ('critical consumption') burst out through a circle with a cross in it.

According to a study published in 2008, almost one billion euros – 1.3 per cent of Sicily's gross domestic product – was finding its way into the hands of the Mafia each year.

Shops paid an average of 457 euros a month, while hotels and restaurants were charged an average of 578 euros. Construction companies typically paid 2,000 euros a month.

In March 2008, *Supermercato Punto Antipizzo* – a *pizzo*-free supermarket – opened. By that time, the names of 241 companies who had refused to pay the *pizzo* appeared on the *Addiopizzo* website. *Addiopizzo* Travel was then set up, so that tourists visiting the island would not have to pay money to the Mafia.

The movement also spread to Germany where the 'Mafia? *Nein danke!'* campaign started after six Italians were murdered by 'Ndrangheta killers in front of a restaurant in Duisberg. *Addiopizzo* was soon joined by a number of Italian restaurants that had been forced to pay protection money.

In Sicily women have been at the forefront of the movement and have endured constant threats by mafiosi. Some members' homes have even been letter-bombed.

Nevertheless, young Sicilians are now ready to stand up to the Mafia. They openly mock local gangsters when they are arrested.

New laws mean that jailed mafiosi are stripped of their property. Some of it is handed over to the *Addiopizzo* movement or to farming co-operatives. The Provenzano family home is occupied by Church groups, who work the fields and vineyards confiscated from the Mafia around Corleone.

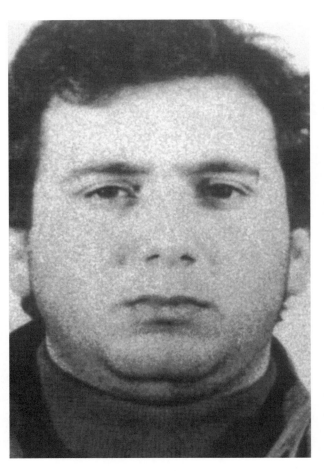

Mafia member Giovanni Brusca who was convicted of murdering Italian magistrate Giovanni Falcone who died when a large bomb exploded underneath his car in Palermo 1992, 13th November 1993. His wife Francesca Morvillo and body guards Rocco Dicillo, Antonio Montinaro and Vito Schifani were also killed in the blast

THE PIG

Giovanni Brusca is known quite simply as 'the Pig' for his unkempt appearance and unbridled appetites, which include a thirst for blood. He once admitted killing at least a hundred people, but couldn't remember the precise body count; he tortured and murdered the 11-year-old son of a fellow Mafioso who had turned state's evidence; and he also detonated the bomb that killed crusading prosecutor Giovanni Falcone, resulting in a huge anti-Mafia backlash. Then Brusca turned state's evidence himself.

There was never any doubt that Brusca would become a Mafioso. In the 1940s, his grandfather had given refuge to Salvatore Giuliano, the bandit and fugitive leader of the Movement for the Independence of Sicily. His father, Bernardo Brusca, had risen through the ranks to become a local boss. The young Giovanni Brusca first set foot in a prison at the age of five when his father was in jail. Bernardo would eventually serve several life sentences for his numerous killings and died in prison in the year 2000.

At the age of 12, on the instructions of his father, Brusca was delivering food and clothing to fugitives, including Bernardo Provenzano and Leoluca Bagarella, who were hiding out near his home in San Giuseppe Jato, a town halfway between Palermo and Corleone.

COLD BEFORE A MURDER

A local woman who had known Brusca as a youth said: 'He was a very normal teenager. He went out for pizza and to discotheques like everybody else.'

However, his free time was usually spent cleaning his father's weapons which were kept buried in the fields. At 18 he was already overweight and had sloping shoulders. It was then that he committed his first murder. He was not told why the person had to die, but he and two others loosed a hail of bullets as the mark drove by. The victim was fatally wounded and died later in hospital.

The following year, Brusca ambushed a thief who had challenged the Mafia's authority. When the miscreant came out of the cinema, Brusca carefully fired into the crowd with a double-barrelled shotgun, hitting only his target. Rushing home, he hid the gun, changed his clothes, and raced back to relish the mayhem he had caused.

'I've always been very cold before, during and after the crime,' he confided in his memoirs. 'I might sometimes be reluctant to become "operative". But once I'd decided, all the worries, the fears and the doubts disappeared.'

At 19, he was fast-tracked into the organization and initiated by Totò Riina himself, whom Brusca already called *padrino* or 'godfather'. He then went to work as a driver for Bernardo Provenzano.

Mafia turncoat Tommaso Buscetta remembered the young Brusca as 'a wild stallion but a great leader'. Another informant, Salvatore Barbagallo, said: 'Giovanni was an excellent soldier, but he doesn't know how to think politically.' But mostly he was remembered as a ruthless butcher with little charisma.

NEVER UPSET BY TORTURE

In his memoirs, Brusca himself admitted: 'I've tortured people to make them talk;

The aftermath of the Falcone bombing, 24 May 1992

I've strangled both those who confessed and those who remained silent; I've dissolved bodies in acid; I've roasted corpses on big grills; I've buried the remains after digging graves with an earthmover. Some *pentiti* say today they feel disgust for what they did. I can speak for myself: I've never been upset by these things.'

Brusca's torture sessions would usually last for only half an hour. He would break the victim's legs with a hammer and pull his ears with pliers – 'but only enough to hurt him and make him understand that we were serious'. This was rarely effective, because the victims knew that they were going to be killed anyway.

'The condemned showed superhuman strength,' he said. 'We realized that and we'd say the fateful word: "*Niscemuninne*" ("Let's get out of here"). The torturers would then strangle the victim.'

Brusca did not even have to know his victims. Once a boss from the neighbourhood of Agrigento asked him for a favour – to kill anyone on a certain type of tractor, in a certain place, at a certain time. Three tractors drove by and he killed all three drivers. On another occasion, he rushed a job because the victim was about to get married and he did not want to leave the would-be wife a widow.

THE MURDER OF FALCONE

During the Second Mafia War in the early 1980s, Brusca became a member of Riina's death squad, which introduced terrorist tactics. He would travel escorted by a truck containing men carrying AK-47s. If they were stopped by the police and the back doors were opened for a routine check, they were told to open fire immediately.

In July 1983, the death squad blew up Palermo chief prosecutor Rocco Chinnici outside his home. The car bomb they used also killed Chinnici's two bodyguards and the porter of the apartment block and injured another 20 people. The car itself was blown three stories high, before crashing back to earth.

Two weeks after the murder of Chinnici, Riina ordered Brusca to prepare another car bomb. This time the target was to be Giovanni Falcone, who was working on indictments for what would become the Maxi Trial, where Riina would be sentenced, *in absentia*, to life.

'The death squad blew up Rocco Chinnici. The car was blown three stories high, before crashing to earth'

Brusca tried to keep watch on Falcone's home but, following Chinnici's assassination, the police were stopping anyone parking outside the homes of prosecutors or other prominent officials. Instead Brusca stationed himself outside the law courts, where he noticed a truck that brought coffee and pastries to the prosecutors each morning. He planned to pack an identical truck with explosives, but could not work out how to make his getaway without being caught in the blast, so Riina told him to leave it for another time.

His next target was Salvatore Lima, a former mayor of Palermo who had become

Mafia boss Salvatore Riina following his arrest in Palermo, 15 January 1993

a member of the Italian chamber of deputies. He was in the firing line for having failed to protect Mafiosi from the Maxi Trial or use his influence to get their convictions overturned on appeal. Lima was on his way to make arrangements for a dinner in honour of former Italian prime minister Giulio Andreotti, who was visiting Palermo, when gunmen on motorcycles blew the tyres out on his car. Lima tried to escape on foot but was shot through the head.

Brusca was then contracted to kill Falcone. The judge had made the mistake of falling into a routine. Every Saturday he would fly in from Rome with his wife, then drive down the autostrada to their home near Palermo. The original plan was to blow up a bridge on the freeway, but Brusca thought that it would not work. He also vetoed a plan to blow up a pedestrian underpass, because the main force of the blast would come out of the exits. Instead he

Burned-out cars litter the street following the bomb attack that killed Paolo Borsellino as he pulled up outside his mother's house in Palermo on 19 July 1992

chose to pack the explosives into a narrow metal drainpipe that ran under the road near the exit to Capaci. The bomb would be detonated by a remote control device normally used in conjunction with model aircraft. Brusca tested it by setting off old-fashioned flash bulbs, working out precisely when he had to flick the switch to blow up a speeding car.

Simulations were performed on a quiet country road outside Corleone. Metal tubes were buried and concreted over to see just how effective the explosives were going to be. After successful tests, Brusca reported back to Riina that he was 'operational'.

Twelve drums containing 770 pounds of explosive in all were placed under the freeway, transported beneath the road on a skateboard. Then for weeks Brusca and his men kept watch, looking out for Falcone. Twice they missed him. Once he was with his friend and fellow prosecutor Paolo Borsellino.

'If we'd known, we'd have killed two birds with one stone,' said Brusca.

But on the afternoon of 23 May 1992, Falcone and his wife Francesca were spotted by Mafia lookouts while driving down the autostrada that runs along the coast, after leaving Punta Raisi airport. Their armour-plated car was one of a convoy of three. Brusca flicked the switch to the remote control. There was a huge explosion that registered on the earthquake monitor on the other side of the island. The first car was blasted into an olive grove 60 yards away, killing the three bodyguards inside. Falcone's car teetered on the edge of a huge crater in the road. The judge, his wife and their driver were badly injured.

Falcone was heard to say: 'If I survive, this time I'll make them pay . . . '

He and his wife died shortly after they arrived in hospital. Only the driver survived.

When Brusca arrived back in Palermo, the television news channels were still reporting that Falcone was fighting for his life.

'That cuckold, if he doesn't die he will make life hell for us,' said Brusca.

Then came the news flash: 'Falcone is dead.'

Brusca was paid handsomely and celebrated with champagne.

CRACKDOWN

The murder of Falcone and, soon after, Borsellino provoked an unprecedented crackdown on the Mafia. In January 1993, Riina was arrested after 23 years as a fugitive. Brusca, Bagarella and Provenzano decided to continue the war against the state that Riina had begun. They discussed poisoning children's snacks, planting HIV-infected syringes on the beaches of Rimini and toppling the Leaning Tower of Pisa. Instead they opted for a series of bomb attacks.

First a bomb went off in Rome which aimed to kill TV host Maurizio Costanzo, who had rejoiced at the arrest of Riina. Costanzo was unhurt, but 23 bystanders were injured. Two weeks later a bomb exploded outside the Uffizi Gallery in Florence, killing five, wounding 40 and damaging dozens of priceless works of art. The following month, there was an attack on the Gallery of Modern Art in Milan, followed by another on Rome's Basilica of St John Lateran, killing another five people. Then a bomb was planted in the Olympic Stadium in Rome. It was timed to go off during a soccer match, but it failed to detonate.

Mario Santo Di Matteo, one of Brusca's accomplices in the Falcone bombing, was arrested and became a *pentito*. Brusca sent six of his soldiers to kidnap Di Matteo's 11-year-old son Giuseppe. They were dressed as policemen and told the boy they were taking him to see his father. Giuseppe, whom Brusca knew personally, was held for 18 months and tortured. Grisly photographs were sent to his father in an attempt to make him recant. In the end, Brusca strangled the boy with his bare hands and threw his body into a vat of acid.

Following the murder of more relatives of Mafia informants – and direct attacks on the Church and Italy's vaunted artistic heritage – the race to capture Brusca was on. He began disguising himself, either sporting a beard or moustache or shaving his head. With his girlfriend Rosaria and their five-year-old son, Brusca frequently moved hideouts and sent coded messages, to avoid using the phone. In January 1996, police swooped on a villa near Palermo to find Brusca gone, but his dinner still warm on the table.

INTERRUPTED TV DINNER

Then Brusca grew careless. Having moved to Agrigento on the southern coast of Sicily, he was using a mobile phone to conclude a million-dollar drugs shipment when a plainclothes policeman rode through the neighbourhood on a scooter without a silencer. This enabled police phone tappers to pinpoint his hideout.

Two hundred black-hooded men from the anti-Mafia squad surrounded the house. They burst in to find Brusca eating a steak and, ironically, watching a TV movie about the Falcone killing. He also had a copy of Falcone's book on the Cosa Nostra.

Brusca quickly turned state's evidence. The prosecutor supplied him with a list of unsolved murders and Brusca went through it, ticking those he was responsible for. He was sentenced to life imprisonment, which was then reduced to 26 years as a reward for this collaboration. Then, in 2004, a court ruled that he should be let out for a week every 45 days to visit his wife and son.

> **'Brusca strangled the boy with his bare hands and threw his body into a vat of acid'**

EPILOGUE

On 20 January 2011, 800 FBI agents swooped on 127 alleged Mafia members in New York, New Jersey and New England. Members of all five New York families were arrested, along with leaders of the New Jersey-based DeCavalcante family and the Patriarca clan who operate out of Providence, Rhode Island and Boston. Particularly hard hit was the Colombo family which had its entire leadership arrested with the exception of those who were already in jail. The FBI called it one of the 'largest Mob round-ups in FBI history'. The charges ranged from loan-sharking, through arson, extortion, drug trafficking, union racketeering, money laundering and illegal gambling, to murder, some of them dating back to the 1980s.

The US Attorney General Eric Holder said he hoped the arrests would at least disrupt Mafia activity which persists despite years of government efforts to stamp it out. 'We are committed and determined to eradicate organized crime in the US,' said Holder.

One of the biggest catches was 83-year-old Luigi 'Baby Shanks' Manocchio, the reputed head of New England's Patriarca crime family, who was arrested in Fort Lauderdale, Florida. The indictments alleged that Manocchio collected payments from strip-club owners in return for Mafia protection.

Holder said that the murders included not only 'classic Mob hits to eliminate perceived rivals' but also senseless murders. Charges were brought against Bartolomeo Vernace, a Gambino captain, for his alleged role in a double shooting in the Shamrock Bar in the Queens district of New York in 1981 that started with a spilt drink. Prosecutors believe that, in retaliation, Vernace unloaded the bullets that led to the deaths of John D'Agnese, who was behind the bar, and Richard Godkin.

The arrests marked a change in strategy by the FBI who, since 9/11, had been concentrating their efforts on fighting terrorism, affording the Mafia freedom to regroup.

Like terrorism, organized crime is now a global phenomenon. According to diplomatic cables released by Wikileaks in December 2010, Russia is seen as a 'virtual mafia state'. The political establishment, including Prime Minister Vladimir Putin, was viewed by US diplomats as being in cahoots with the oligarchs and organized crime to profit from arms trafficking, money laundering, protection rackets, extortion and other kickbacks. According to the leaked US cables, bribery alone was running at an estimated

The cables accused Putin himself of amassing money from his time in office and hiding it overseas.

Organized crime sprang up in Russia before the collapse of Communism. It began in 1988 when the Soviet Union began to allow private enterprise, without putting in place the laws to control a market economy that exist in the West. For example, a market opened next to Rizhsky railway station in Moscow was taken over by street hooligans. As central control collapsed, corrupt officials hived off state enterprises for their personal gain. Veterans of the KGB and the Afghan and Chechen wars found themselves out of work and turned to crime.

By 1993, most of the banks were owned by the Russian Mafia and over three-quarters of businesses were paying protection money. Kidnapping, bombing and gangland slayings soared. That year, 1,400 people were murdered in Moscow. Criminals had no compunction in killing businessmen who would not pay protection, or bank owners, politicians or journalists who opposed them. According to Alexander Litvinenko, the whistle-blower who was poisoned with polonium in London in 2006, the biggest criminal cartel was formed by former KGB men. He called it the Lubyanka Gang, after the KGB's headquarters in Lubyanka Square. Members included former KGB officer Vladimir Putin. He was associated with the property company SPAG, thought to have been used by St Petersburg mobsters to launder money.

The funeral of Russian godfather Vyacheslav Ivankov at Vagankovskoye cemetery, Moscow, October 2009. He died in hospital after a sniper attack

$300 billion a year. Suitcases full of money find their way to secret offshore bank accounts in Cyprus and it is often hard to distinguish between the activities of the government and the Russian Mafia.

Law enforcement agencies including the police, state security and the prosecutor's office actively protect the criminal networks. Russian spy agencies use Mafia bosses to carry out criminal operations such as arms trafficking. Unbridled bribery acts like a parallel tax system for the enrichment of policemen, officials and officers of the KGB's successor, the federal security service (FSB).

Through the KGB's overseas contacts, the Russian Mafia went international, controlling the drug traffic out of Afghanistan and making connections with the Sicilian Cosa Nostra, the Chinese Triads and the Latin American drug cartels. They also set up operations in the Brighton Beach area of Brooklyn in the US. However, in 1997, the head of the New York operation Vyacheslav Ivankov, also known as Yaponchik or 'Little Japanese', was convicted in a $5.6 million extortion case.

The Russian Mafia is thought to have taken over the underworld in Israel, with Russian gangsters producing bogus proof of Jewish ancestry to settle there.

Like organized crime in America, the Russian Mafia is not a single entity. The Izmaylovskaya gang from the Izmaylovo district is thought to be the oldest and most important Mafia group in Moscow. It also has tentacles in Tel Aviv, Berlin, Paris, Toronto, Miami and New York City. With quasi-military ranks and strict internal discipline, it is involved in extortion and murder-for-hire, and has infiltrated legitimate businesses.

The Solntsevskaya Brotherhood operates out of the Solntsevo district of Moscow. It is involved in money laundering, prostitution, credit-card fraud, human trafficking, arms dealing and other illegal activity.

It also has a presence in Toronto and San Francisco, and is thought to have over 5,000 members. In the 1990s, it merged with the Orekhovskaya gang to counter the encroachment of the Chechen Mafia. In 2005, 11 of its members were sentenced to up to 24 years for 18 brutal murders.

The Tambov gang has taken over businesses in St Petersburg. In 2008, members were arrested in Spain, Bulgaria and Berlin. The police operation in Spain also bagged $307,000 in cash and 23 luxury cars, and froze €12 million in bank accounts there. The Bulgarian prosecutor said that more than €1 billion from drug trafficking, prostitution and protection rackets had been laundered through Estonia and Bulgaria.

Crime gangs have sprung up in other parts of the former Soviet Union. The Potato Bag gang were a bunch of conmen from Odessa that operated among the émigré community in Brighton Beach. The largest of the non-Russian gangs is the Chechen Mafia who, as well as drug trafficking, have links to Islamic fundamentalists.

In the 1990s, the Russian Mafia also infiltrated the Afghan Veterans' Association – the Russian equivalent of the Vietnam Veterans' Association or the British Legion. Its head was murdered and the association split into two factions.

The head of one branch, Valery Radchikov, survived an assassination attempt in 1995. The following year, the leader of the other faction, Sergei Trakhirov, his wife and 11 others were killed when a bomb exploded in the cemetery during a funeral.

With the Cosa Nostra having their wings clipped both in Sicily and the US, the Russian Mafia are well placed to take over.

THE YAKUZA

A member of the Yakuza with shortened fingers

Japan has its own home-grown Mafia, the Yakuza. It sprung up among peddlers in the Edo Period, 1603–1868, when the country was run by the Shogun in Tokyo. They were granted permission to carry swords, alongside the nobility and the samurai class. After they took over illegal gambling and loan-sharking, they assumed the name Yakuza, from *ya-ku-za* or eight-nine-three, a losing hand in *oichi-kabu,* the Japanese version of blackjack. It then expanded to take in the *burakumin,* the descendants of the former outcast class that were considered impure because of their association with death – executioners, undertakers, butchers and leatherworkers.

Like the Cosa Nostra, the Yazuka is organized along quasi-family lines with ordinary members considering themselves the foster children of the gang's boss. 'Foster child and foster parent' drink saké from the same cup. Recruits then abandon their ties to their biological family.

Discipline is strict. As penance, members are forced to cut off parts of their own finger and hand the severed portion to their boss. This begins with the tip of the little finger for a first offence, then progresses joint by joint across the hand.

The ritual punishment is a hangover from the days when Yakuza carried swords as the progressive amputation gradually weakened the victim's sword grip. Full-body tattooing is also widespread among Yakuza. They keep these covered in public but play *oicho-kabu* bare-chested to show their tattoos off to other members.

The structure of the Yakuza is complex with a strict hierarchy of boss, section heads and their advisers. There are five principal gangs with the largest being the Yamaguchi-gumi, founded by Harukichi Yamaguchi, a Japanese with Korean ancestry. It started in 1915 in Kobe and is thought to have over 55,000 members – more than the other four syndicates put together. It is divided into 850 clans and many thousands of other affiliate members. Operating across Asia and in the US, the Yamaguchi-gumi make billions from extortion, gambling, prostitution, guns, drugs, real estate scams, construction kickbacks, stock market manipulation and internet pornography. Its turnover is now estimated to be as much as $20 billion a year.

The Sumiyoshi-kai or Sumiyoshi-rengo is the second-largest Yakuza group in Japan with an estimated 20,000 members. Founded in 1958, it operates out of the Sumiyoshi district of Osaka. On the morning of 5 January 2007, its boss Ryoichi Sugiura was shot dead in his car in Tokyo. Within hours the offices of the Yamaguchi-gumi were fired upon in retribution.

The Inagawa-kai has 15,000 members and was founded in Yokohama in 1958, though the headquarters is now in Tokyo. Traditionally, it has made its money from illegal gambling.

Recently the police have begun a crackdown on the Yazuka since its involvement in sumo wrestling came to light. In November 2010, 63-year-old Kiyoshi Takayama was arrested for extorting $400,000 from construction firms.

Abbandando, Frank 'the Dasher' 136

Abbatemarco, 'Frankie Shots' 261

Accardo, Clarice 80

Accardo, Linda *82–3*

Accardo, Tony *78*, 78-83, *83*, 85, 217, 289

Adonis, Joe 105, 108, 109, 110, 113, 114, 135, 136, 137, 214, 219

Aglieri, Pietro 328

Aiello, Giuseppe 'Joe' 72, 89, 104, 105

Aiuppa, Joe 80, 306, 309

Alberti, Gerlando 192

Alderisio, 'Milwaukee Phil' 306

Alfano, Enrico 'Erricone' 47-8

Alfano, Pietro 237, 239

Alo, Vincent 'Jimmy Blue Eyes' 219

Alongi, Giuseppe 22

Amato, Baldassare 236, 239

Amato, Gaetano 'Tommy Scars' 265

Amatuna, Samuzzo 'Samoots' 72, 89

Ambrosoli, Giorgio 200

Ammaturo, Umberto 207, 209

Amuso, Vic 313, 315

Anastasia, Albert 80, 105, 109, 110, 115, 121, 123, 127, 130, 132, 133, *134*, 135-8, *140–1*, 141, 153, 226, 311

Anastasia, Salvatore 141

Andreotti, Giulio 195, 198, 199, 200, 323, 327, 339

Angersola, George 97

Angersola, John 97

Angleton, James Jesus 159

Annenberg, Moses 137

Anselmi, Alberto 70, 71, 72, 75, 79, 85–6

Antonori, Ignacio 234

Arena, Vito 301

Ashcroft, John 285

Avena, John 277

Badalamenti, Gaetano 171, 173, 185, 194-5, 199, *235*, 236, 237, 238

Badalamenti, Vito 237, 239

Bagarella, Antonietta 'Ninetta' *166*, 168, 170, 171, 173–4, 176, *177*

Bagarella, Calogero 167, 168, 171, 191

Bagarella, Guiseppe 167

Bagarella, Leoluca 174, 176, 330

Bagarella, Salvatore 167

Bala, Jorge Asaf y 234

Balistrieri, Frank 309

Barbagallo, Salvaore 337

Barbara, Joseph 'Joe the Barber' 80

Barko, Louis 74

Barrel Murders 55, 57, 99

Bartolomeo, Carmelo 148

Basciano, Vincent 'Vinny Gorgeous' 285

Basile, Frank 96

Batista, Fulgencio 211

Batters, Joe *78*, 78-83

Bauer, H.G. *92*

Berlusconi, Silvio 200

Berman, Otto 'Abbadabba' 120, 123

Betillo, David 123, 126

Bianchi, Giuseppe 33

Bianco, Antonio *28-9*

Bilotti, Thomas 242, *242–3*, 245, 248, 259

Bingham, Theodore A. 51

Binion, Benny 221

Bishop, William H. 53, 54-5

Bocchino, Felix 272

Boccia, Ferdinand 127, 153

Bollettino della Sera 48

Bonnano, Joseph 'Joe Bananas' 11, 12, 104, 108, 110, 115, 117, 119, 164-5, *165*, 184, 185, 226, 251, 293, *293*

Bonnano, Salvatore 'Bill' 164-5, 294

Bononolo, Paolo 48

Bontade, Stefano 'the Prince' 171, 173, 194, 195, 199, 200, 323

Bonventre, Vito 104

Bonventure, Cesare 236, 237–8, 284

Bordonato, Lucio Tasca 156, 159

Borelli, 'Dirty' Henry 299, 300

Borelli, Vito 283

Borgesi, Georgie 271

Boriello, 'Bobby' 246

Borsellino, Paolo 176, 323, 324, *324*, 325, 329, 331, *340–1*, 342

Boscaglia, Giovanni 209

Bozzuffi, Antonio 43

Bozzuffi, John 43

Brancato, Tony 217

Branchi, Giovanni 53

Breen, David W. 8

Bresciano, Maria 293

Brown, 'Cokey Flo' 126

Bruno, Angelo 223, 224, 272, *276*, 277–9

Brusca, Bernardo 329

Brusca, Giovanni 328, 329, 330–1, 334, *336*, 336-9, 342–3

Buccieri, Fiore 'Fifi' 288

Bulger, James 'Whitey' 268

Buonomo, Amadio 58–9

Buscemi, Giuseppe 'Pidduzzo' 24

Buscetta, Tommaso 16, *16*, 159, 176, *180*, 181, 185, 187, 190, 195, 196, 199, 323-4, 325, 337

Byrne, Brendan 222

Caifano, Marcello 220–1

Cain, Richard 220, 288–9

Calabrese, Nick 290

Calabro, Paul 258, 259

Calderone, Antonio 145, 147

Calderone, Giuseppe 194

Callinbrano, Salvatore 'Sally' 311–12

Calò, Giuseppe 200, 201, 326

Calvi, Roberto 200–1, *201*, 326

Camorra 29, 30–1, 36, 58–65, 99, 100

Campbell, Judith 229, 230

Cannon, Howard 289

Capezio, Anthony 'Tough Tony' 78

Capone, Al 50, 68, *68*, 69, 70, 71, 72, 73–6, 78–9, 85–7, *87*, 89, 95–6, 104, 105, 110, 117, 118, 126, 137, 164

Capone, Frank 73

Capone, Ralph 86, 96

Caponigro, Antonio 'Tony Bananas' 223, 224, 278, 279

Caponnetto, Antonio 324–5

Cappiello, Nicolo 34, 36

Carey, Estelle 220

Carillo, Tom 62

Carmenciti, Stephen 39

Carneglia, John 248

Carnevale, Corrado 326

Carollo, Benedetto 18, 19

Carter, Eunice 123

Carter, Jimmy 301

Caruso, Damiano 190, 191

Caruso, Giuseppe 24, 25

Casella, Peter 224, 277, 279

Casino 305, 309

Cassarà, Antonio 196

Casso, Anthony 'Gaspipe' *310*, 311–15

Castellano, G. *154-5*, 156

Castellano, Paul 'Big Paul' 224, 226, 239, 241, 242–3, *243–4*, 245, 248, 259, 279, 283, 300, 301, 312, 314

Castellano, Peter 226

Castro, Fidel 211, 229, 230, 234

Catalano, Salvatore 236, 237, 239

Catania, Giuseppe 39, 43

Catena, Gerardo 'Jerry' 219, 223

Cavataio, Michele 'the Cobra' 171, 190-1

Cellini, Dino 211-12, 223

Chapman, Lyle 92

Chiesa, Carlo Alberto 199, 200, 323, *323*

Chilante, Felice 100

Chinnici, Rocco 15, 324, 338

Chiodo, Peter 24, 315

Ciancaglini, Joseph 'Joey Chang' 271

Ciancaglini, Michael 'Mikey Chang' 271, 273

Ciancimino, Vito 198, 199

Cina, Salvatore 44

Circella, Nick 220

Cirillo, Ciro 31

Ciulla, Antonio 326

Cloonan, Barney 92

Cohen, Mickey 216, 217

Cohen, Sam 218

Colgan, Patrick F. 282–3

Coll, Vincent 111, 120

Colletta, Frank 245–6

Colombo, Joe 120, 164, *250*, 251, 262, 263

Colombo, John Jnr. 251

Colonna, Niccolò Turrisi 16–17

Colosimo, 'Big Jim' 68-9, 73

Conigliaro, Antonio 179, 180

Conta, Frank 95

Contorno, Salvatore 'Totucco' 196, 323–4, 325

Coppola, Agostino 174

Coppola, Anthony 141

Coppola, Frank 'Three-fingers' 162, 174, 182

Coppola, Leonardo 'Nina' 236, 237

Corallo, Tony 'Tony Ducks' 239, 241, 314–15

Cornero, Tony 219

Corozzo, Nicholas 'Little Nicky' 249

Cosmano, 'Sunny Jim' 68

Costa, Gaetano 195

Costnazo, Maurizio 318, 342–3

Costello, Frank 'the Prime Minister' 57, 109, 113, 114, 123, 127, 128, 129, 130, *131*, 132, 135, 137, 138, 141, 153, 219, 236, 262

Cotroni, Francesco 'Frank' 293, 294, 295

Cotroni, Giuseppe 'Pep' 233, 293, 294–5

Cotroni, Vincenzo 'the Egg' 233, *292*, 293–7

Cottone, Antonio 180, 182

Craxi, Bettino 200, 201, 325

Crimaldi, Charles 'Chuckie' 307

Crimi, Questore 145

Crispi, Francesco 26

Cuccia, Ciccio 143

Cuiringione, Anthony 74

Cullotta, Frank 305, 306, 308

Cutolo, Raffaele 31, 207, *208*, 209

D'Agnese, John 344

D'Agostino, Antoine 233

D'Alba, Antonia 24

D'Alba, Vincenzo 23, 24

D'Aleo, Tommaso 24, 26

D'Alessandro, Nicola 181, 182

D'Amuro, Pasquale J. 284

D'Andrea, Antonio 89, 100

D'Andrea, Phil 89

D'Antonio, James 'Legs' 289

D'Aquila, Salvatore 99, 100, 101

D'Arco, 'Little Al' 315

Daley, Richard 228–9, *229*

Dalitz, Morris 'Moe' 97, 219

Daniello, Ralph 'the Barber' 62–3, 64

Davis, J. Richard 'Dixie' 120

Davis, O.T. *92*

De Marco, Frank 'Shoes' 312

De Marco, Joe 59–60, 62

De Marco, Salvatore 62

De Niro, Robert *44–5*

De Priemo, Giuseppe 38–9, 40

DeChristopher, Fred 263

DeCicco, Frank 246, 313, 314

Del Gaudio, Gaetano 59, 62

Del Gaudio, Nicolo 59, 62

Dellacroce, Aniello 'the Lamb' 226, 241, 242

Dellacroce, Buddy 243

DeLuca, Louis 'Louie Irish' 272

DeMeo, Roy 242, 256, 257, 259, *298*, 299–301, 313

DeMora, Vincenzo 78

Denaro, Francesco Messina 317–18

Denaro, Ignazio 'Natz' 277

Denaro, Matteo 'Diabolik' *316*, 317–21

DeStefano, 'Mad' Sam 221–2, 306, 307

DeStefano, Mario 307, 308

Dever, William 73

Dewey, Thomas E. 120–1, *121*, 123, 126–7, *128*, 129, 133, 137

Di Cristina, Giuseppe 'the Tiger' 191, 194

Di Girolamo, Giacomo 319, 320–1

Di Maggio, Baldassare 329

Di Maggio, Balduccio 176

Di Matteo, Domenico 167, 168

Di Matteo, Giuseppe 331, 343

Di Matteo, Mario Santo 343

Di Pisa, Calcedonio 184, 190

Di Sano, Emanuela 22–3

Di Sano, Giuseppa 22–4

DiAddorio, James 'Jimmy Brooms' 272

Diamond, Jack 'Legs' 120

DiBella, Tommy 263

DiBernardo, Robert 248

DiBono, Louie 248

DiFronzo, John 'No Nose' 287–8

DiGregorio, Gaspar 164–5

DiNome, Freddy 299

DiNunzio, Carmen 'the Big Cheese' 269

DiSimone, Frank 164, 251

Doherty, Brendan 268–9

Doherty, James 73

Domingo, Bastiano 103, 104–5

Dorfman, Allen 288, 289–90

Doto, Giuseppe 'Joe Adonis' 57

Dovi, Joseph 'Bruno' 277

Dragna, Jack 214

Drucci, Vincent 'the Schemer' 71-2, 74, 89

Duffy, John 70

Durante, Jimmy 215

Eisenhower, Dwight D. *154–5*

Enemy Within, The (Kennedy) 230

Eppolito, James 301

Eppolito, James Jnr. 301

Esposito, Antonio 205–6

Esposito, Giuseppe 65

Esposito, Johnny 'Lefty' 59, 60, 62, 64

Fabrizio, Francis Anthony 213–14

Falcone, Giovanni *7*, 176, 181, *239*, 318, 323, 324, *324*, 325, *326*, 327–8, 329, 331, 334, 336, *337*, 339, 340

Fanaro, Giuseppe 99

Fanfani, Amintore 197–8

Favara, John 243, 258

Fecarotta, John 290

Ferland, William J. 269

Ferrantelli, Domenico De Michele 55

Ferrarello, Gaetono 145

Ferriola, Joseph 'Mr Clean' 308

Ferro, Vito Cascio 40, *41*, 47, 53, 55–7, 104, 145

Ferrugia, Salvatore 'Sally Fruits' 283

Fetto, John 'the Painter' 60

Fevrola, Frank 62, 64

Fischetti, Charlie 73

Flemmi, Stephen 'the Rifleman' 267–8

Florio Jnr., Ingazio 24–5, 26, 30

Foceri, Vincent 'Vinnie Beans' 313

Fontana, Giuseppe 30, 99

Foreman, Leo 307

Fowler, George *92*

Francese, Mario 174

Frankos, Donald 'Tony the Greek' 231

Frasso, Dorothy di 214

Fratianno, Aladene 'Jimmy the Weasel' 308

Freeman, Harry 132

Friel, Tom 92

Frugone, Frank L. 48

Furnari, Christopher 'Christy Tick' 241, 312, 313–14

Gaggi, Anthony 'Nino' 299, 300–1

Gagliano, Tom 110, 115, 117

Galante, Carmine 130, 182, 185, 233, 234, 236–7, *238*, 241, 283, 293–4, 295

Galati, Gaspare 18–19, 22, 26

Galatolo, Gaetano 182

Gallo, Albert 262

Gallo, Joey 'Crazy Joe' 251, 262, 263

Gallo, Larry 262

Gallo, Willie 153

Gallucci, Frank 68

Gallucci, Gennaro 58

Gallucci, Giosue 58, 59, 62, 63

Galucci, Luca 59, 62

Gambino, Carlo 130, 164, 226, *227*, 234, 241–2, 251, 277, 300, *302–3*

Gambino, John 196

Gambino, Thomas 226

Gambino family 100, 236

Ganci, Giuseppe 237–8

Gardner, Bill 92

Garibaldi, Giuseppe 12

Geller, Kenneth 265

Gelli, Licio 200–1

Genna, Angelo 70, 71–2, 89

Genna, James 72–3

Genna, Mike 'the Devil' 72

Genna, Tony 72

Genna brothers 70, 71, 72–3

Genovese, Carmine 255

Genovese, Michael 153

Genovese, Vito 57, 64, 103, 105, 109, 110, 113, 115, 127, 130, 135, 136, 141, 150, *152*, 153, 154, 164, 226, 255

Genovese family 57

Gentile, Nick 'Zu Cola' 89, 99, 100, 101, 156, 182

Getty III, John Paul 194

Giacalone, Anthony 'Tony Jack' 231

Giammona, Antonio 17, 18, 26

Giancana, Sam 80, 219, 220, 229, 230

Gigante, Vincente 'the Chin' 130, 246, 249, *312*, 313, 315

Giglio, Salvatore 233, 294

Gioia, Giovanni 198

Gioè, Gino 334

Giolitti, Giovanni *54*, 55
Giuliani, Rudolph *240*, 241, 264
Giuliano, Nunzio *9*
Giulaino, Salvatore 16, *16*, *158*, 159–62, *162–3*
Giunta, Joe 85–6
Godkin, Richard 344
Godfather, The, Part II 44–5
Goldstein, Buggsy 137
Gordon, Waxey 213
Gotti, Frank 242
Gotti, John 241, 242, *244–5*, 245, 246–7, 248–9, 258, 259, 282, 283, 301, 314
Gotti, John Jnr. 246, 249
Gotti, Peter 249
Grado, Gaetano 191
Grassi, Libero 327
Gravano, Sammy 'the Bull' 245, 247, 249, 258, 259, 313, *314*
Greco, Francesco 182
Greco, Giuseppe 179
Greco, Giuseppe 'Piddu the Lieutenant' 179, 180, 185, 192
Greco, Giuseppe 'Pino' 195, 196, 323, 324
Greco, Luigi 'Louie' 294, 295
Greco, Michele 'the Pope' 192, 194, 195, 196, 199, 326
Greco, Pietro 179
Greco, Salvatore 179, 180–1, 184, 185, 191, 192, 194
Greco family 179
Greenbaum, Gus 217–18
Greenberg, Harry 'Big Greenie' 215
Guarrasi, Vito 156
Guérini, Antoine 233, 236
Guglielmo, Joseph 'Dracula' 299
Gurino, Vito 'Chicken Head' 133, 136
Gusenberg, Frank 76
Guttadauro, Giuseppe 318
Guzik, Jake 'Greasy Thumb' 75–6, 86
Guzik, Sam 'Big Bell' 87
Haffenden, Charles R. 127, 128–9
Hennessy, David C. 65
Hill, Virginia *214*, 215, 216, 217
Hoffa, Jimmy 219, 230–1, *231*, *287*, 288
Hoffman, Paul 259

Holder, Eric 344
Hoover, Herbert 86
Hoover, J. Edgar 133
House, Percy 258
Hughes, Howard 219–20
Hydell, James 314
Hymes, Charles J. 265
Ida, Joseph 277
Impastato, Giuseppe 'Peppino' 194, 195
Indelicato, Anthony 'Bruno' 241
Inserro, Vinnie 'the Saint' 306
Invisible, The (Di Girolamo) 318
Inzerillo, Pietro 195
Inzerillo, Salvatore 'Totuccio' 194, 195, 323
Ivankov, Vyacheslav *345*, 346
Jackson, William 'Action' 80
John Paul II, Pope 200
Johnson, Jerome 251
Johnson, Nucky 137, 222
Juin, General 151
Kane, Pat 259
Katz, Andrei 299–300
Kefauver, Estes 130
Kelley, John 'Red' 267
Kelly, Kevin 247
Kennedy, Jackie *228*, 229
Kennedy, Joe 228
Kennedy, John F. 80, 129, *228*, 228–30
Kennedy, Robert F. 230
King, Alan 219
King, Mike 92
Krakower, Whitey 215
Kuklinksi, Barbara 257, *258,* 259
Kuklinski, Richard 231, *252,* 253–9, 301
La Barbera, Angelo *183*, 185, 191, 198
La Barbera, Salvatore 185
La Guardia, Fiorello 121, 130
La Torre, Pio 323
Labruzzo, Frank 164
Laduca, Vito 40
Lahart, Marty 92
Lane, Charley 253
Langella, Gennaro 'Gerry Lang' 239, 241
Lansburgh, Morris 218
Lansky, Meyer 79, 105, 108, 122–13, *113*, 117, 118, 128, 129,

130, 135, *136*, 137, 141, 211–12, 213, 214, 215, 216, 217, 218–19, 223, 226, 233–4
Lanza, Joseph 'Socks' 127–8
LaPenta, Stephen 274–5
LaPluma, Frank 103
LaRocca, Charlie 312
LaSalle, Steve 60
Lauritano, Leopoldo 59, 60, 64
Laxalt, Paul 219
Leach, John A. *94–5*
Lecchi, Antonio 36
Lee, Charles 141
Leeson, Joe 92
Leggio, Luciano 167, 168, 170–1, 173–4, *175*, 188, 190, 194, 326, 330
Leonardi, Francsco 53
Leonetti, Phil 225, 248
Lepke, Louis *132,*132–3, 136, 137, 164
Levine, Samuel 'Red' 111, 132–3
Li Causi, Girolamo 157, 161
Li Destri, Baron 145
Licandro, Salvatore 182
Ligambi, Joseph 'Uncle Joe' 225, 275, 279
Ligammari, Giovanni 239
Lima, Salvatore 176, 198-9, 200, 326, 327, 329, 338–9
Limone, Peter 'Chief Crazy Horse' 269
Lino, Edward 246
Litvinenko, Alexander 345
Lo Cicero, Calogero 165
Lo Piccolo, Salvatore 333, *333*, 334
Lo Piccolo, Sandro 334
Lo Porto, Vincenzo 24, 25
Lo Verno, Stefano 332
LoCascio, Frank 248, 249
Lolordo, Pasqualino 'Patsy' 89
Lombardi, Charles 60
Lombardo, Antonio 'the Scourge' 74–5, 89
Lombardo, Joseph 222, *286*, 287–91, 306
Lonardo, 'Big' Angelo 97
Lonardo, Joseph 100
Lopipero, Pasquale 36
Luca, Ugo 161
Lucchese, Giuseppe 196

Lucchese, Tommy 105, 106, 108, 110, 111, 115, 164, 226, 251
Luciano, Charles 'Lucky' 57, 100, 101, 105–6, 108–9, 110, 111, 112–15, 117, 118–19, 123, *124–5*, 126–7, 128–9, 130, 135–6, 137, *139*, 150, 154, 156, 157, 164, 168, 182, 184, 194, 205, 213, 216, 226, 233, 234
Lumia, Domiano 151, 154
Lupo the Wolf 40, 41–5, 48, 57–8, 59, 89, 99
Luppino, Giacomo 295
Maas, Peter 103, 247
Macri, Benedicto 138, 141
Macri, Vincent 138, 141
Madden, Owney 111, 118, 123
Maddox, 'Screwy' Claude 78
Madonia, Benedetto 40, 43
Maffia in its factors and its manifestations; study of the dangerous classes of Sicily (Alongi) 22
Mafia-Camorra war 58–65, 99
Magaddino, Stefano 117, *118*, 164, 251
Maggio, Michael 277
Magliocco, Joe 164, 262, 263
Maione, Harry 'Happy' 136, 137
Malliband, George 258
Man of Honor, A (Bonanno) 165
Manfredi, Alfredo 'Al Mineo' 99
Mangano, Philip 138
Mangano, Vincent 100, 110, 117, 137-8
Manna, Louis 246
Manocchio, Luigi 'Baby Shanks' *266*, 267-9, 344
Manzella, Cesare 184, 185, 194
Manzella, Salvatore 43-4
Maranzano, Salvatore 100, 103, 104, 105, 106, 108, 109–11, *111*, 113, 114, 117, 130, 164, 226
Marchese, Filippo 196
Marchese, Giuseppe 330
Marcinkus, Paul 200
Maresca, Assunta 'Pupetta' *202*, 203, 205–7, 209
Maresca, Camorrista Vincenzo 203
Marfeo, Rudolph 'Rudy' 267
Marino, Donald 312
Marino, Giovanni 334

Martelli, Claudio 318
Mascarello, Joseph 39
Mashay, Louis 258
Masseria, Giuseppe 'Joe the Boss' 57, 89, 100, 101, 103, 104, 105, 106, 108–9, *110*, 113, 114–15, 130, *135*, 135–6, 153, 213, 226
Massino, Joey 'the Ear' 241, 246, *280*, 281–5
Mattarella, Bernando 160–1, 184, 197, 199
Mauro, Salvatore 100
Mazzara, Gaetano 237–8
Maxi Trial 8, 31, 176, 181, 196, 198, 239, 325–7
McCarthy, Bill 306
McClellan, George B. 51
McClellan, John *102–3*, 103, 230
McElroy, James 247
McGurn, 'Machine Gun' Jack 76, 85, 78
McIntosh, Hugh 265
McQuade, J.D. *92*
McSwiggin, William 73–4
Mealli, Michael 62, 63
Meany, George 230
Meli, Rosario 33
Merlino, Joseph 'Skinny Joey' 225, *270*, 271–5
Merlino, Lawrence 'Yogi' 271
Merlino, Salvatore 271, 272
Merlo, Mike 70, 71, 89
Messino, Salvatore 33
Miceli, Salvatore di 15
Milazzo, Gaspare 104
Milazzo, Vincenzo 318
Milito, Louis 248
Mineo, Al 103, 105
Miraglia, Jimmy 306
Mirra, Anthony *294*, 295
Modica, Philip 246–7
Molinelli, Pascal 236
Mollica, Carmine 59
Moncada, Filippo 191, 192
Moncada, Girolamo 191
Monosco, Joe 312
Moran, George 'Bugs' 70, 71–2, 73, 76, *77*, 79, 85
Morano, Pellegrino 59, 60, 63–4
Morello, Calogero 57
Morello, Ciro 40

Morello, Giuseppe 40, 42–3, 44, 57–8, 99, 100, 101, 104–5, 115
Morello, Nicolo 40, 43
Morello, Salvatore 42
Morello family 59–63, 64, 99, 100
Moresco, Victoria 68
Moretti, Willie 110, 138, 153
Mori, Cesare 143, *144*, 145
Moro, Aldo 199
Mursuneso, Carmine 39
Mussolini, Alessandra 209
Mussolini, Benito 127, *142*, 143, 148, 153
Natale, Ralph 272–3, 274
Navarra, Michele 167, 168, 170, 188
Navy Street gang 59, 60, *60–1*, 62, 63, 64, 99, 100
Nazzaro, Generossi 'Joe Chuck' 59, 62
'Ndrangheta 29, 30–1
Ness, Eliot *90*, 90–7
Nicoletti, Charles 'Chuckie' 306
Nicotera, Giovanni 20
Nitti, Frank 'the Enforcer' 86, *88*, 89#
Nixon, Richard 228, 231
Notarbartolo, Emanuele 26–7, 30
Notarbartolo, Leopoldo 27, 30
Notaro, Mike 62, 64
Noto, Francesco 24–5, 26
Noto, Pietro 24–5, 26
Nuzzolese, Raniero 148
O'Banion, Dean 69–71, 75
O'Connor, John 246–7
O'Donnell, Myles 73
O'Donnell, William 223
Orena, Vittorio 'Little Vic' 246, 264, *264*, 265
Orlando, Gaetano 207
Ormanni, Italo 207
Oswald, Lee Harvey 129
P2 200–1
Pagano, Tom 60, 62
Palermo, Michael *82–3*
Palizzolo, Raffaele 26, 27, 30, 51
Panico, Salvatore 295
Pantaleone, Michele 56, 151, 157
Papalia, Johnny 'Pops' 295, 296

Paretti, Aniello 64
Paretti, Antonio 'Tony the Shoe-maker' 62, 64
Parkerson, William S. 65
Passananti, Antonio 43
Pastoia, Francesco 'Ciccio' 332–3
Pate, Herbie 'Blue Eyes' 314
Pati, Pasquale 48-9
Patriarca, Raymond 219, 267, *268*
Pecorelli, Carmine 199, 200
Pedrici, Barbara 255–6
Perone, Sam 165
Perrano, Joseph 105
Persico, Alphonse 'Little Alley Boy' 261, 263, 264, 265
Persico, Carmine 'the Snake' 241, *260*, 261–5, 283
Persico, Theodore 261, 265
Petacco, Arrigo 56–7
Petrosino, Giuseppe 'Joe' *38*, 39, *46*, 47, *49*, 51, 52–4, 55
Petrelli, Dominick 'the Gap' 115
Petto, Tomasso 'the Ox' *38*, 40, 43
Piacenti, Peter 'Petey 17' 301
Piancone, Michael 336
Piazza, Angela 57
Piazza Montalto family 20
Piccolo, Anthony 'Tony Buck' 225
Piecyk, Romual 245–6
Pinzolo, Joe 115
Pisciotta, Gaspare 161
Pistone, Joseph 241, 283–4, 295
Polakoff, Moses 126
Poletti, Charles 154, 156
Polifrone, Dominick 259
Polizzi, Charles 97
Pollaro, Gaspare 105
Pollina, Antonio 'Mr Miggs' 277–8
Prestifilippo, Mario 326
Prisco, Aniello 'Zopo the Gimp' 58
Profaci, Joe 108, 109, 110, 115, 117, 180, 182, 251, 262, 263, 299
Profaci, Salvatore 264
Pronge, Robert 258
Provenzano, Anthony 'Tony Pro' 231
Provenzano, Bernardo 167,

168, 170-1, 176, 188, *189*, 191, 194, 317, 318, 320, 326, 329, 330-3, 334
Puccio, Pioggio 53–4
Puccio, Vincenzo 196
Putin, Vladimir 344, 345
Puzo, Mario 165
Radchikov, Valery 346
Raft, George *213*, 214, 215, 217, 219
Rampino, Anthony 248
Rastelli, Phil 'Rusty' 239, 241, 281, 283, 284
Rava, Armand 'Tommy' 226
Reginelli, Marco 277
Reina, Bernardina 101
Reina, Gaetano 'Tommy' 104, 114–15, 153
Reles, Abraham 'Kid Twist' 133, 137, 215
Ricca, Paul 'the Waiter' 79
Ricci, Andrea 59, 62
Riccioli, Angelo 148
Riccobene, Harry 'the Hunch-back' 224, 279
Ricord, Auguste Joseph *232*, 234
Riina, Antonietta 'Ninetta' *166*, 168, 170, 171, 173–4, 176, *177*
Riina, Francesco 167
Riina, Gaetano 167
Riina, Giovanni 167, 176
Riina, Salvatore 'Totò' 167–8, 170, 171–2, 173, 174, 176, 188, 189, 191, 194, 195, 196, 199, 317, 318, 326, 327, 329, *329*, 330, 337, 339, *339*, 340, 342, 343
Rio, Frank 74, *75*, 85
Rizzotto, Giuseppe 15
Rizzotto, Placido 188
Rizzuto, Nicolo 296
Robsky, Paul 92
Roche, Pat *88*
Romano, Salvatore 36
Romano, Tony 59
Roosevelt, Franklin D. 71, 129
Rose, John Forester 19, 20, 65
Roselli, Johnny 229, 230
Rosen, Joseph 123, 133
Rosenberg, Harvey 'Chris' 299, 300–1
Rosenthal, Frank 'Lefty' 288, 306, *307*

Ross, Tommy 74
Rothenberg, Paul 257, 300
Rothstein, Arnold 113, 118, *119*
Rotolo, Antonio 'Nino' 333, 334
Rotolo, Salvatore 326
Ruby, Jack 129
Ruggerio, Angelo 247
Rupolo, Ernest 'the Hawk' 153
Russo, Andy 'Fat Man' 263, 265
Russo, Giuseppe Genco 'Zu Peppi' 150, 151, 184, 185, 186–7, 197
Russomano, John 58, 59
Russon, Joseph 156
Ryan, Raymond J. 220
Sabella, Salvatore 277
Saietta, Ignazio 40, 41–5, 48, 57–8, 59, 89, 99
St Valentine's Day Massacre 79, *84–5*, 85
Salemi, Lieutenant-Colonel 147–8, 151
Salemi, Vincenzo 101
Salemme, Francis 'Cadillac Frank' 267-8
Salerno, Alfred 223, 224
Salerno, Anthony 'Fat Tony' 239, 279s
Salvemini, Gaetano 55
Salvo, Ignazio *197*, 198
Salvo, Nino 198
Sangiorgi, Ermanno 22, 23, 24, 25, 26, 27, 30, 179
Santoro, Salvatore 'Tom Mix' 241
Sassi, Nick 60
Satarano, G. 37
Scafidi, Gaetano 'Tommy Horsehead' 271
Scafidi, Salvatore 'Tori' 271
Scaglione, Pietro 190
Scalise, Giovanni 70, 71, 72, 75, 79, 85–6, 105
Scalvo, Philly 306
Scalvo, Ronnie 306
Scarfo, Nicodemus 'Little Nicky' 223, 224–5, *225*, 248, 271, 278
Scarfo, Nicky Jnr. 271, 272
Scarpa, Gregory 'the Grim Reaper' 264–5, *265*, 313
Scarpato, Gerardo 109
Scelba, Mario 161
Schiro, Nicolo 'Cola' 99, 104, 164

Schlereth, Joseph 247
Schultz, Dutch 110–11, 120–1, *122*, 123, 132, 137, 214
Schuster, Arnold 138
Schwimmer, Reinhardt 76
Sciacca, Paul 165
Scialo, Carmine 'Mimi' 222
Sciara, Pietro 296
Sciascia, Gerlando 'George from Canada' 285
Scirra, 'Little' Angelo 97
Scopo, Ralph 241
Scordato, Giuseppe 15
Scorsese, Martin 309
Seager, Sam 92
Sedway, Moe 217
Seifert, Daniel 289, 291, 308
Senter, Anthony 299, 314
Sessa, Carmine 264
Sferlazza, Don 14
Sferrazzo, Tano 36
Sgroia, Alphonso 'the Butcher' 62, 64
Sicilian Vespers *10*, 11–12
Siegel, Benjamin 'Bugsy' 105, 106, 109, 112, *112*, 113, 115, 135, 136, 138, 212–17
Siino, Francesco 25–6
Simonetti, Pasquale *202*, 202, 205
Simonetti, Pasqualino 206
Sinagra, Antonio 326
Sinagra, Vincenzo 'the Tempest' 326
Sinatra, Frank 79–80, 219, 226, 229, 251
Sindona, Michele 200
Sliwa, Curtis 249
Small, Len 73
Smiley, Allen 216–17
Sollena, Matteo 236
Sollena, Salvatore 236
Spano, Antonio 'Cavallero' 72
Spatola, Rosario 324
Spilotro, John 222
Spilotro, Michael 222, 290, 308–9
Spilotro, Tony 'the Ant' 83, 221, *221*, 222, 288, 289, 290, *304*, 305–9
Spina, Chris 'the Nose' 290
Spinelli, Pasquarelli 58–9

Spinelli, Salvatore 50–1
Spingola, Henry 72
Stacher, Joseph 'Doc' 219
Staley, Edna 96, 97
Stanfa, Giovanni 'John the Dour Don' 225, 272, 278-9
Stanfa, Joseph 273
Stenson, Joseph 69
Strauss, Harry 'Pittsburg Phil' 133, 136, 137
Strauss, Louis 'Russian Louie' 221
Streva, Paolo 170
Sugiura, Ryoichi 347
Sullivan, Daniel 231
Sullivan, Manley 86
Sutera, Francesco 191
Sutton, Willie 138
Svodada, Steve 95
Takayama, Kiyoshi 347
Tancl, Eddie 73
Tannenbaum, Albert 'Allie' 215
Terranova, Bernardo 57, 59
Terranova, Cesare 190, 323, 326
Terranova, Ciro 40, 43, 57, 60, 64, 103, 109
Terranova, Lucia 101
Terranove, Nicolo 57, 59, 60, 62, 63, 64, 99
Terranova, Salvatrice 42–3, 57
Terranova, Vincenzo 40, 43, 57, 59, 64, 101
Testa, Joey 299, 300, 314
Testa, Patrick 299, 314
Testa, Phil 'Chicken Man' 224, 279
Testa, Salvatore 224-5, 271
Thompson, 'Big Bill' 73
Tieri, Frank 'Funzi' 223, 224, 278, 279
Tobey, Charles W. 215
Tombino, Tony 218
Torello, Jimmy 'the Turk' 306
Torino, Joe 135
Torrio, Johnny 68–71, 72, 73, 105, 113, 137
Trafficante, Santo 230, 234
Trafficante, Santo Jnr. 234
Trakhirov, Sergei 346
Trapani, Ignazio 33
Tresca, Carlo 153
Trigona, Giovanna d'Ondes 25

Truman, Harry S. 129, 160
Turano, Giuseppe 236, 237
Turra, Louis 273
Tuzzio, Louis *285*
Ubriaco, Camillo 'Charles' 62, 63
Unione Corse 233
Unione Siciliana 70, 74, 85, 88–9, 100
Untouchables, The (Ness) 97
Valachi, Joseph 'Joe Cargo' 103, 104, 110, 185–6, 263
Valachi Papers, The (Maas) 103
Valente, Rocco 60, 62
Valenti, Umberto 99, 100, 101
Valvo, Amelia 62
Verizzano, Giuseppe 60, 62, 64
Vernace, Bartolomeo 344
Vernotico, Anna 153
Victor Emmanuel, King 12, 143
Violi, Francesco 296
Violi, Paolo 295, 296-7
Viserti, Diamond Joe 101
Vitale, Salvatore 'Good Looking Sal' 281, 284
Vizzini, Calogero (Don Calò) 148, *149*, 150-151, 156-7, 159, 184, 197, 199
Vizzini, Giovanni 148
Volini, Carlo 50
Vollero, Alessandro 59, 60, 62, 63
Volpe, Paul 295
Wean, Ray 283, 284
Weinberg, Abraham 'Bo' 111, 120, 214
Weiss, Earl 'Hymie' 70, 71–2, 73, 74–5, *75*
Weiss, Emmanuel 'Mendy' 123, 137
Welch, Neil 278
Whalen, Grover 114
Whitaker, Audrey 24, 26
Whitaker, Joshua 24, 26
Wilkerson, Herbert 87
Wilson, Frank 86, 90, 96, *97*
Winchell, Walter 133
Winter, Dale 69
Workman, Charlie 'the Bug' 123
Yakuza, The 347
Yale, Frankie 68, 69, 71
Yamaguchi, Harukichi 347
Zaraca, Antonio 58
Zwillman, Abner 'Longy' 219